POLITICS AND SOCIETY

An Introduction to Political Sociology

by

MICHAEL RUSH

New York London Toronto Sydney Tokyo Singapore

First published 1992 by
Prentice Hall Harvester Wheatsheaf
Campus 400, Maylands Avenue
Hemel Hempstead
Hertfordshire, HP2 7EZ
A division of
Simon & Schuster International Group

Typeset in 10pt Plantin by
Mathematical Composition Setters Ltd, Salisbury, Wiltshire

Printed and bound in Great Britain by
T. J. Press (Padstow) Ltd, Padstow, Cornwall

British Library Cataloguing in Publication Data

Rush, Michael
Politics and society: an introduction to political sociology.
I. Title
323

ISBN 0-7450-1214-0
ISBN 0-7450-1215-9 pbk

5 96

CONTENTS

List of figures ix
List of tables xi
Preface xii

PART I INTRODUCTION

1 WHAT IS POLITICAL SOCIOLOGY? 3
Sociology and political science 3
The origins and development of political sociology 8
The remit of political sociology 12

PART II THE STATE, POWER AND AUTHORITY
INTRODUCTION 17

2 THE STATE AND SOCIETY 20
Introduction 20
The origins of the state 23
The development of the modern state 29
The Marxist concept of the state 39
Conclusion 42

3 POWER, AUTHORITY AND LEGITIMACY 43
Defining and analysing power 43
Authority and legitimacy 50
Legitimacy and compliance 55

4 THE DISTRIBUTION OF POWER 58
Introduction 58
Elite theory 59
Pluralism 67
Totalitarianism 70
Democracy 78
The distribution of power: an overview 83

PART III POLITICAL BEHAVIOUR AND SOCIETY
INTRODUCTION 89

5 POLITICAL SOCIALISATION 92
Introduction 92
A theory of political socialisation 96
A critique of political socialisation theory 108

6 POLITICAL PARTICIPATION 110
Introduction 110
Forms of political participation 111
The extent of political participation 116
Explaining political participation 120
Conclusion 127

7 POLITICAL RECRUITMENT 128
Introduction 128
A model of political recruitment 130
Problems of political recruitment theory 147

PART IV POLITICAL COMMUNICATION, PUBLIC OPINION AND IDEOLOGY
INTRODUCTION 151

8 POLITICAL COMMUNICATION 153
Introduction 153
Theories of communication 154
The characteristics of political communication 160
The factors influencing political communication 161
Conclusion 163

9 PUBLIC OPINION AND SOCIETY 166
Defining public opinion 166
The characteristics of public opinion 169
The formation of public opinion 173
Political communication and public opinion 179

10 IDEOLOGY AND SOCIETY 181
What is ideology? 181
The characteristics and functions of ideology 182
The Marxist view of ideology 183
Ideology, political culture and the end of the ideology thesis 186
Ideology, values and attitudes 190
Ideology and society 193

PART V REVOLUTION, DEVELOPMENT AND MODERNISATION
INTRODUCTION 197

11 REVOLUTION 200
Introduction 200
The Marxist view of revolution 202
A non-Marxist view of revolution 206
The causes of revolution 211
Revolution and societal change 217

12 DEVELOPMENT AND MODERNISATION THEORY 219
Introduction 219
The political-development school 220
The nation-building school 222
The modernisation school 223
Underdevelopment and dependency theory 227
Modernisation and development as industrialisation 229
Changing society: an overview 236

PART VI CONCLUSION

13 WHITHER POLITICAL SOCIOLOGY? 241
Introduction 241
The achievements of political sociology 241
What remains to be done 243

Bibliography 247

Index 259

FIGURES

Figure 3.1 A continuum of social and political obedience or compliance (Source: Held (1984), pp. 301–2) 56
Figure 4.1 Classifying elite theorists (Source: based on Parry (1969), Chapter II) 61
Figure 4.2 Pareto's types of elites (Source: Pareto, *Mind and Society*, Vol. 4, Sec. 2178, 2227, 2274, 2275) 64
Figure 4.3 Democracy: consent and control mechanisms 81
Figure 5.1 A model of political socialisation 97
Figure 5.2 The stages of childhood political socialisation (Source: Easton and Dennis (1969)) 98
Figure 6.1 A hierarchy of political participation 112
Figure 6.2 Socio-economic characteristics and political participation (Source: Milbrath and Goel (1977), pp. 86–122) 118
Figure 6.3 A model of political participation 122
Figure 7.1 A model of political recruitment 136
Figure 7.2 The primary, secondary and tertiary opportunity structures 138
Figure 8.1 A basic communication model 159
Figure 8.2 Maletzke's communication model (Source: Maletzke (1963), as adapted by McQuail and Windahl (1981)) 164
Figure 9.1 The formation of opinion: a model 173
Figure 9.2 A typology of media effects (Source: McQuail (1987), p. 258) 176
Figure 9.3 A typology of media effects: definitions (Source: McQuail (1987), pp. 258–9) 177

Figures

Figure 11.1 The causes of revolution 212
Figure 12.1 Political development: variables and crises (Source: Binder *et al.* (1971)) 221
Figure 12.2 Theories of modernisation (Sources: Rostow (1950); Organski (1965)) 223
Figure 12.3 Apter's two models of modernisation (Source: Apter (1965)) 226

TABLES

Table 6.1 A hierarchy of political participation in Britain, 1989 116
Table 6.2 Types of political participation in Britain, 1984–85 121
Table 7.1 The socio-economic background of British MPs, 1987 146
Table 9.1 Proportion of 'don't knows' on devolution proposals for Scotland, 1976 167
Table 9.2 Changes of opinion on MPs' pay in relation to respondents' information 168
Table 9.3 Intensity of party preferences in Britain, 1990 169
Table 9.4 Salience of problems facing Britain, February 1990 171
Table 9.5 Consistency of opinion on Race Relations Bill, 1968 172

PREFACE

Rush and Althoff's *An Introduction to Political Sociology* was published in 1971 and has been out of print for some years. In the meantime, the scope of political sociology has broadened considerably and a number of its traditional concerns have benefited from further research and publication, although some have suffered from relative neglect. A more wide-ranging volume therefore seemed appropriate, building and drawing on the earlier work reported in Rush and Althoff, but, much more importantly, seeking to incorporate new ideas and developments. The present volume is not therefore a revised edition of the original book, but a new and much more comprehensive piece of work, covering a number of major themes not previously included. Its purpose is to introduce students to the wide range of concepts, themes and ideas now regarded as central to political sociology and to draw on the extensive research available.

Not all observers, whether political sociologists or not, will agree with the choice of areas covered or the emphasis placed on some concepts and theories rather than others. For example, some political sociologists would place much greater emphasis on electoral behaviour than I have done, but I have chosen to weave material on that subject into discussions of political socialisation, political participation, public opinion, and ideology, because that seems appropriate in the context of political sociology. Apart from that, however, there is a widespread and increasingly sophisticated literature on electoral behaviour in its own right to which the attention of readers is drawn and to which reference can and should be made. The general approach is eclectic, but one person's eclecticism can easily be seen as reflecting bias or neglect: more could always be said about some ideas and theories, while others which have been omitted could have been included. This is almost inevitable in subject areas like political sociology that straddle traditional disciplines and draw on many others; it is all too easy to say, 'If I were going there, I wouldn't start from here!'

This book owes much to many people, not least to the many students who have taken the course in political sociology that I have taught at the University of Exeter for many years. The course itself has gone through a number of versions, reflecting changes in political sociology, but also benefiting a great deal from the contributions made by students in tutorial and seminar discussions, and from the dissertations and assessed work submitted. A greater debt, however, is due to my colleagues from the Department of Sociology at Exeter with whom I have had the good fortune to share the course. They are Stephen Mennell, now Professor of Sociology at Monash University, Anne Witz, now at the University of Birmingham, and my current collaborator, Paul Keating. All have made contributions, often unwittingly, extending my knowledge, improving my understanding, arousing my curiosity, correcting my misconceptions. However, they bear no direct responsibility for the contents of *Politics and Society*; any errors and misconceptions that remain are entirely my responsibility.

I should also like to express my thanks to my colleagues in the Department of Politics, who have been so supportive in helping me shoulder the burden of being Head of Department while this book was being written. It is also likely that the book would not have been completed without the patient encouragement of Clare Grist, the commissioning editor of Simon & Schuster – grateful thanks are therefore due to her. My greatest debt, however, is to my wife, Jean, without whose unfailing support projects like this would either not get finished or would take even longer than this one already has; her tolerance of the remorseless and inane chatter of my PC printer seems to know no bounds!

Michael Rush
University of Exeter
September 1991

PART I

INTRODUCTION

Chapter 1

WHAT IS POLITICAL SOCIOLOGY?

SOCIOLOGY AND POLITICAL SCIENCE

Sociology is the study of human behaviour within a societal context. A society is therefore the basic unit of analysis, in that sociology differs from psychology, whose basic unit of analysis is the human being. A society may be defined as a distinctive and coherent grouping of human beings living within some degree of proximity, whose behaviour is characterised by various common practices, norms, and beliefs that distinguish it from other human groupings with clearly different practices, norms, and beliefs.

The term 'sociology' was coined by Auguste Comte (1798–1857), one of the founding fathers of the discipline. Both Comte and Herbert Spencer (1820–1903), another of the founding fathers, stressed that society was the basic unit of sociological analysis. Nominating the founding fathers of one of the more recently established academic disciplines might seem a fairly simple business, but it is always a matter of opinion and some observers might wish to add – even substitute – one or more of the names of Karl Marx (1818–83), Emile Durkheim (1858–1917), or Max Weber (1864–1920). Founding fathers or not, however, all three made massive contributions to sociology, both theoretically and empirically. Marx was a polymath – historian, political philosopher, and economist, and, of course, actively involved in politics. His exploration of and theories concerning the relationship between politics, economics and society, to which he involuntarily gave his name, are an eloquent testimony to his contribution to sociology. Durkheim's development of the division of labour or the specialisation of roles in society was of great importance and his studies of religion and of suicide were models of sociological investigation, especially in the use of statistics. Weber was both a critic of Marx and the progenitor of a remarkable range of concepts concerning the state, power, authority, and legitimacy, and of the role of ideas or value-systems in the development of and changes in society. In the cases of Marx and Weber, however, significant as their contributions were to the development of sociology, an even better case can be made for calling them the founding fathers of political sociology, but that is to anticipate later discussion.

By definition, sociology could be said to encompass political science. After all, politics takes place within a societal context, but as an academic discipline it developed almost entirely separately from sociology. The study of politics, particularly in Europe, grew out of legal studies, especially, and not surprisingly, constitutional law. In Britain, and to a lesser extent the United States, it developed mainly from the study of history. Both, of course, were perfectly logical developments, but they led to a situation in which the study of politics had little in common with sociology. Moreover, whatever disputes may have arisen over the rights of disciplines such as sociology, psychology and economics to claim to be social *sciences*, there was little dispute over their subject matter. Not only has political science been more frequently accused of being a pseudo-science, but its subject matter his always been in greater dispute.

Definitions of politics are legion and no one definition has been universally accepted. In order to solve this definitional problem it has frequently been circumvented by trying to delineate the essence or central concept of political study. Politics, it is argued, is the resolution of human conflict; it is the process by which society authoritatively allocates resources and values; it is the process by which society makes decisions or evolves policies; it is the exercise of power and influence in society. In practice, this merely shifts the definitional problem. None the less, each of these concepts focuses on a particular question: how, within a society, do human beings solve their problems with their fellow human beings and with their environment? Viewed this way political science is concerned with the study of the problems themselves, of the means that may be evolved to deal with them, of the factors that influence individuals and groups of individuals in seeking their solution, and, by no means least, with the ideas and values which influence human beings in dealing with those problems. Bernard Crick (1966, p. 683) argues that 'political science is a subject-matter, not an autonomous discipline ... The subject-matter is defined by a problem', and that problem is the role of government, which he defines as 'the activity of maintaining order'. The reference to order is meant in the sense of the regulation of relations between individuals and groups of individuals, not merely in the narrow sense of the phrase 'law and order'. Political science is therefore the study of the function of government in society.

Although political scientists like Crick and sociologists like Gary Runciman (1965) see an essential unity of the social sciences, academically they have largely developed separately. The study of politics in particular exhibited a strong tendency to concentrate on the study of political institutions, such as executives and legislatures, political parties and bureaucracies, and of central and local administration, only later venturing into the study of areas such as the electoral, legislative, policy-making, and organisational and administrative processes. Political scientists were also slow to develop an interest in other areas now regarded as crucial to an understanding of politics. For example, although A. F. Bentley published a pioneering book on pressure or interest groups in 1908, it was not until the 1950s that political scientists paid significant attention to pressure politics. However, it was two other related developments that gave rise to the growth of modern political sociology.

The first of these was the development in the social sciences of the behavioural approach to the study of social phenomena. Behaviouralism developed initially and most strongly in the United States and grew out of what were known as behaviourist studies in psychology. As the term 'behaviourist' implies, these studies concentrated on observing and analysing individual and group behaviour, often using animals in laboratory experiments. There was a strong emphasis on systematic and precise measurement and on seeking to establish the existence of behavioural patterns which could form the basis for hypothesising laws of behaviour. Other social scientists, especially in sociology and later in political science, began to use similar methods, stressing the importance of intellectual rigour, precise measurement, the development of empirically based generalisations, and objectivity (see Eulau 1963, 1969).

The second and subsequent development was a particular concern among American political scientists about the problem of studying the politics of the Third World or developing countries – those parts of the world in Africa, Asia, and Latin America that, in most cases, had been subject to colonial rule or, like China, to extensive Western influence. Earlier comparative studies had tended to follow the traditional pattern of institutional analysis, with relatively little consideration of the socio-cultural milieu in which those institutions operated and the differences that this might make. The criticisms of the traditional approach were sometimes exaggerated, but were far from unfounded.

These two developments brought many political scientists much closer to their colleagues in other social sciences, especially sociology. In particular, a number of political scientists were attracted by the development of systems theory, notably though not exclusively through the ideas of Talcott Parsons, whose book *The Social System* (1951) had a considerable impact beyond the realm of sociology. Parsons argued that all societies constituted a social system, within which operated a number of subsystems. In addition, he argued a social system was self-regulating or self-adjusting, adapting itself as circumstances changed. Its normal state was one of equilibrium and, in response to demands made upon it, the social system adjusted itself in order to restore a state of equilibrium. The latter state was normally attained and maintained by the adequate and necessary performance of a number of functions, each performed by a different part of the system. Thus the pattern-maintenance function (i.e. managing tension within the system) is performed by its cultural subsystem, the adaptation or distributive function by the economic subsystem, the integration function (i.e. co-ordinating interrelationships between members of the system) by the legal and regulatory subsystem, and the goal-attainment function (i.e. mobilising people and resources to achieve collective ends) by the political subsystem. Parsons' theory of the social system is also known as structural functionalism, since the functions necessary for the survival of the system are performed by the structures or patterns of behaviour which constitute each subsystem.

The application of systems theory in political science was not exclusively Parsonian and one of the leading political scientists in the systems field, David Easton (1953, 1965a, 1965b), did not develop his ideas about the political system in structural–functional terms.

However, Easton placed great stress upon the relationship between the political system and its environment, developing what he called input–output analysis. In Easton's scheme of things the environment produced inputs into the political system in the form of demands – desired political decisions on particular policy matters, and supports – attitudes and actions by individuals and groups of individuals which sustained the political system. The latter processed these inputs, producing outputs in the form of decisions and actions, which, operating through a feedback loop, produced more demands and supports.

Subsequently, Gabriel Almond adapted Easton's input–output analysis to structural functionalism, describing certain functions as inputs and others as outputs. Almond's purpose was to provide a basis for comparative political analysis, particularly of developing countries. In collaboration with James S. Coleman and a number of other political scientists, Almond produced *The Politics of Developing Areas* (1960) and later, with G. Bingham Powell, *Comparative Politics: A developmental approach* (1966). Meanwhile, Almond and another political scientist, Sidney Verba, wrote another influential book. *The Civic Culture* (1963), which, based upon a detailed five-nation survey, developed the concept of political culture – the ideas and attitudes that underpin a given political system.

Systems theory, structural functionalism, and concepts such as political culture were not accepted universally, but the work of Easton, Almond and others was part of and also itself stimulated much research into comparative politics in general and Third World politics in particular. Systems theory was criticised as lacking empirical support, difficult to apply in the conduct of research, and as being theoretically unable to give an adequate explanation of major or fundamental changes in societies. Structural functionalism was similarly criticised, particularly in respect of accounting for societal change and for its inadequate conceptualisation of its key terms, 'structure' and 'function'. These criticisms applied equally to the developmental approach, but Almond's conceptual scheme of types of political systems within a developmental framework was also seen as value-laden and ethnocentric by appearing to fit best and imply development towards the American political system.

It would be misleading, however, to attribute the development of modern political sociology to Easton and Almond and their colleagues, and even more so to describe them as the founding fathers of political sociology. The latter's roots not only significantly predate this work, but are far more disparate.

THE ORIGINS AND DEVELOPMENT OF POLITICAL SOCIOLOGY

All disciplines or subjects produce their subdisciplines or more specialised areas of study and research, but political sociology, while not unique in this respect, seeks to straddle two important social sciences. Essentially political sociology seeks to examine the links between politics and society, to place politics within its societal context by analysing the relationship between social structures and political structures and between social behaviour and political behaviour. It is what Giovanni Sartori (1969, p. 19) has called 'an inter-disciplinary hybrid'. As such it draws heavily upon both disciplines it seeks to inform, but given their respective histories, it is perhaps appropriate that the two men who have the strongest claims to be the founding fathers of political sociology were more closely associated with sociology than with political science. These are, of course, Karl Marx and Max Weber, both of whom regarded politics as inextricably embedded in society.

Marx's contribution was massive and varied and falls into three areas: general theory, specific theory, and methodology. Following Hegel, Marx developed a theory of historical inevitability, but unlike Hegel he based his theory on the material conflict of opposing economic forces arising out of the means of production, resulting in the ultimate overthrow of capitalism and the creation of a classless society. Basically, Marx argued that the nature of any society depended upon the predominant mode of production, which determined the relationship between individuals and groups of individuals and the ideas and values predominant in that society. It therefore followed that fundamental change in society was consequent upon major changes in the mode of production. Marx's interpretation of history was based on the twin pillars of economic and sociological theory. He developed David Hume's labour-value theory into theories of surplus value and the exploitation of labour, and these formed the basis of his major sociological theory, the class struggle. He also developed a theory of alienation, which argued that the subordinate class or classes in society come to reject the ideas and values of the ruling class and develop alternative and eventually revolutionary ideas and values, which formed the basis of the class struggle. This had to be preceded, however, by the development of class consciousness – another of Marx's important concepts, the realisation by subordinate classes of their true position in the means of production and therefore in society.

Many criticisms have been levelled at Marx's theories, some based on their general validity, others on their predictive value. For example, although he did not ignore the importance of ideas as sociological factors, Marx regarded them as dependent rather than independent variables, thus subordinating them to his economic interpretation of history. The role of Marxism as an ideology in many parts of the world would suggest that Marx over-emphasised the economic subordination of ideas. Similarly, the failure of a number of his predictions and his failure to anticipate the adaptive capacity of capitalism, have cast doubt on the validity of his theories. These criticisms do little, however, to diminish his contribution to political sociology. Indeed, Marx's theories have shown themselves to be extremely adaptable, and later Marxists and neo-Marxists have interpreted and reinterpreted them in the light of subsequent research and events. Both his general and his specific theories have stimulated an enormous amount of work, some of it seeking to support Marx's ideas, some to refute them. The result has been a vast contribution to knowledge, which in turn has often stimulated yet further research.

Quite apart from this, however, Marx made a further vital contribution in the field of methodology. His development of 'scientific socialism' laid down standards of scholarship and methods which were an example to subsequent social scientists. Marx endeavoured to give his theories a firm basis in fact by amassing a vast amount of evidence which he sought to examine in a systematic and rigorous fashion. How successful he was remains a matter of dispute, but the very fact that he claimed this for his theories meant that both his followers and critics had to make similar endeavours (see McLellan 1970, 1974, 1979, 1983; Giddens 1971; Bottomore 1979; Bottomore *et al.* 1983).

Perhaps inevitably, the second founding father of political sociology, Max Weber, was one of Marx's leading critics. Weber's contribution consisted not only of a major critique of Marx, but of a considerable number of specific studies and concepts of importance to political sociology. In his work *The Protestant Ethic and the Spirit of Capitalism* (1930 [1904–5])*, and in his studies of India, China and the Jewish people, Weber sought to demonstrate that non-economic factors, especially ideas, were important sociological factors. Moreover, in examining social stratification in various societies he argued that social strata could be based not only on an individual's 'class' or economic position in society, as Marx asserted, but also upon status or social position in society, or upon an individual's position in the societal power structure. These could, Weber acknowledged, be overlapping, but were not necessarily identical.

Weber also contributed several important conceptual and methodological ideas to political sociology: he focused attention on the importance of power as a political concept, particularly within the context of the state, and on the authoritative exercise of power or legitimacy. In the latter case he suggested three major bases for legitimacy – the traditional, the charismatic, and the legal–rational, which are the most famous of his 'ideal types'. Weber's concept of the ideal type is simply the construction of historically observable facts into a model or bench-mark against which other similar phenomena can be measured. The term 'ideal' is not meant as a judgement, but rather as a means of plotting points on a sociological graph, and the ideal type remains a useful tool in sociology generally.

Weber's other methodological legacy was the concept of sympathetic (or subjective) understanding or *Verstehen*, as applied to sociology. Weber felt that human behaviour could be better understood if account were taken of the motives and intentions of those directly involved in that behaviour. It was natural that Weber should stress such a concept, given the importance he attributed to the force of ideas as sociological factors. He acknowledged that the choice of subjects for investigation inevitably reflected the values of the researcher, but that once chosen it was possible, through the application of *Verstehen*, to be objective. None the less, there has been criticism of Weber's work on the grounds that, regardless of his claims that it was value-free, the examination of human motives involved an interpretative element which could not be ultimately objective. His work has also been criticised on other grounds, such as historical accuracy, but his work and ideas, like those of Marx, have proved

* Dates within square brackets denote original date of publication.

a stimulus to subsequent generations of sociologists and political scientists (see Weber 1947, 1948, 1949; Giddens 1971).

Marx and Weber laid the foundations of political sociology, but a considerable period was to elapse before anything remotely resembling a complete edifice was to rise on those foundations. What did occur was the development of work on particular aspects of what are now regarded as integral parts of political sociology, such as the development of elite theories by Gaetano Mosca (1858–1941) and Vilfredo Pareto (1848–1923) and related studies of political parties by M. Ostrogorski (1854–1919) and Robert Michels (1876–1936). Subsequently, others, such as Stuart Rice in *Quantitative Methods in Politics* (1928), Paul Lazarsfeld *et al.* in *The People's Choice* (1944), and Rudolf Herbele, *From Democracy to Nazism* (1945), analysed electoral behaviour. Meanwhile, a small number of political scientists, notably Harold Lasswell in *Psychopathology and Politics* (1930) and *Politics: Who gets what, when, how* (1936), turned their attention to the role of personality in politics and to its psychological dimension; and after the Second World War Theodor Adorno and his colleagues published their influential *The Authoritarian Personality* (1950).

The period after the Second World War saw a massive burgeoning of research and publications in the social sciences generally, much of it in the United States, but later spreading into Europe and elsewhere. A great deal of this literature was highly relevant to political sociology, none more so perhaps than the work of the American sociologist, Seymour Martin Lipset, particularly *Political Man* (1960), which explored among other things the relationship between economic development and democracy and between ideology and politics, and his *First New Nation* (1963), an account of the development of national identity in the United States.

Other areas also began to receive attention, such as political socialisation, participation, and recruitment – seeking to explain how people acquired their political beliefs, how they became involved in politics, and how those who secured political office came to do so. Yet others examined the role of political communication – how political information and ideas were transmitted within society. Gradually political sociology assumed a more coherent whole, although early texts and collections of readings tended to focus on limited and selected aspects of the subject area.

Meanwhile, the existence of the USSR as a self-proclaimed communist state and the establishment of similar states in Eastern

Europe and mainland China, the continued survival of advanced capitalist states in Western Europe and North America, and the emergence of the Third World in the aftermath of post-1945 decolonisation, stimulated much activity in Marxist studies. Neo-Marxist theories developed to explain these phenomena and to revise Marx's own predictions about the inevitable collapse of capitalism and the circumstances in which it would occur. The work of Lenin, Trotsky and Mao Zedong as theorists and revolutionary practitioners played a crucial part, but others such as the members of the Frankfurt School (e.g. Adorno, Horkheimer, Marcuse, and Habermas), existentialists (e.g. Sartre), and structuralists (e.g. Althusser, Poulantzas) all made important contributions.

Marxist theorists also focused renewed attention on the role of the state in society (see Althusser 1972; Anderson 1974; Jessop 1982; Miliband 1973), discussion of which had often become arid and largely abstract in non-Marxist writings. Yet in a world of states it was a concept that political sociologists could hardly ignore. The state, actually or ostensibly, provides the framework for the exercise of political power, especially in its legitimate form and it is within the confines of the modern state that much political behaviour takes place. The development of neo-Marxist theories also played an important part in the attention paid to the role of ideology in politics, not least in that non-Marxists regard Marxism itself as an ideology.

THE REMIT OF POLITICAL SOCIOLOGY

Marx and Weber were of the same mind in believing that politics could only be explained and understood within a societal context, a context which was deeply historical. The strong tendency towards compartmentalism in academic studies and teaching resulted in the haphazard and piecemeal development of political sociology, leading to a concentration on some aspects of the subject and the neglect of others, and the eclecticism that pervaded the work of both men largely disappeared under the weight of specialisation. Different aspects of what may properly be claimed to be the province of political sociology were nevertheless explored and developed – elite and pluralist theories of the distribution of power, political parties (especially electoral behaviour and the conditions which appeared conducive to the development and sustenance of liberal–democratic regimes), political socialisation and political culture, political participation, political recruitment, theories of revolutionary and evolutionary change in society, renewed interest in the state, in ideology, and in the relationship between values and society. Increasing attention was also paid to the formation of public opinion and its impact on the political process and, more recently, a revived awareness of the importance of the psychological dimension of politics. None of these areas should be seen as the exclusive province of political sociology, but taken together they contribute powerfully to political sociology being seen as a coherent area of study.

The task, then, of political sociology is to explore and explain the relationship between politics and society, between social and political institutions, and between social and political behaviour. The breadth of such a task is daunting, but no less necessary for that. For any society to be understood, so must its politics; and if the politics of any society is to be understood, so must that society. Ultimately, of course, the focus of political sociology is on those aspects of societal structures and behaviour that contribute to and explain politics. This involves exploring four major themes: the role of the state and the exercise of power; how political behaviour is related to its societal context; how values are related to a society's politics; and how societies change. These themes constitute the four main sections of the book. Within each, more particular aspects are examined in greater depth: in the first, the development of the state and its relationship to the concepts of power, authority and legitimacy; in the second, the concept of political socialisation, participation and recruitment; in the third, theories of communication, public opinion and the role of ideology; and in the fourth, theories of revolution, development, modernisation, and dependency. The final section is an assessment of what political sociology has achieved and what remains to be done.

If the remit of political sociology seems a large one, then perhaps, just as the Liberal politician Sir William Harcourt proclaimed in 1892, 'We are all socialists now', so it might be appropriate to proclaim as the theme of this book, 'We are all political sociologists now'.

PART II

THE STATE, POWER AND AUTHORITY

INTRODUCTION

We live in a world of states: with the exception of parts of Antarctica, there is no part of the world which is not claimed by, territorially part of, or subject to the domination of a sovereign state. In 1991 the United Nations had 159 member states, all claiming an exclusive right of control or sovereignty over defined territories and, commonly and where appropriate, over areas of sea and the ocean floor. Some states belong to larger, international organisations to whom implicitly or explicitly they have surrendered some of their sovereign powers and therefore accept a higher authority on some matters. Indeed, the UN itself was intended and aspires to be such a supra-national body, notably in seeking to maintain peace or settle conflicts between member states, but also through its various agencies, such as the World Health Organisation, the Food and Agricultural Organisation, the UN Educational and Scientific Organisation, and the World Bank. Military alliances also limit sovereignty and impose obligations on their members – NATO and the former Warsaw Pact being obvious examples, but one of the most important examples of supra-national organisation is the European Community (EC), which has developed detailed policies on a wide range of matters to which member states are expected and usually do conform. Organisations like the EC present problems to the traditional definition of the state, of which much the best known is Weber's (1948, p. 78): 'a human community that successfully claims the monopoly of the legitimate use of physical force within a given territory.'

In the modern world the state is a major and crucial part of the political structures of society. A few societies, which in the past anthropologists would have described as 'stateless', still exist in remote parts of the world, such as New Guinea and the Amazonian rain forest, but they are at least nominally within the confines of a modern state. There also exist some religious groups which can be described as societies in their own right, because they are sufficiently remote from the wider society that surrounds them and little touched by the state. But most modern societies are closely associated with a particular state, and therefore to understand politics in most societies means examining the role of the state.

By arguing that force and its legitimate use constitute crucial characteristics of the state Weber points to the need to consider three other, related concepts – power, authority and legitimacy. For the moment power may be defined as the ability to impose one's will. For many social scientists the exercise of power is the distinguishing characteristic of political activity and power is seen as the key concept in the study of politics. In fact, Weber (1948, p. 78) defined politics as: 'striving to share power or striving to influence the distribution of power, either among states or among groups within a state.'

As Weber points out, power may be exercised between or within states. Political sociology, however, is primarily concerned with the exercise and distribution of power within the context of the state, although the ability of one state to exert power or influence over another may be a significant variable in the exercise of power within a particular state.

Ultimately, power must be discussed in relation to claims by individuals or groups of individuals to a right to exercise power – a claim to authority, the right to be obeyed. Whether such authority is accepted and on what grounds are yet further key questions. Authority may be recognised in the sense that those claiming it are obeyed, but such authority may or may not be recognised as legitimate, namely, that the claim to be obeyed is accepted as a rightful one by those to whom it applies. It is therefore important to examine other reasons why people obey those in authority, and to seek explanations for political and social compliance in society.

Who exercises power in society is a matter which has probably received more attention than any other in political science, both empirically and normatively. Empirically, arguments tend to centre

around whether power is concentrated in the hands of a small gro
– an elite – or whether it is dispersed among many, as pluralis
theory argues. Normatively, arguments about the authoritarian, totalitarian, and democratic distribution of power have received most attention. The distribution of power is not a simple matter, however, even though there are many occasions when the exercise of power is starkly, even brutally evident. The modern state is normally a powerful actor in the equation, but it is neither a neutral actor nor an all-powerful one. It is in Held's words (1984, p. 354), 'deeply embedded in socio-economic relations' and is subject to significant constraints, some internal (the administrative structure, economic factors, and competing interests), some external (both political and economic). Part II therefore examines the origins and development of the state in its societal context, the related concepts of power, authority and legitimacy, and the distribution of power in the modern state.

Chapter 2

THE STATE AND SOCIETY

INTRODUCTION

For Weber the modern state was characterised by much more than power and its legitimate use: it was also distinctive in having an administrative organisation through which it maintained its day-to-day existence, leading Weber (1947) to offer a somewhat more elaborate definition of the state: 'A compulsory political association with continuous organisation will be called a "state" so long as it and insofar as its administrative staff successfully claim the monopoly of physical force in the enforcement of its orders.' This definition also makes it clear that for most individuals belonging to a particular state is not a matter of choice but of accident; only those who move, usually voluntarily, from one state to another are able to exercise any real choice. It may well be that most individuals accept their membership of a particular state with little or no question, but this in no way derogates the compulsory nature of the state, since it is in the name of the state that individuals are taxed, laws passed, and policies determined and implemented.

The emphasis that Weber (and others seeking to define the state) laid on a monopoly of the *legitimate* use of physical force clearly links the concept of the state with the concept of legitimacy. How far individuals subject to the domination (to use Weber's term) of the state actually accept that domination as legitimate is a matter for empirical analysis, but for non-Marxists the state is inextricably linked with legitimacy for its existence and its survival. Thus the collapse of the regimes in Eastern Europe in 1989 is inevitably interpreted as evidence of a loss of legitimacy, not merely for those holding office but for the communist states they represented. That these regimes lacked legitimacy at the time of their collapse can hardly be doubted, but it is pertinent to ask to what extent they enjoyed legitimacy in the forty or so years of their existence. In the eyes of some of their citizens, perhaps a significant number, they may have been seen as legitimate, but it is a considerable assumption that quiescence denotes legitimacy.

Thus the acceptance of the state may rest on factors other than legitimacy, and ultimately on the individual's unwillingness to accept the consequences of not obeying the law and of defying the policies promulgated and implemented by the state. These consequences may well be fear of imprisonment, even torture or death, but also of less – a loss of employment, a decline in living standards, some form of discrimination or social stigma – but acceptance may also stem from apathy – a sheer lack of interest – or from cynicism – a feeling that resistance is useless or not worth the effort. On the other hand, the perceived material advantages of the state to the individual may also form the basis for its acceptance, so that its advantages appear to outweigh its disadvantages. Acceptance of the state may therefore be less a matter of legitimacy and more a matter of grudging acquiescence or material advantage. A major factor in the events in Eastern Europe in 1989 was, with the important exception of Romania, the ultimate unwillingness of the regimes to use force to maintain themselves in power, backed crucially by the knowledge that the Soviet Union had made it clear it would not itself use force to maintain communist rule in its satellite states, as it had done in Hungary in 1956 and Czechoslovakia in 1968. The ability of the state to maintain its existence is a crucial question for political sociology, but whether it should be explained wholly in terms of legitimacy is a different matter. It would seem more sensible to suggest that legitimacy is one explanation for the persistence of the state, but not an exclusive one, a question which is explored further in Chapter 3.

Bodies like the EC may appear to challenge the traditional definition of the state in that they possess many of the attributes of the state – 'a human community' within clear territorial boundaries, with a political and bureaucratic apparatus which determines particular policies and sees to their implementation – but they lack a monopoly of the legitimate use of physical force. Indeed, the EC possesses no coercive forces of its own, relying on the political will of its members and, occasionally, the judicial authority of the European Court of Justice to enforce its policies within the Community. However, the EC and other similar organisations differ in another crucial aspect from the state: it is a voluntary association, whereas the state, as Weber points out, is a compulsory association. Some states were in origin voluntary associations, resulting from a willing and desired coming together of individuals and territories, or a desire to break away from an existing state, or the consequence of a struggle for independence from a dominant power. The United States and Canada are clear examples of states which are the product of a willing union of a number of smaller political entities; the Republic of Ireland and Bangladesh are illustrations of successful breakaways from existing states, from the United Kingdom and Pakistan respectively; and the many former colonies of the European powers, especially Britain and France, are clear cases of states resulting from demands and, more often than not, struggles for independence. But once established such states become compulsory associations in Weber's sense of the term.

The Marxist view of the state (and therefore of power, authority and legitimacy) differs significantly from that of Weber and other non-Marxists. Marxists do not deny the territorial nature of the modern state, but they view its *role* very differently. For some non-Marxists the state is the necessary but politically neutral apparatus through which a society maintains order, settles internal conflicts, and achieves its economic and social goals. Marxist theory, however, assigns to the state the crucial role of representing and operating in the interests of the dominant class in a society. In the words of Engels (1990 [1884] vol. 26, p. 271) the state is the instrument by which 'the most powerful, economically dominant class . . . becomes also the politically dominant class, and thus acquires new means of keeping down and exploiting the oppressed class.' Similarly, and with brutal directness, Lenin defined the state as 'a special force for the suppression of a particular class' (1960 [1917], p. 52). Thus, far from being neutral, the state is the product of historical class struggles; its legitimacy and authority are irrelevant and exist only in the minds of the ruling class and the false consciousness of those unaware of its true nature. Moreover, according to Marxist theory the state will eventually 'wither away' or cease to exist, since the classless society characteristic of communist society will, by definition, not produce a state.

However, whether conceived of in Marxist or non-Marxist terms the state is of central concern to political sociology. Its origins and development need to be explored and the place of the state in the modern world understood.

THE ORIGINS OF THE STATE

Modern states are characterised by clearly defined geographical boundaries within which a widely acknowledged political and administrative apparatus operates exclusively and is ultimately able to enforce its authority through the use of physical coercion. The fact that territorial or boundary disputes between states are not uncommon acknowledges the principle of clearly defined boundaries. Furthermore, modern states are largely characterised by contiguity of territory, including offshore islands. Cases such as Alaska being part of the United States are exceptions to the general rule, but historically the relationship between territory and political and administrative apparatus is less clear in pre-modern states. Indeed, many primitive societies are described as 'stateless' in that they have an ill-defined territory and lack a clearly defined political and administrative apparatus. The empires of the ancient world had much of their territory clearly defined, although its extent varied considerably and at the peripheries of imperial rule the boundaries were anything but clearly defined. However, with their elaborate political and administrative structures the Mesopotamian, Egyptian, Greek, and Roman Empires had much in common with modern states. The same was true of the ancient civilisations of the Chinese, the Hindus, the Maya, the Aztecs, and the Incas. These were all recognisably states in the Weberian sense.

Feudal societies present a more complex picture, however: they normally had clearly defined territories, but these were often scattered over a wide area in piecemeal fashion and lacked clearly defined political and administrative institutions applicable to all the territories concerned. Thus a feudal lord might control various territories, but owe allegiance to different feudal overlords for each. Norman and later kings of England, for instance, were vassals in respect of Normandy of the king of France and therefore owed allegiance to and had feudal obligations to the latter as far as

Normandy was concerned. In fact, maps showing the territorial divisions of early medieval Europe are a complex and seemingly haphazard patchwork reflecting the results of inheritance, inter-marriage and conquest characteristic of the time.

The great colonial empires that developed out of feudal Europe and the two great European empires of Austria-Hungary and Russia were all recognisably states, even though their boundaries were sometimes uncertain (especially beyond Europe) and their authority not always recognised or enforced. The relationship between the component parts of these empires differed, with varying degrees of autonomy and varying political and administrative structures. They lacked the extensive bureaucracies which Weber associated with the modern state, but appropriate if limited political and administrative structures existed.

Of the existence of these early states there is no doubt – apart from the broader historical record, many of them maintained elaborate records of their procedures and activities. What is less clear is how they came into existence and how, eventually, the modern state emerged. A good deal of research has addressed the first of these two questions and even more the second.

The concept of politics used by political anthropologists has a remarkably modern ring to it. Radcliffe-Brown (1940, pp. xiv and xxiii) argued that politics was concerned with 'the maintenance or establishment of social order' and 'the control and regulation of the use of force'. The real question is not whether primitive or early societies have politics, but whether they have government in the sense of having political and administrative structures. Lucy Mair, in her book *Primitive Government* (1977, p. 33), summarises the situation succinctly: 'People argue whether primitive societies have government. They also argue whether they have laws. But nobody questions that they have rules of some kind which everyone thinks it right to obey.' Also, there is no doubt that primitive societies had means of settling disputes or conflicts, as studies of the Nuer, with their 'leopard-skin chiefs', and the Dinka, with their 'masters of the fishing spear' illustrate. These were individuals who acted as mediators in and settlers of disputes. In addition, these and other early societies also developed rules about the circumstances in which force could legitimately be used. All these are examples, however, of what Mair calls *minimal politics* – the existence of a recognised means of settling disputes, but no more.

The next stage is that of *minimal government*, in which leadership positions emerge, whether individual or collective, sometimes for particular purposes, such as hunting, fighting, or seeking water, when different leaders emerged for different purposes, but culminating in the emergence of a single leader or group of leaders with more general authority. Territory was generally ill-defined, but extensive and supporting small groups at or about subsistence level. This did not mean that groups were constantly on the brink of starvation so much as existing in a situation which combined survival with sufficiency. To proceed beyond survival and sufficiency, other related developments were necessary.

The first was the production of a surplus to enable such societies to turn their attention to matters other than survival. Some societies lived in relative abundance, but continued to lead a nomadic or semi-nomadic life, moving as often as necessity dictated or, commonly in the case of pastoral societies, seasonally to meet the needs of their herds. The production of a surplus facilitated the second development – what Herbert Spencer called 'specialisation' and Durkheim 'a division of labour', in which different individuals or groups of individuals performed different tasks for the society more or less exclusively. This process was helped by and helped the development of the transition from small family groups to much larger, extended families and to tribes, but the crucial impact of the production of a surplus depended on the development of agricultural societies and settlement. Even before settlement societal organisation in some cases became more complex, with the emergence of lineages and age-sets providing a basis for leadership dependent on factors such as wealth, status, inheritance, and privileges. The division of labour in particular not only produced a greater surplus, since it was a more efficient means of production, but created opportunities for more extensive political activity, including the establishment of control over a particular territory and, in many cases, for territorial expansion. Thus politics and territory, never far apart, became inextricably linked.

Theories of state formation

Much is known about the world's ancient civilisations, not least because of the elaborate and detailed records they developed and maintained. Of their specific origins less is known, partly because in many instances this preceded any form of written records, but more particularly because each developed their own mythical and mystical account of their beginnings. The transformation from primitive society through pastoralism and agricultural settlement to nascent states is not easily traced, nor can it necessarily be explained by a single theory of state formation. However, two basic theories of state formation have emerged – conflict theories and integrative theories (see Service 1975; Claessen and Skalnik 1978; and Cohen and Service 1978).

Conflict theory, as the term suggests, argues that states developed as a consequence of clashes between individuals or groups of individuals or between societies. Cutting across the various conflict theories is the argument that the conflicts that gave rise to states were about the exercise of power. For example, drawing on anthropological studies some observers have argued that the transformation from stateless societies to states was initially the result of power struggles between kinship groups in settled societies, leading to a concentration of power in the hands of a particular group who then consolidated their position by setting up political and administrative structures. Not far removed is the Marxist explanation that the state is the product of an historical class struggle arising out of the prevailing means of production. Both focus on power and on intra-societal conflicts, but the anthropological argument sees power as the objective of the struggle, whereas the Marxist argument sees power as the means of the struggle. That conflicts between kinship groups have occurred, leading to the domination of one over others, is not difficult to establish. Similarly, control of the means of production is a credible basis for the possession and the exercise of power. In neither case, however, is it readily apparent that one or the other is the sole explanation of or the principal factor in explaining the development of the state.

A second type of intra-societal conflict focuses on individual conflicts. One of the oldest is contract theory: the state, it is asserted, is the product of the individual's need for protection from the inevitable conflicts found in society, a view held by both Hobbes and Locke and historically manifested most clearly in the development of feudalism, which regularised into an elaborate contractual relationship the rights and obligations between lord and vassal, resting ultimately on protection in return for agreed services. Magna Carta, for example, is essentially a feudal document reasserting in considerable detail mutual rights and obligations, in spite of its justifiably greater historical fame as a foundation of English liberties. Another major type of individual conflict theory focuses on social Darwinism, in which the strongest individuals in society would eventually prevail and form a state to strengthen and maintain their dominance. The problem with both types of individual conflict theory is that they are plausible, but not easily tested. Except for feudalism, for which there is a good deal of supporting evidence, much is assumed and little direct evidence can be brought to bear. Even in the case of feudalism, where much is known about the contractual relationships involved, the evidence is causally extrapolated into the past. No one doubts that individual conflicts existed, as they continue to exist, nor that the 'fittest' or more powerful emerged as the dominant group, but the links with state formation are far more difficult to establish.

Inter-societal conflicts appear to offer more sustainable explanation of state formation. Simple conquest is the most obvious, but Darwinian selection again emerges as an alternative and offers a more flexible approach by encompassing conquest, but adding to it the possibility of other strengths or weaknesses – economic, leadership, ideological and geographical. However, the same sort of problems arise: one state may have replaced or subjugated another by one such means or a combination of them, but pushing back causal factors to origins is a difficult process.

Perhaps the most obvious limitation of conflict theory is the apparent unwillingness to acknowledge any cause other than conflict, so that however much co-operation and agreement may be involved in the development of the state, its origin rests solely on conflict. Integrative theories of state formation offer a different perspective, without necessarily excluding conflict as a factor. They tend to fall into two types: integration resulting from the circumscription of society and integration bringing organisational benefits. Circumscription theory argues that a society which cannot shed its surplus population through emigration because of geographical barriers such as mountains, seas and deserts, will seek to organise itself more effectively in the form of a state. Conflict may well play a part, either internally because of the pressures that the inability to expand have created, or externally from rival societies or nomadic marauders. Similarly, the benefits that may accrue from greater organisation may also, it is argued, lead to the establishment of a state. For instance, the expansion of trade, both internally and externally, is likely to be of benefit not only to those directly involved but much more widely in a society, increasing the overall wealth available and extending the benefits of that wealth. Alternatively, benefits may accrue to particular strata or groups in society, giving them an incentive to organise more complex political and administrative structures. The building of public works, such as irrigation systems or great monuments, requires considerable organisation and mobilisation of resources normally beyond the scope of a single leader or a small, but loosely organised group, but becomes feasible with more formal and elaborate organisation. The same may be said of developing a society's military capability.

All state formation theories that seek to explain the origin of the state itself as a social and political phenomenon tend to suffer from the same problem when it comes to testing their accuracy – a reliance on largely circumstantial evidence and hindsight. Ancient civilisations, such as those of Egypt and Mesopotamia, which developed sophisticated irrigation systems and built great monuments, clearly developed complex political and administrative structures, but what was the causal relationship between such public works and the development of the state? Was the state created to facilitate public works, or did the building of public works lead to the formation of the state? The latter explanation seems more likely, so that, as irrigation schemes became more elaborate and buildings larger and more complex, the development of appropriate organisational structures became desirable, even necessary. Indeed, it is possible to suggest a degree of parallel development involving an interspersing of cause and effect, in which, for instance, developing an irrigation system demands greater organisation and greater organisation facilitates a more sophisticated irrigation system.

Theories of state formation are difficult to prove or disprove, especially in respect of societies with no written records or of states formed before the development of such records. Evidence often depends on oral history, which is invariably shrouded by mythical beliefs, often of a supernatural type obscuring rather than illuminating such oral history as may exist. Darwinian theories may help to explain the survival of states more than their formation, since they do not explain why a state was established at a particular time. Marxist theory of the class struggle offers a credible explanation of the development of the capitalist state, but in seeking to explain the origins of the state itself it is no less reliant than other theories on little hard evidence and much speculation.

There is, however, far less difficulty in tracing and explaining the formation of later states, from those that developed in medieval Europe, through modern, capitalist states, to those of the Third World. Records are widely available and hypotheses more easily tested. Thus the development of most European states is not difficult to trace and, though specific explanations vary, they are not lacking. Two major factors were conquest and inter-marriage. The English state was expanded into the United Kingdom of Great Britain and Ireland by the conquest of Wales and Ireland and the incorporation of Scotland through the inter-marriage of the English and Scottish royal families, which eventually resulted in a common monarch – James VI of Scotland and the I of England. The latter, however, was not by intent, but was the consequence of the marriage of the Scottish king, James IV and Margaret, daughter of England's Henry VII, and the extinction of the Tudor line with the death of Elizabeth I in 1603. Indeed, James IV died at the Battle of Flodden in 1513, following a Scottish invasion of England, and even after the uniting of the crowns Scottish incorporation was by no means inevitable and was the subject of periodic military conflict. The ability of various rulers to impose their rule by force within their territories or to extend their territory was extremely common in medieval Europe, but so also were territorial consolidation and expansion by inter-marriage, as the well-known Latin couplet makes claim in the case of Austria:

> Bella gerant alii, tu, felix Austria, nube
> Nam quae Mars aliis, dat tibi regna Venus
>
> Let others war, thou, happy Austria, wed;
> What some owe Mars, from Venus take instead.

However, the development of European states and subsequently of a world divided into states is dominated by the twin developments of the modern capitalist state and the nation-state.

THE DEVELOPMENT OF THE MODERN STATE

There are three key strands in the development of the modern state: the development of capitalism, the coming of the industrial revolution, and the development of the nation-state. Together they are responsible for the world of states which characterises modern society. Whether the modern state is the inevitable product of inexorable forces in society, as Marxist theory asserts, is a matter of opinion, but there can be little doubt that the modern state is the product of the twin forces of economics and nationalism.

The development of the capitalist state

Fernand Braudel, in his monumental and comprehensive study *Civilisation and Capitalism* (1981/1985 [1979]), argues that the capitalist economy was preceded by the development of two other economies, the market economy and the monetary economy. A market economy is one based on the widespread and regular exchange, circulation and distribution of goods and a monetary economy is economic activity based on convertible wealth rather than exchange or barter. The development of a monetary economy facilitated the accumulation of wealth from profit, in short the creation of capital. However, Braudel does not argue that the development of market and monetary economies led inevitably to the development of capitalism wherever they developed. In fact, he points out that market and monetary economies developed in various parts of the world, but that capitalism developed ultimately only in Europe – not, however, in states but in towns and cities, described by Braudel as 'outposts of modernity' (1979, vol. I, p. 512). Capitalism could have developed in other world civilisations, but did not; these included the Chinese, Islamic and Indian civilisations, which were developed significantly earlier than European civilisation and which were highly sophisticated.

In his study *Powers and Liberties* (1985) John Hall concluded that each of these civilisations developed what he called 'blocking power' (1985, pp. 22–3), in which different types of power – political, economic and ideological – conflict with each other and militate against or block societal change. China had developed a number of important innovations, especially in agriculture, but never developed market autonomy and therefore a substantial degree of social and political dynamism. No serious external challenges had confronted China before significant European penetration occurred in the nineteenth century. Its political system was feeble and lacked impetus. Hall described China as a 'capstone state' (1985, p. 51) in which, in Braudel's words, 'the bureaucracy lay across the top of Chinese society as a single, virtually unbreakable stratum; any damage was spontaneously repaired' (1979, vol. II, p. 595).

Islamic and Indian societies presented a similar picture. Islam provided society with the powerful unifying force of religion and universal law, but with the important exception of the Ottoman Empire, only weak states developed. Even the Ottoman Empire was only a partial exception, since its economic growth was based on territorial expansion and when that expansion ceased so did economic growth. Moreover, cities in Islamic societies did not develop the economic autonomy characteristic of many of those in Europe and there was a lack of continuity amongst the upper strata in society, which also hindered economic development. Hinduism in India created rigid social stratification. In contrast to Islam, however, the Hindu religion organised social but not political life, which lacked organisation and direction, and was further undermined by the failure to develop a ruling dynasty.

By comparison, in Western Europe autonomous political units which competed with each other developed, notably but not exclusively in towns and cities. The political strength of these units rested on their development of market autonomy and, crucially, they were never fully under the control of the state.

Braudel argues that three developments were necessary for the growth of capitalism: first, the survival of dynasties and families to allow the accumulation of wealth through inheritance and marriage; second, stratified society with sufficient social mobility to allow for the regeneration of the existing upper strata and the encouragement of the lower strata in society; and third, the development of world trade to raise profit levels. However, as Braudel points out (1979, vol. II, p. 533), 'until the nineteenth century the rest of the world outweighed Europe both in population and, while the economic *ancien regime* lasted, in wealth . . . it is virtually beyond question that Europe was less rich that the world it was exploiting.' What made the vital difference was that capital accumulation was the key to bringing about the industrial revolution.

The industrial revolution

The industrial revolution depended on the coming together of a range of requisites in addition to capital – resources, manpower, food, entrepreneurs, markets, and ideological support. Capital alone was not enough, but it was the key factor. It was needed in particular to exploit the resources – the raw materials and energy – without which industrial development could not take place. And it was needed also to support a workforce paid in cash, not kind; to invest in food production to feed and maintain that workforce; and to develop and maintain an infrastructure of transport and communications, and of educational and, more gradually, welfare systems. Entrepreneurs also played a vital role: the ability to recognise the possibilities of industrial development, to organise the resources and manpower, and, perhaps above all, to risk the necessary capital, was crucial. Similarly, the prevailing ideology and the political structures needed to be supportive by being open to innovation and change, at best encouraging, at worst not obstructive. Last and by no means least, markets needed to be developed and expanded, both at home and overseas.

All these requisites were present in Europe, most markedly and effectively in Britain. The shift from a subsistence and barter economy to a cash economy, opening up the way to a market economy occurred more extensively in Europe than elsewhere, especially in the wealthy cities of Italy, such as Venice and Florence, in the towns of the Hanseatic League, and various cities and ports in England. Capitalist economies could have and did develop in various parts of Europe, but England (later Britain) advanced more rapidly towards such an economy because it held a number of advantages.

The breakdown of feudalism, particularly as a form of land tenure, occurred earlier, bringing in its train enclosure – the break-up of the old open-field system and the consolidation of much larger agricultural units, new methods of cultivation and crop rotation, and the use of fertilisers; in short, what became known as the agricultural revolution. Increased crop yields facilitated population growth, but new agricultural methods were less labour intensive, creating a surplus population to provide manpower for labour-intensive industry. England and Scotland were well endowed with appropriate natural resources, such as iron ore, wool, and clay, whilst cotton was readily available from overseas. Coal and water provided the energy and were also in abundant and easily exploited supply. The development of a market economy in the towns and of England as a major trading nation provided both capital and markets, domestic and overseas.

The break-up of feudal society in England did not isolate the aristocracy, as in a number of other European countries, especially France, but led to its partial integration with the rest of society under the impact of primogeniture, its depletion through civil war during the Wars of the Roses, and a willingness on the part of monarchs to regenerate its ranks from lower strata in society. The result was a marked degree of social mobility, downwards as well as upwards. Merchants and traders were not exclusively drawn from the lower ranks of society and an innovative and enterprising middle class or bourgeoisie emerged, providing the entrepreneurial impertus necessary for the industrial revolution. The early stages of that revolution were accompanied by the building of canals, roads and railways, the telegraph, and, in due course, the development of education – the underpinning infrastructure of economic development.

England also possessed the considerable advantage of early unification and the establishment of effective political structures, while many of its rivals struggled to achieve this or were more seriously damaged by conflicts in Europe and elsewhere. England was not infrequently embroiled in Europe but, earlier than its rivals, shed its *territorial* commitments on the European mainland, confining itself to overseas conflicts, which were often ultimately profitable, and military activity in Europe itself.

In England the conflict between church and state was basically resolved in favour of the latter by the Reformation and, although religious conflict continued for more than a century, the state was never subordinated to religion and the established church was the church of the state. Though the English state in turn struggled for survival against the absolutist ambitions of Charles I and James II, it survived to provide a political framework within which individualism and enterprise could flourish, thus giving ideological underpinning to industrialisation.

England was undoubtedly well placed to nurture the industrial revolution, both materially and ideologically, not least as a naval and trading power based on a unified state, and well served by the accidents of history and, perhaps even more, of geography. However, what was true for England was only to a lesser extent true for many other parts of Europe and for the newly established United States, which at various intervals and varying pace followed suit. Those parts which did not, most obviously the earliest beneficiaries of European colonialism – Spain and Portugal – languished economically, while the development of others, such as Italy and Germany, was delayed. For England, the industrial revolution was a relatively prolonged process, beginning with the age of discovery in the fifteenth century and the Reformation; for other European states it was somewhat shorter, but nevertheless spread over a number of generations. Furthermore, not all the changes occurred simultaneously and, without necessarily suggesting a causal chain of events, there was time for societal adjustment and adaptation. Even so, much of that adjustment and adaptation was socially painful and achieved at considerable human cost.

What was possible in Europe over several hundred years could not automatically be transferred to other societies at other times, for the simple reason that the industrial revolution in Europe and the United States transformed the world politically and, above all, economically. Europe, and more particularly the major European powers, came to dominate much of the world, initially through colonialism, while the western hemisphere came largely to be dominated by the United States. It remains a matter of argument whether, if left to themselves, the societies of what is commonly now called the Third World would have developed on capitalist lines; what is undisputed is that they have not done so. Marx paid only limited attention to the Third World, but later Marxists developed theories of imperialism and dependency to explain the relationship between it and capitalist societies. These theories will be discussed at greater length in Chapter 12. For the moment it is sufficient to argue that it is a considerable assumption that the European model of industrialisation is available, let alone applicable, to other societies, whether historically or contemporaneously. The development of capitalism in Europe eventually transformed the world, but it also led to the development of other models of industrialisation. These too will be discussed in Chapter 12. But European capitalism was accompanied by another force, *nationalism*, which led to the emergence of the nation-state.

The rise of the nation-state

If one of Europe's major legacies to the world is capitalism, its other is the nation-state. Nationalism as a modern social and political force is not, of course, peculiar to Europe, but historically its origins lie in Europe. Certainly, in the later medieval period England and

France could be described as nations in the sense that the overwhelming majority of their populations belonged to common ethnic, linguistic and cultural groups. How far it is accurate to translate this commonality into a sense of community or national identity is a different matter, but appeals to patriotism were not unknown. Even so, most of the states in post-medieval Europe were not nations, even in the sense of commonality, let alone in the sense of sharing a national identity. The great conglomerate empires of the Spanish and Austrian Habsburgs, Russia and Turkey occupied vast territories, while Germany and Italy consisted of a multiplicity of states. The four Scandinavian states of Denmark, Norway, Sweden and Finland have for most of their history been united with one or other of their neighbours and, after securing independence from Spain, modern Belgium and Holland were united until the earlier part of the nineteenth century.

As a social and political force nationalism became increasingly important from the end of the eighteenth century onwards. The internationalism of the French Revolution was fairly rapidly transformed into nationalism when revolutionary France sought to export its radical ideas, but it was the hundred years from 1815 to 1919 that was to be the century of European nationalism. In that period the map of Europe was redrawn by the break-up of the old empires, culminating in the Bolshevik Revolution in Russia in October 1917, the defeat of Germany and Austria-Hungary in the First World War in 1918, and the Treaty of Versailles in 1919. Long before Versailles, however, various parts of the Turkish Empire in Europe had successfully broken away – Greece early in the nineteenth century, Romania, Serbia, Montenegro, and Bulgaria somewhat later, while Belgium separated from Holland in 1830 and soon after the turn of the century, in 1905, Norway separated from Sweden.

Meanwhile, abortive nationalistic revolutions had occurred in Poland in 1830 and throughout Europe in 1848, 'the year of revolutions'. The setting up of the Dual Monarchy of Austria-Hungary in 1848 was an open acknowledgement of Austrian and Hungarian nationalism, particularly the latter, but was accompanied by a continuing refusal of Austria and Hungary to recognise the aspirations of the many other nationalities under their control. However, the most significant examples of European nationalism in the nineteenth century were the unifications of Italy and Germany, powerfully manifesting the idea that the most appropriate basis for the state is the nation as defined ethnically, linguistically, culturally, and historically. This idea achieved its apotheosis in the Treaty of Versailles, with its enormous emphasis on the principle of national self-determination.

It was as a consequence of the chaos in Europe following the end of the First World War and the Versailles settlement that many of the states now a familiar part of Europe were created or, in cases like Poland and Finland, recreated. Drawing boundaries was a nightmare, since some ethnic minorities were invariably left the 'wrong' side of any border and the compromise states of Czechoslovakia and Yugoslavia were set up. A Yugoslav historian, Matja Duric, has described Yugoslavia as 'an ungovernable stew of two alphabets, three religions, four languages, five nationalities, and six constituent republics'. There is ample evidence that a strong sense of national identity played an important, even crucial part in the establishment of many of the states of modern Europe, in that resentment against alien rule was very strong and the political rhetoric used by those who led movements for self-determination and independence in various parts of Europe was frequently couched in nationalistic terms; but the extent to which nationalism was the ideology of the elite, on the one hand, and a grass-roots ideology, on the other, is less clear. As it is, nationalism can be seen as a unifying force in the face of a state's neighbours, providing an external identity without necessarily providing a majority of the population with an identity within the state.

Nationalism was a force which Marx and Engels acknowledged but largely underestimated. Engels, however, did argue that in cases like Poland freedom from alien rule must precede a proletarian revolution. Other Marxists acknowledged the claims of different nationalities to cultural self-determination or expression and, in a pamphlet published in 1913, Stalin defined a nation in recognisably nineteenth-century terms, in that while denying that nationality was a racial phenomenon, he argued that a nation was characterised by 'a stable, continuing community, a common language, distinct territory, economic cohesion, and a collective character' (Bottomore *et al.* 1983, p. 344). Ultimately, Marx and his successors expected that working-class consciousness would be a more powerful force than nationalism, so that on the outbreak of the First World War many socialists, Marxists and non-Marxists alike, expected the working classes of the belligerent states to reject bourgeois patriotism in favour of proletarian solidarity; but for the most part socialist leaders were as solid in their support of the war as non-socialists. In this respect attitudes towards the First World War could be seen as strong evidence of widespread nationalism in Europe.

The essentially European concept of the nation-state thus became the model for the modern state and where a national identity did not exist it became necessary to create one. This was done nowhere more successfully than in the United States, which became what Seymour Martin Lipset (1964) called 'the first new nation'. Although the populations of the colonies which formed the first thirteen members of the United States of America were of largely common ethnic stock and had English as a common language, they were by no means united in other respects, not least in terms of religion. Historians have suggested that during the American War of Independence one-third of the colonists supported the break with Britain, one-third opposed it and the remaining third waited to see what happened. Much bitterness resulted, not a little persecution of those who had chosen the 'wrong' side ensued, and a substantial number of colonists resettled in Canada, which remained under British rule. The task of creating and sustaining a new identity was helped by the fact that independence had been won by force of arms and that the victorious colonists had brought about a 'revolution', but there followed nearly a decade of a looser, confederal association before the present federal system was adopted in 1789. Continued recognition of the states as separate entities was an important part of the American identity, and that identity was firmly established before the great waves of European immigration occurred in the nineteenth and early twentieth centuries.

The immigrants were therefore confronted with an established national identity and, coming as many of them did from circumstances of economic deprivation and, not infrequently, persecution, they tended to be receptive to adopting a new national identity as Americans. Culturally, and to a degree linguistically, the immigrants were allowed to retain their previous identities, but the United States was aptly described as a melting pot in which the newcomers were expected to become first and foremost Americans.

The pattern set by the United States was, in essence, that which the 'new nations' of the post-colonial era sought to follow. The contrast between the 'old nationalism' of Europe and the 'new nationalism' of what is now known as the Third World was aptly summarised when 'old nationalism' was defined as 'nations seeking boundaries' and 'new nationalism' as 'boundaries seeking nations'. The boundaries of many newly independent states after 1945 were arbitrary, reflecting the ability of the colonial powers to impose their will on indigenous peoples and on each other, since the fate of particular peoples and territories often depended on events far from their location. Consequently, many of the new states lacked a common culture, language and history and were divided rather than united by ethnicity. They therefore embarked on what has been called the *nation-building* process, seeking to establish a sense of national identity where it was previously weak or non-existent (see Deutsch and Foltz 1963; Bendix 1964; and Eisenstadt and Rokkan 1973).

Wherever possible a common language was adopted, a common 'history' and 'culture' developed, and a unifying ideology embraced. A common language often meant that of the 'colonial oppressor', but in some cases alternatives were available, such as Arabic in North Africa and the Middle East, while in the case of Indonesia the nationalist leadership deliberately rejected Dutch and adopted Indonesian Bihasa, a Malay-based language. Many new states looked for roots in their pre-colonial past, claiming links with ancient cultures and civilisations untainted by the colonial experience. This was sometimes reflected in the choice of names for new states – Zimbabwe for Rhodesia and Ghana for the Gold Coast, for example. Others later adopted new, indigenous names – Zaïre for the Congo, Burkina Faso for Upper Volta, Mynamar for Burma. Many also sought unity through ideology, such as Marxism or socialism, not infrequently seeking to give it an indigenous or domestic flavour – African socialism in Tanzania, Arab socialism in Nasser's Egypt, for instance, or emphasising village democracy in India – the Hindu *panchyat*, or 'guided democracy' in Indonesia – drawing on the concepts of *musyawarah* (deliberation) and *mufakat* (consensus). The most powerful ideology, however, was usually nationalism itself: the claim to be a nation and to identify the interests of the state with those of the nation.

Language, culture, history, and ideology were, and in many cases remain, the symbols of national identity, along with a national flag and national anthem. A key role in the nation-building process is invariably played by political leaders who claim to represent the 'nation' and who, in many instances, led the 'nation' in its struggle for independence from colonial rule. In some cases that struggle involved prolonged and bitter conflict in which the colonial power was defeated, or at least pressured into conceding independence. Thus the French were decisively defeated in Indo-China in 1954, the position of the Belgians in the Congo by 1960 and the Portuguese in Angola and Mozambique by 1974 rendered militarily untenable, while armed opposition and violence played a significant role in British decisions to grant independence to, for example, the Gold Coast (Ghana) in 1957, Cyprus in 1960, and to withdraw from Aden in 1965. In the event, often the reality was less important than the ability of national leaders to develop and sustain a widespread belief that victory over the colonial power had been achieved, independence won – not granted, and the new nation's 'revolution' proclaimed. The myth and reality of achieving independence became powerful symbols in the 'new nationalism'.

Nation-building also involves other means: the socialisation of the population through education and the media; the need to defend the nation against external threat, real or imagined; the use of war as a unifying force; membership of regional organisations, such as the Arab League or the Organisation of African Unity (OAU), or generic associations, such as non-aligned states, and the Organisation of Petroleum Exporting Countries (OPEC); but above all in policies of economic development. Few new states adopted policies of economic isolation in order to preserve traditional ways of life; most embarked on programmes of industrialisation and agricultural modernisation, claiming that independence would bring material benefits denied by colonial rule. Success in these areas, particularly economic development, has varied considerably, and some theorists, notably neo-Marxist and dependency theorists, have argued that the Third World has been incorporated into a world capitalist system. These views will be explored further in Chapter 12. What it is important to acknowledge is that not only has the Third World been inexorably drawn into the world of states, but also the model of nation-state has been universally adopted or imposed.

THE MARXIST CONCEPT OF THE STATE

It was noted earlier that the Marxist concept of the state is distinctive in that the state is defined as the product of the historical struggle between classes and as an institutional superstructure resting on the economic base. It can therefore only operate in the interests of the dominant class. Once the class struggle has been resolved, following the proletarian revolution and the emergence of a classless society, the state will wither away. Neo-Marxists such us Gramsci (1971 [1929–35]) and Althusser (1972 and 1977 [1965]) explained the persistence of the state in capitalist societies through its ability to elicit consent from members of society, as well as the incipient threat of force. Gramsci argued that the bourgeoisie helps to maintain its dominance by making concessions to the working class, by accepting compromises which do not fundamentally undermine its position and therefore that of the state. Althusser stresses the importance of ideology and the ability of the bourgeois state to secure the acceptance of its values through what he terms 'ideological state apparatuses', such as the education system, the church, and trade unions, as distinct from repressive state apparatuses, such as the armed forces and the police.

Miliband (1969) draws a distinction between the government and the state, arguing that the government is the most visible, but not necessarily the most important, part of the state. The state also includes the bureaucracy, the police, the judiciary, regional and local authorities, various economic institutions (such as banks and public corporations), and national, local and regional representative institutions – a view with which many non-Marxists would concur. But Miliband goes on to suggest that the state has a significant degree of autonomy which helps it operate in the interests of the dominant class because it appears neutral and then, following Gramsci, argues that it is able to make concessions to subordinate classes which help preserve the position of the dominant class. However, ultimately the persistence of the state rests not on its repressive capacities, nor on its institutional pervasiveness, but on the fact that the dominant class is drawn from those with similar socio-economic characteristics and therefore similar economic and social values. Poulantzas (1969 and 1973), on the other hand, regards the socio-economic characteristics of the dominant class as irrelevant and, while agreeing with Miliband that the state develops a degree of autonomy, argues that this is so because the structures of the system reflect the extent to which the institutions of the state are embedded in society.

Once in power, however, the state presents a problem to Marxists. Lenin was quite clear in stating that the state would wither away immediately after the proletarian revolution and be replaced by the dictatorship of the proletariat. In practice, after the October Revolution the dictatorship of the proletariat, if it ever existed, rapidly gave way to the dictatorship of the Party. Once the civil war had been won the Soviet Union certainly possessed all the characteristics of a state defined in non-Marxist terms – a clearly defined territory, a monopoly of the legitimate use of force, and an administrative apparatus to implement the policies of the state. Indeed, in 1921 Lenin himself described the Soviet Union as 'a worker state with bureaucratic distortions' (McLellan 1979, p. 101). This was taken much further by Stalin, who argued that the USSR was 'a state of a new type' (Bottomore *et al.* 1983, p. 468) representing the whole people, and although a later Soviet leader, Khrushchev, predicted the withering away of the state, it patently did not occur.

What has happened is that the communist states of Eastern Europe and the Soviet Union have not withered away but collapsed. Economic pressures in the USSR initiated a process in which the role of the state changed, but did not disappear in the Marxist sense. In the Soviet Union Mikhail Gorbachev's policy of *perestroika* resulted first in the Communist Party losing its 'leading role' in society and therefore in the operation of the state, and then in its collapse following an unsuccessful coup. The outcome was not a 'withering away' of the state, but the creation of a multiplicity of new states.

Marxist critics of the Soviet Union have described Soviet-style states as 'deformed workers' states' and those like the Yugoslav dissident, Milovan Djilas, have asserted that communist states became dominated by a 'new class' of party *apparatchiks* and bureaucrats, who gave themselves privileged status and better material conditions than those they ostensibly served. None the less, the concept of the state leaves Marxists with a problem, not of explaining its role and nature *prior* to a proletarian revolution, but after. It is not sufficient to explain away the state by terms like 'dictatorship of the proletariat', 'dictatorship of the Party', 'state of the whole people', or 'the administration of things'; complex modern societies require administrative structures and, whether or not these constitute a state, it remains open to question whether they, any more than the state, can be neutral.

It is, perhaps, the argument that the state is not neutral that is the most important contribution of Marxism to the debate on the role and nature of the state. Social and political institutions do not operate in a vacuum; they themselves reflect particular values, but they can also be put to different purposes by different groups who from time to time control them.

CONCLUSION

The state provides the basic linkage between politics and society in virtually all polities in the modern world. The development of the state in Europe provided the role model for the development of the state throughout the world, not always, of course, in the capitalist form, or in the pure form of the nation-state, but the concept of a higher authority than those currently exercising power and of the exercise of that power within an established institutional framework is almost universal. The fact that much controversy still surrounds the state and its role, not merely between Marxists and non-Marxists but more widely, is powerful evidence of its importance.

However, the role of the state is more than that of providing an institutional framework; its role is much more extensive and pervasive in some societies than others. It is therefore important to consider variations in and theories about power and its distribution within particular societies, since it is invariably through the state that power is ultimately exercised, and this is the subject of Chapters 3 and 4. Neither the state itself, nor the political and social institutions that constitute a given state, are immutable, and how societies change is dealt with in Part V.

Chapter 3

POWER, AUTHORITY AND LEGITIMACY

DEFINING AND ANALYSING POWER

Much has been written about power as a concept, but there is no generally agreed definition and it remains a subject of much dispute. Media usage of the term is common: phrases like 'winning power', 'seizing power', and 'power struggle' abound. Historians frequently refer to the 'great powers' and the 'balance of power'; political analysts and others describe the United States (and formerly the Soviet Union) as 'superpowers'. All the usages fit a simple dictionary definition of power as 'an ability to do or act' in the sense that possession of power enables individuals or groups of individuals to carry out their will. 'Winning power', 'seizing power', and 'power struggle' clearly relate to acquiring the ability to act; 'great powers' or states ostensibly have a greater ability to act than lesser powers or states; a 'balance of power' implies that the ability of one state or group of states is matched by that of another state or group of states; and presumably the 'superpowers' have a much superior ability to act compared with other powers or states. Yet merely to examine the media usage in relation to what seems a concise definition of power illustrates the difficulty of conceptualising it.

'Power', argued Bertrand Russell (1938, p. 35), 'is the production of intended effects.' In the context of 'balance of power', 'great powers' and 'superpowers' Russell's definition is easily illustrated and understood. Not only has much modern history been viewed as one of alliances between different states, often involving the notion of a balance of power, but ultimately power has invariably been measured in terms of military capacity. Military force has frequently been used, and continues to be used, to produce intended effects, not merely in the military sense but also to achieve wider objectives. Bismarck's almost clinical use of military force to bring about German unification and create the German Empire under the leadership of Prussia is a vivid case in point.

The key to Russell's definition is the phrase 'intended effects', easily understandable in a military context: the use of military force is usually deliberate and has intended effects, but what of unintended effects, of which there may well be many, even where the original objectives have been achieved? It can, of course, be acknowledged that unintended effects may be important (even more important than intended effects), but that they are incidental to the use of power. Unintended effects are therefore consequential upon the use of power, but because they were not foreseen or were not part of the original objectives, do not amount to the exercise of power. Such a response will not satisfy neo-Marxist critics, especially structuralists, a point that will be taken up later in the chapter. Important as intended effects undoubtedly are, it seems logically perverse to ignore the unintended effects of the exercise of power.

Russell's definition also sees power as a process or an activity rather than as a commodity or resource, so that the question arises whether power exists only when it is used. Of course, it is understandably common to measure military power *before* it is used by counting numbers of troops, guns, missiles, tanks, ships, and aircraft, and by trying to measure its likely effectiveness by assessing quality of leadership, likely strategy and tactics, and relevant non-military resources. Power needs to be seen in terms of its potential as well as its use, and unsuccessful attempts to exercise power are as much part of social and political behaviour as its successful use.

Weber (1947, p. 152), in what is certainly the best-known definition of power, offers a solution to this problem: '"Power" (*Macht*) is the probability that one actor within a social relationship will be in a position to carry out his own will despite resistance, regardless of the basis on which this probability exists.' His use of the word 'probability' is crucial because it allows power to be seen potentially, rather than await its use and, more importantly, in relative rather than absolute terms. This means that while there are circumstances in which power operates in a zero-sum context – one individual's gain is proportionate to another's loss – it operates more often in a variable-sum situation, in which power changes and develops according to circumstances and the distribution of the resources on which its rests. Thus Weber rejects any suggestion that power rests solely on the use or threat of physical force, but that other factors can determine whether the will of one individual or group of individuals prevails over that of another individual or group of individuals.

Much social science theory, whether statistically based or not, is couched in terms of probability and power should not be an exception. It is also helpful to see power as both a resource and a process, since the one inevitably complements the other and also allows for the unsuccessful application of power.

All this leaves many questions about power unanswered and at this point it would seem appropriate to reduce these to three fundamental questions. *Who* exercises power? *How* is it exercised? And *why* is it exercised? Given the lack of an agreed definition of power itself, categorical answers can hardly be expected. Nevertheless a useful exploration can be attempted.

There are three broad answers to the question of *who* exercises powers: the elitist, the Marxist, and the pluralist. The simplest is that of the elite theorists, such as Mosca (1939 [1896]), Pareto (1935 [1916]), and Mills (1956): a socially identifiable, cohesive group within a given society wields power based on conscious self-interest. To a significant extent the elite theorists were offering an alternative explanation to that of Marx and his followers, who identified power as being exercised by the social class which controlled the means of production in society. Historically this class varied, but in a capitalist society it is the bourgeoisie or capital-owning class, who will in due course be superseded by the proletariat or working class once it controls the means of production. The third broad answer is the pluralist response of writers like Dahl (1956, 1961, 1982 and 1985) and Polsby (1963), who argued that neither a particular elite or social class held power, but that it was exercised by competing groups and varied from issue to issue.

These theorists will be examined further in Chapter 4, but they can be subsumed under an even broader question about who exercises power by asking, to what extent is power concentrated or diffused in society? And to what extent does it operate hierarchically? Equally important questions arise in respect of whether those individuals or organisations in a society formally designated as the holders of power – such as kings and emperors, prime ministers and presidents, generals and police chiefs, judges and juries, mayors and magistrates, governments and legislatures, bureaucracies and courts – actually exercise power, or, as is alleged by some theorists, are facades behind which 'real' power is wielded by court favourites, *éminences grises*, vested interests, faceless bureaucrats, party *apparatchiks*, corrupt officials, and the like.

The arguments between elite theorists, Marxists and pluralists and the question of who exercises power depends on *how* it is exercised, that is, the *bases* on which power rests. Power is perhaps most often associated with force, or physical coercion, but it may be based on other resources, notably wealth, status, knowledge, charisma, and authority. In many instances power may rest on more than one of these bases. Power may also take different forms, such as coercion, influence, and control. Coercion includes not only the use or threat of physical force, but also extortion, blackmail, expropriation and confiscation; influence includes not only rational persuasion, respect and deference, but also bribery and corruption; and control involves the acceptance, for whatever reason, that those seeking to exert power have the means to do so.

Conceived as a commodity or resource power becomes a means to an end: *why* is power exercised? To what purposes or ends is power put? Power may be used for individual or collective ends, for political, economic or ideological ends. As noted in Chapter 2, Hall (1985) usefully combines types of power with ends by positing three types of power – political, economic, and ideological – each drawing on particular resources in society. Political power is seen as the capacity of some individuals in society to organise and dominate their fellows, economic power as the capacity to organise and develop resources in society, and ideological power as the capacity to rationalise the organisation of society through belief or value systems. Hall regards military power as part of political power, drawing, as it does, on economic and ideological resources and used primarily for political purposes. Hall's approach does not confine power to the political sphere, arguing that economic and ideological power are not necessarily used exclusively for political purposes, and by doing so he places power, as does Weber, in a broad societal context. Above all, however, power is seen as a motive force in society, used to achieve particular ends, whether selfish or altruistic, material or spiritual, maintaining the status quo or impelling change. This leads Hall to argue that '[w]here ideological, political and economic power move in the same direction, it is extremely likely that great social energy will be created...' resulting in societal change – this he calls 'enabling power' (Hall 1985, pp. 22–3), but where there is conflict between different types of power societal change will not occur, will be less likely or much slower in taking place – this, as already noted, he calls 'blocking power' (1985, pp. 22–3).

There are yet other answers to why power is exercised, many of which relate to more immediate ends, such as acquiring wealth, status, control of people or territory, or extending or imposing spiritual or ideological beliefs, but most of these are historically self-evident and widely documented. Less well explored is the meeting of psychological needs. Lasswell in *Psychopathology and Politics* (1930), Adorno and his colleagues in *The Authoritarian Personality* (1950), and Eysenck in *The Psychology of Politics* (1954) have examined various aspects of the role of personality in politics. As in a number of areas of political behaviour, there is a growing awareness of the significance of psychological factors, but much remains to be explored (see Hermann 1986).

In practice the exercise of power involves costs and benefits, both for those who exercise it and those who are subject to it. These costs and benefits may be individual or collective, or both, and may involve the imposition or threat of sanctions or the receipt or promise of rewards. What is less clear is how far the exercise of power involves rational choice. No doubt in many instances it does, at least within the limits of the knowledge and information available to those involved; but, as will be discussed later in the chapter, power may take the particular form of authority – an acceptance of the right to exercise power, ultimately comprising unquestioning obedience, rather than a rational analysis of advantages and disadvantages. More importantly, however, there is the question of whether power is exercised only knowingly and overtly on both sides of the power equation.

With the important exception of unintended effects, power has thus far been discussed in terms of its overt exercise, that is where the will of one individual or group of individuals has clearly and intentionally prevailed over that of another individual or group of individuals, or what pluralists have called observable decisions. Thus Robert Dahl's classic study of decision-making in New Haven,

Who Governs? (1961), examined how decisions were made and, crucially, *who* made them in respect of three case studies, one on urban redevelopment, one on political education, and one on political nominations. In so doing, Dahl concentrated on isolating, through observation, who had the power of initiative, decision and veto in each policy area. Critics of Dahl, notably Bachrach and Baratz (1962 and 1970) pointed out that he neglected what they termed 'non-decision-making', or the power to control the political agenda, in particular to keep issues off the agenda. Their argument was particularly well illustrated by a later study by Crenson (1971) of air pollution as a political issue in the United States. He first examined how the issue had been dealt with in two similar cities in Indiana, East Chicago and Gary. Crenson found that action to curb air pollution had been taken in East Chicago as early as 1949, but not until 1962 in Gary. His explanation was twofold: first, that United States Steel, which was the principal employer in Gary and therefore dominated the town, successfully played down its role as the cause of air pollution, and, second, that Gary had a strong party organisation which showed little or no interest in pollution as an issue; the combination of these two factors kept air pollution off the political agenda. Crenson tested and confirmed his findings against the experience of other American cities.

By definition the pluralist approach concentrates heavily on the activities of organised interests, but governments can also play an important role in controlling the political agenda. This happens most frequently for ideological reasons: as long us a particular party or group holds power certain issues will either be kept off the political agenda or have very low priority on it; other issues will figure very high on the agenda and have a very high priority.

Subsequently, Lukes (1974) described the pluralist approach, as criticised by Bachrach and Baratz and tested by Crenson, as a two-dimensional view of power, arguing that power was used to deal with issues (i.e. observable or overt conflict) and with potential issues (i.e. observable, but covert conflict), but that power also operated in a third dimension concerned with what he termed 'latent conflict' and 'real interests'. This raises the question of whether the exercise of power can be unconscious, leading Lukes to argue what he calls a radical view of power: 'A exercises power over B when A affects B in a manner contrary to B's interests' (1974, p. 27). In such a situation B may well be aware that A is not acting in his interests, but is unable to prevent A from acting against them, but Lukes goes on to argue that B may not be aware of his real interests: 'The radical ... maintains that men's wants may themselves be the product of a system which works against their interests, and, in such cases, relates the latter to what they would want and prefer, were they able to make the choice' (1974, p. 34). Lukes thus draws a clear distinction between subjective interests – what someone thinks they want – and objective interests – what someone would want if they could experience the results or be made aware of alternative courses of action.

This concern with real interests shifts the focus away from power (*Macht*) to what Weber calls *Herrschaft*, that is, lordship or domination. In fact, in spite of providing one of the best-known definitions of power, Weber wrote mainly in terms of domination, which he defined as: 'the probability that a command with a given specific content will be obeyed by a given group of persons' (1947, p. 152). Similarly, Marxist theorists have come to be interested far more in domination than power. In a sense, Marx, Engels and their earlier followers tended to take power for granted: it was implicit in the concept of a ruling or dominant class and it was only later, when capitalist societies showed a tenacious ability to survive, that Marxist theorists showed an explicit interest in power in order to explain how the capitalist class continued to dominate society. One answer was imperialism – a polemical and much-abused term, but in this context meaning economic exploitation of less-developed areas of the world by economically developed or industrialised societies. A far more subtle answer was through the control of ideas, sometimes called the mobilisation of bias. Writing in 1845/6, Marx and Engels argued that 'the ideas of the ruling class in every epoch are the ruling ideas' (1976 [1927], vol. 5, p. 59).

Antonio Gramsci (1971 [1929–35]), writing during his imprisonment under Mussolini between 1926 and 1934, argued that the bourgeoisie dominated society less by force and more by eliciting consent through using cultural institutions to ensure that its view of the world prevailed, using the term 'hegemony' to describe the situation in which the ruling class was able to represent its interests as the interests of society as a whole. This leads directly to the structuralist arguments advanced by Nicos Poulantzas, who defined power as: 'the capacity of a social class to realise its specific objective interests' (1973 [1968], p. 104), combining the unconscious exercise of power with unintended effects in that by definition a social class will act in its own interests whether fully aware of them or not. Similarly, Louis Althusser (1972) linked such ideological domination to the state through what he called 'ideological state apparatuses' – the education system, trade unions, political parties, the churches, even the family.

The control of ideas, the mobilisation of bias, and hegemony can be linked to socialisation theory, which suggests that societal values and norms of behaviour are transmitted from generation to generation by a conscious and unconscious learning process. Political values and norms are thus the product of political socialisation, which, some theorists argue (Almond and Verba 1963, 1980; Pye 1966), creates a distinctive *political culture* in every society. Ideas about socialisation can also be linked to the extent to which those exercising power or dominating a society seek to control it. This is clearly central to Marxist theory and to theories of totalitarianism, which argue that all aspects of societal activity are actually or potentially subject to control by those who exercise power. However, the question of control is also central to other sets of values, such as liberalism, socialism, and democracy.

Power was initially conceived of simply as an ability to act or impose one's will, but eventually as an infinitely more complex concept concerning domination of others by some individuals or groups of individuals in society, taking a variety of forms, drawing on a variety of resources, and having costs and benefits for those involved on both sides of the power equation. Its exercise may be overt or covert, conscious or unconscious, and, while often having intended effects, will invariably also have unintended effects. However, it remains open to argument whether power or domination is always exercised by the same group of individuals in a given society, exactly how it is exercised, and for what purposes. It is also open to argument whether the exercise of power or domination is accepted by those who are subject to it; in short, whether power is exercised with *authority*.

AUTHORITY AND LEGITIMACY

Political philosophers have devoted much time and effort to explaining the question of political obligation. In practice, this raises two questions. First, why *do* people obey? And second, why *should* people obey? Political philosophers mainly offer answers to the second question, why should people obey? Jean-Jacques Rousseau's answer in *The Social Contract* (1913 [1762]) is that the 'general will' or common good can be elicited through direct, participatory democracy and that laws which express the general will should be obeyed. Such a state of affairs was brought about and maintained through a social contract between all individuals in society. Rousseau's ideal was the small city-state in which direct democracy was feasible and, while laws would presumably be administered by a small number of individuals, he conceived power as being shared.

Other contract theorists offered a very different response to the question, notably Thomas Hobbes and John Locke. Both argued that it was in the interests of individuals to accept the domination of a government for their own protection, but differed significantly on the circumstances in which a government could be rejected. Hobbes (1914 [1651]), writing during and in the aftermath of the English Civil War, saw submitting to an all-powerful sovereign or Leviathan as the only means of avoiding the chaotic or anarchic state of affairs epitomised by recent events. Without the protection of a powerful government society would revert to a state of nature, described by Hobbes in a much-quoted phrase as 'solitary, poor, nasty, brutish and short' (1914 [1651], p. 65). Only in the event of a clear failure by the sovereign to provide that protection could allegiance be transferred elsewhere. Hobbes is thus seen as the ultimate justification for an absolutist or authoritarian state, involving no obligation to carry out the wishes of its subjects.

Locke (1924 [1690]) also saw government as a means of providing protection to the individual, but the scope of government was limited by consent. Thus, while government was expected to maintain order, it was also expected to protect the civil rights, liberty and property of the individual, and failure to do so entitled individuals to withdraw consent and, if necessary, overthrow the government. So, where in a Hobbesian view the acceptance of the exercise of power is prudential and does not necessarily signify approval of the use of power other than for protection, a Lockian view allows the use of power to be judged or approved of much more widely. Feudal society illustrates Hobbesian authority to the extent that tenants offered their feudal lord obligation in return for protection, although feudalism also involved complex contractual arrangements of mutual obligation. Rousseau and Locke, on the other hand, with their emphasis on the consent of the governed, provide important bases for the development of democratic theories. Locke is not strictly speaking a democratic theorist, but his ideas of limited and representative government were subsequently incorporated into democratic theory. Similarly, although Rousseau has subsequently and mistakenly been associated with the justification of authoritarian and totalitarian regimes by equating the general will with knowing people's 'real' interests, his ideas can be firmly linked to liberal democracy – ideas about equality, the rule of law, and, in the context of authority, that legitimacy depends on the will or consent of the governed.

Hobbes, of course, also offered an answer to the first question, why do people obey? They do so for their own good and, although in Hobbes' case it was fear of the alternative which prompted obedience, people may accept the exercise of power by others over them because they see it is to their advantage in other ways – back to the costs and benefits equation. This was clearly the view of David Hume: 'There is evidently no other principle than interest; and if interest first produces obedience to government, the obligation to obedience must cease whenever the interest ceases, in any degree, and in a considerable number of instances' (1978 [1739–40], p. 553). Modern theorists see authority – the acceptance of the exercise of power, both by those who exercise it and those to whom it is applied – as a crucial concept in politics. The moral justification of where power should lie is important, but so are the reasons why individuals appear willing to accept power being exercised over them.

Students of jurisprudence draw a distinction between *de facto* and *de jure* authority. *De facto* authority exists when an individual or group of individuals accept the exercise of power over them and obey orders or commands of those possessing that power; *de jure* authority exists when the exercise of power is accepted as right or justified by those to whom it is applied. Modern governments sometimes refuse to accord any form of recognition to a regime they dislike or abhor. However, it is not unusual to grant *de facto* recognition – recognising that the regime concerned has control – but denying it *de jure* recognition – that it has the right to that control. Authority is sometimes defined as *legitimate power* and 'authority' and 'legitimacy' are often used synonymously. In the context of particular governments or regimes this often presents no problem, but in the wider context of social and political organisations it is often more appropriate to talk of *legitimacy*.

Weber's (1947, p. 328) discussion of domination is principally concerned with *legitime Herrschaft* – legitimate domination – and he offered three ideal type bases for legitimacy. These are the traditional, the charismatic, and the rational–legal:

1. *Traditional legitimacy* is based on 'an established belief in the sanctity of immemorial traditions and the legitimacy of the status of those exercising authority under them'.
2. *Charismatic legitimacy* is based on 'devotion to the specific and exceptional sanctity, heroism or exemplary character of an individual person, and of the normative patterns of order revealed or ordained by him'.
3. *Rational–legal legitimacy* is based on 'a belief in the "legality" of patterns of normative rules and the right of those elevated to authority under such rules to issue commands'.

Weber cites gerontocracy – rule by elders – and patriarchalism – rule based on inheritance – as traditional types of legitimacy. History provides many examples of charismatic leaders, those whose personal attributes and ideas enabled them to attract and inspire their followers – individuals such as Alexander the Great, Julius Caesar, Oliver Cromwell, Hitler or, more recently, Gandhi, Nkrumah, Nasser, and Gaddafi. The modern bureaucratic state, based on legal rules and norms, exemplifies rational–legal legitimacy. It is important, however, to remember that Weber put his three bases forward as ideal types and that in practice the legitimacy of particular regimes is often a mixture of all three. Indeed, Weber points out that charismatic leaders seek to stabilise their position by adopting or adapting traditional legitimacy, that more complex forms of traditional legitimacy have a tendency towards the rational–legal forms, and that the latter may retain important vestiges of traditional legitimacy and periodically be subject to charismatic leaders.

Legitimacy – the extent to which social and political norms in a given society are accepted, especially those applying to the exercise of power or the domination of some individuals or groups of individuals by others – is undoubtedly an important concept in understanding the exercise of power and the relationship between politics and society. Structural–functional theorists, such as Parsons (1951) and Almond (1960, 1966), and systems theorists, such as Easton

(1953, 1965a, 1965b) see legitimacy as crucial to the maintenance of social and political systems. In his theory of the social system Parsons argued that one of its major functions is that of pattern-maintenance, which is the system's capacity to maintain its stability through the inculcation of shared values and the existence of widespread cultural norms. Easton, in developing his input–output analysis, speaks of system 'supports', such as various forms of political participation, especially voting, and positive reactions to policy outputs, that is activities which sustain the operation of the political system; and Almond originally regarded political socialisation as one of three input functions in the political system. Almond and Verba (1963) provided evidence of the basic legitimacy of the American political system in the 1960s in that attitudes towards political institutions were strongly positive and there were high levels of political efficacy – a sense by respondents to their survey that they could influence the course of politics.

A very different picture emerges from studies of the Weimar Republic (1919–33), which preceded Hitler's accession to power in 1933. With the bitterness over the defeat of Germany in the First World War (widely regarded as a betrayal of the military by the politicians), the loss of German colonies, and the punitive reparations imposed by the victorious Allies, coupled with periods of hyperinflation culminating in the Great Depression, it is little wonder that the institutions of the Weimar Republic lacked widespread acceptance and were little mourned after Hitler came to power. Similarly, the political instability of the Fourth French Republic (1946–58), combined with a humiliating colonial defeat in Indo-China, the debacle of Suez in 1956, and an increasingly ferocious struggle against nationalist forces in Algeria, severely undermined confidence in its political institutions and paved the way for Charles de Gaulle to become President and establish a significantly different set of institutions under the Fifth Republic.

For most Marxist theorists, however, legitimacy has been largely ignored as an irrelevance, being part of the ideology of the ruling class. More recently some Marxists have effectively seen legitimacy as an important part of the explanation for the survival of the capitalist system – Althusser's concept of ideological state apparatuses is the most relevant example, but, more significantly for Marxist theory, Poulantzas (1973) and Habermas (1976 [1973]) have argued that, in order to stave off economic crises, the capitalist system will need to resort to increasing state intervention. Growing state intervention will, according to Poulantzas, increasingly identify the state with the interests of capital and therefore undermine the popular legitimacy it claims to secure through periodic elections. In his *Legitimation Crisis* Habermas (1976 [1973]) says that such intervention will produce a series of crises – an economic crisis, a rationality crisis, a motivation crisis and, ultimately, a legitimation crisis – in a process effectively summarised by Connolly:

> Habermas perceives the state to be caught within a set of contradictory institutional imperatives: if it responds to one set, it undermines the rationality of the economy, and if it responds to others, it depletes the legitimacy the state itself needs to steer the economy and the motivations people require to carry out the roles available to them in the political economy. (Connolly, 1984, p. 97)

Claus Offe (1984) argues that the state has an institutionalised self-interest in preserving the existing structures of capitalist society rather than simply the interests of the dominant class because, in order to survive, the state has to be 'structurally selective'. This means that in a capitalist society the state favours different groups and interests, including sections of the working class, at different times so it can survive the economic and social crises which continually threaten it. In short, the state seeks to maintain its legitimacy by trying to accommodate the forces of organised labour and monopoly capital.

LEGITIMACY AND COMPLIANCE

Legitimacy is ultimately in the mind of the observer, whether the latter exercises power or is subject to it. The advantage of legitimacy for those exercising or seeking to exercise power is obvious, as Rousseau makes clear in a famous quotation from *The Social Contract*:

> The strongest man is never strong enough to be always master unless he transforms his power into right and obedience into duty. (Rousseau, 1913 [1762], p. 6)

Legitimacy, however, can be seen as only one explanation of why people obey those in power or claiming authority over them.

David Held (1984) has put forward a continuum of obedience or compliance, as shown in Figure 3.1. Held's continuum encompasses the full range of explanations of why people obey those who claim authority over them, from the perception or belief that they have no choice in the matter, to the belief that it is right and proper to do so. However, Held limits legitimacy to his sixth and seventh categories – 'normative agreement' and 'ideal normative agreement', although he concedes that category five – 'instrumental acceptance' – is 'ambiguous [and] could be taken to imply a weak form of legitimacy' (1984, pp. 302–3). These categories are, of course, Weberian ideal types, and social and political compliance in any society will be a mixture of categories, with the emphasis on particular categories varying from society to society. Although Held's particular concern was with legitimacy in Britain in the 1980s, he draws a general conclusion in seeking to explain social and political compliance:

> Political order is not achieved through common values systems, or general respect for the authority of the state, or legitimacy, or, by contrast, simple brute force; rather, it is

---

1. *Following orders or coercion:* there is no choice in the matter.
2. *Tradition:* no thought has ever been given to it and we do it as it has always been done.
3. *Apathy:* we cannot be bothered one way or another.
4. *Pragmatic acquiescence:* although we do not like the situation – it is not satisfactory and far from ideal – we cannot imagine things really being different and so we 'shrug our shoulders' and accept what seems like fate.
5. *Instrumental acceptance or conditional agreement/consent:* we are dissatisfied with things as they are but nevertheless go along with them in order to secure an end; we acquiesce because it is in the long run to our advantage.
6. *Normative agreement:* in the circumstances before us, and with the information available to us at the moment, we conclude it is 'right', 'correct', 'proper' for us as an individual or member of collectivity: it is what we genuinely *should* or *ought* to do.
7. *Ideal normative agreement:* it is what in ideal circumstances – with, for instance, all the knowledge we would like, all the opportunity to discover the circumstances and requirements of others – we would have agreed to do.

Figure 3.1 A continuum of social and political obedience or compliance (Source: Held (1984), pp. 301–2).

> the outcome of a complex web of interdependence between political, economic and social institutions and activities which divide power centres and which create multiple pressures to comply. State power is a central aspect of these structures but it is not the only key variable. (Held, 1984, pp. 361–2)

The matrix of variables to which Held refers are also closely related to concepts discussed later in the book, especially political socialisation (Chapter 5) and ideology (Chapter 10), and to the crucial question of why societies persist and change, discussed in Part V. More immediately, however, the question of social and political compliance needs to be seen in the context of different explanations of the distribution of power in society, which is the subject of the next chapter.

Chapter 4

THE DISTRIBUTION OF POWER

INTRODUCTION

If, as many social scientists argue, power is the distinguishing characteristic of political activity, then a key question is, to what extent does the distribution of power vary from one society to another? This question has exercised philosophers and political scientists, sociologists and psychologists, among many others. Some provide normative, some empirical answers, and not a few a combination of both, in that having described 'reality', they offer a prescription. Efforts to provide answers go back at least to the Greek philosophers, particularly Plato and Aristotle, both of whom presented ideal forms of government and compared them with the reality of their experience. Thus Plato believed that there exists a number of absolute moral truths to which men should aspire and that the perfect society resulting from the application of such truths could only exist where power was in the hands of philosopher-kings, who understood these truths. His views stemmed from his experience of the Greek city-states, and of Athens in particular, where the reality of tyranny, oligarchy, and democracy – power in the hands of an arbitrary individual, a selfish few, or the mob – appalled him. Aristotle also posited government of a single ruler, the few, and the many, but in ideal and perverted versions of each: monarchy was the ideal for a single ruler, tyranny its perverted form; aristocracy the ideal of rule by the few, oligarchy its perversion; and rule by the polity – the responsible citizens – the ideal of rule by the many, democracy – rule by the mob – its perversion.

Later philosophers, such as St Augustine of Hippo and St Thomas Aquinas, brought Christian ideals to bear on politics; others, such as Machiavelli and Hobbes, related their prescriptions to their perceived reality of a dangerous and chaotic world, Machiavelli with his ideal prince and Hobbes with his absolute sovereign or Leviathan. Locke and Rousseau placed greater faith in the ability of men to recognise their mutual self-interests and co-operate in the running of society. Not dissimilarly, utilitarians, like Jeremy Bentham and James Mill, argued that self-interest determined individuals' behaviour and would therefore produce, in Bentham's phrase, 'the greatest happiness of the greatest number'. However, James Mill's son, John Stuart Mill, although strongly influenced by utilitarian ideas, stressed the need to curb the exercise of power, especially to avoid what he termed 'the despotism of public opinion' (1887 [1838], pp. 376–8). Marx, of course, was in no doubt where the power lay: it lay with the class that controlled the means of production, but once this was understood Marx and his successors tended to take the distribution of power as a given dependent variable, which needed no further discussion other than to explain how the dominant class maintained its position and in what circumstances that position could be overthrown. Marxist views apart, however, modern theories about the distribution of power may be divided into four basic types – elite theory, pluralism, totalitarianism, and democracy.

ELITE THEORY

The word 'elite' is widely used socially to denote a superior group in terms of ability or privilege. Furthermore, in a social context it often has a pejorative connotation, leading it to be associated with other terms like 'the establishment', 'the powers that be', and 'the chosen few'. However, while such usages give something of the flavour of its meaning, elite theorists are concerned only with the distribution of power in society, with the distinction between rulers and ruled. In the words of one writer on the subject: 'The core of elitist doctrine is that there may exist in any society a minority of the population which takes the major decisions in the society' (Parry, 1969, p. 30). Elite theorists are mainly anti-Marxist, and two of the classical theorists, Gaetano Mosca and Vilfredo Pareto, set out specifically to disprove Marx's theories of economic determinism and the class struggle. Elite theorists are also largely anti-democratic, since they argue that democratic theory is at variance with reality and, in practical terms, an inherently weak form of government. In a frequently cited passage Mosca clearly stated the basic premise of elite theorists: 'In all societies – from societies that are very meagrely developed and have barely attained the dawnings of civilisation, down to the most advanced societies – two classes of people appear – a class that rules and a class that is ruled.' He goes on to elaborate:

> The first class, always the less numerous, performs all political functions, monopolises power and enjoys the advantages that power brings, whereas the second, the more numerous class, is directed and controlled by the first, and in a manner that is now more or less legal, now more or less arbitrary and violent, and supplies the first, in appearance at least, with material means of subsistence and with the instrumentalities that are essential to the vitality of the political organism. (Mosca, 1939 [1896], p. 50)

Implicit in elite theory is that the dominant group or elite is conscious of its existence, cohesive in its behaviour, and possesses a common sense of purpose (see Meisel 1965). Above all, elite theory is regarded as historically and universally applicable, except for one theorist, C. Wright Mills (1956), who concentrated on the distribution of power in the United States and conceded that the power structure in other societies might differ radically from the American model.

Parry divides the elite theorists into four types, as shown in Figure 4.1, each having a different approach or emphasis

The organisational approach – Mosca and Michels

According to Mosca, 'the individual ... stands alone before the totality of the organised minority' (1939 [1896], p. 53) and both he and Michels (1915 [1911]) believed that the existence of the elite and its domination of society rest on its organisational position and abilities. In short, the organised minority will invariably outmanoeuvre

Elite theorist	Principal works	Approach
A. Gaetano Mosca (1858–1941)	*The Ruling Class* (1896, rev. 1923, trans. 1939)	Organisational
Robert Michels (1876–1936)	*Political Parties: A Sociological Study of the Oligarchical Tendencies of Modern Democracy* (1911, trans. 1915)	Organisational
B. Vilfredo Pareto (1848–1927)	*The Mind and Society* (1916, trans. 1935)	Psychological
C. James Burnham (1905–87)	*The Managerial Revolution* (1941)	Economic
D. C. Wright Mills (1916–62)	*The Power Elite* (1956)	Institutional

Figure 4.1 Classifying elite theorists (Source: based on Parry (1969), Chapter II).

the less organised or unorganised majority in society. Mosca divided the elite into upper and lower strata, the upper stratum consisting of a small group of political decision-makers and the lower stratum performing lesser leadership functions, such as opinion leaders and political activists. Not surprisingly the more numerous lower stratum provided the main recruitment pool for the upper stratum.

The relationship between the elite or ruling class and the rest of society is measured in terms of authority and elite recruitment and varies according to two pairs of variables. The authority relationship depends on either the autocratic principle, in which authority flows from the elite to the masses, or the liberal principle, in which it flows from the masses to the elite. Recruitment depends on a similar dichotomy: the aristocratic tendency, in which movement is restricted to within the elite, moving from the lower to the upper stratum; and the democratic tendency, in which there is movement from the masses into the elite. These are, however, Weberian ideal types and particular societies will invariably exhibit elements of several variables. For example, an elected executive, such as the President of the United States, fulfils the liberal principle, but the President's Cabinet, all of whom are appointed, fulfils the autocratic principle. Similarly, an autocratic society might recruit members of its bureaucracy on merit, thus fulfilling the democratic tendency. Although Mosca argued that the recruitment or regeneration of the elite came mainly from within its lower ranks, he acknowledged that a more fundamental change in the elite could occur. Thus the masses or non-elite might become sufficiently discontented or disaffected to overthrow the elite, but in such cases it was likely that an organised minority within the non-elite would be responsible and, in any case, an organised minority would rapidly form a new ruling class.

Mosca was originally strongly anti-democratic, but later shifted his ground and accepted that representative government was the best way to articulate interests in a society, to which the elite should respond, and of controlling the autocratic authority of the bureaucracy through the liberal authority of a representative assembly. None the less, Mosca remained firmly elitist in his views: a ruling class was necessary to provide leadership and to manipulate the rest of society for its own good. In fact, Mosca would have restricted the franchise to the middle and upper classes, but conceded that historically it was too late to reverse the trend towards universal suffrage.

Although Michels' principal work was much narrower in scope than that of other elite theorists in that it concentrates on political parties, his famous 'iron law of oligarchy' (1915 [1911], pp. 377–92) has much wider implications and applications. Michels sought to test his theory of oligarchy – self-perpetuating dominance by the few – by examining the organisation of European socialist parties, especially the German Socialist Party, since he argued that if his 'iron law' really existed then there could be no better test than finding out who exercised power in parties that claimed that their mass membership controlled the party. Michels concluded that organisation was the inevitable consequence of the scope and complexity of human activity. Once established an organisation becomes dominated by its leadership: 'who says organisation, says oligarchy' (1915 [1911], p. 418). In order to function successfully in the modern conditions of mass electorates a political party needs a mass membership to raise funds, promulgate its policies, and, above all, to fight elections. This was not a new observation: M. Ostrogorski (1854–1919) had made the same point in detail in his *Democracy and the Organisation of Political Parties* in 1902, but Michels took it an important stage further.

Arguing that parties are essentially machines for winning and retaining power, Michels says that in order to do this they need to moderate their ideologies and policies to win support beyond the confines of their party activists. The initiative in all this lies largely with the party leadership and they, and the party's bureaucrats and legislative representatives, have a clear organisational advantage over ordinary party members. This advantage is reinforced by a psychological factor – the apathy of the majority of the population, who are basically ignorant of and uninterested in politics, except when it directly affects their interests. Here Michels anticipates one of the ideas of Kornhauser (1959), whose theory of the mass society posits circumstances in which the non-elite is available for manipulation by the elite and vice-versa, which will be examined later in this chapter. Michels, of course, regards the manipulation of the non-elite by the elite as the normal state of affairs in society.

The psychological approach – Pareto

Pareto and Mosca were contemporaries and rivals; they differed on the constitution of the elite, the reasons for its existence, and the manner of its recruitment or regeneration. Like Mosca, Pareto says the elite is divided into two sections, but Pareto draws a distinction between what he terms 'the governing elite' and 'the non-governing elite'. The governing elite are those who directly or indirectly influence political decisions, and the non-governing elite those who hold leadership positions in society, but who do not influence political decisions. This means that Pareto's elite is a larger group than Mosca's and that he comes closer to the commonplace concept of a social elite.

There are, however, more important distinctions between the two theorists in explaining the existence of the elite. Pareto explicity rejects the Marxist notion that the dominant group in society is the product of economic forces, or social forces for that matter, and asserts that the elite stems from human attributes, from individual abilities and instincts. Human beings, according to Pareto, do not act logically but seek to justify their actions logically through ideologies or values, which Pareto calls 'derivations'. These values or derivations produce instincts or states of mind that Pareto calls 'residues' and it is these that form the basis of human activity. Pareto divides the residues into two types or classes – 'instincts of combination' and 'persistence of aggregates'. The former involves the use of ideas and imagination, and Pareto dubs those who operate on this basis as 'foxes'; the second stresses permanence, stability and order, and those who operate on this basis Pareto calls 'lions'. In this

Pareto is reminiscent of Machiavelli, whose ideal in *The Prince* is a combination of wisdom and ruthlessness, similar to Pareto's ideal elite of a mixture of 'foxes' and 'lions' (see Figure 4.2).

Pareto acknowledges that his ideal elite of 'foxes' and 'lions' seldom materialises and that the balance between the two changes, so that there is a 'circulation of elites'. Thus 'foxes' replace 'lions' and 'lions' replace 'foxes', but 'foxes' gradually replace 'lions', whereas 'lions' suddenly replace 'foxes'. Recruitment or regeneration, therefore, can be either by evolution or revolution, but in either case the downfall of one elite is brought about by its own inherent vices: 'foxes' become over-manipulative or compromise once too often; 'lions' become too self-important and unacceptably ruthless, for example.

Pareto also differs from Mosca, and other elite theorists, in that he does not subscribe to group coherence and common purpose amongst the elite, but argues that individuals act as individuals and for this reason often fail to foresee the consequences of their own actions, as well as those of others.

The economic approach – Burnham

James Burnham agrees with Marx that power lies with those who control the means of production and acknowledges that, whereas in

Class I 'Instincts of combination' 'Foxes'	Class II 'Persistence of aggregates' 'Lions'
Intelligent	Strong-minded
Imaginative	Reliable
Manipulative	Possessing integrity
Persevering	Ruthless
Consensual	Confrontational
Compromiser	Inflexible
Patient	Impatient
Ideal = political fixer, wheeler-dealer	Ideal = determined, charismatic leader

Figure 4.2 Pareto's types of elites (Source: Pareto , *Mind and Society*, Vol. 4, Sec. 2178, 2227, 2274, 2275).

the aftermath of the industrial revolution this was the capitalist owners, in advanced industrial societies control of the means of production has passed to those with managerial and technical expertise, including leading members of the bureaucracy. These, according to Burnham, constitute the new elite. The state becomes subordinated to the needs of the managerial elite and industrial societies will become increasingly centralised and subject to bureaucratic control. Burnham saw a convergence between the already state-dominated USSR and advanced capitalist societies and, in a sense, posits what some observers were later to describe communist systems as – administered societies.

The institutional approach – Mills

Wright Mills argues that the American elite is embedded in the structures of society and that power is therefore institutionalised. He concludes that the United States is dominated by an industrial-military-political complex of overlapping elites, with movement from one elite to another and that the key members of this complex constitute a *power elite* – those in 'positions to make decisions having major consequences . . . in command of the major hierarchies and organisations of modern society' (1956, p. 4). The elite may be based on a conscious conspiracy or simply shared values, but its power stems from its position, rather than from status, wealth, class, or ability.

Testing elite theory

The most common type of evidence presented to support elite theories seeks to answer two questions: who is selected for particular positions in society and how are they selected? The first question is usually answered by examining the socio-economic backgrounds of those who hold or secure positions regarded as designating membership of the elite, such as members of legislatures, holders of political and administrative office in the state, and, in some cases, holders of offices in political parties and other organisations thought or known to be important in wielding or influencing the exercise of power. In some ways the evidence thus adduced is very compelling, since it is a common finding that, regardless of how they are defined or constituted, elites are unrepresentative in socio-economic terms of the populations from which they are drawn. With few exceptions they tend to be drawn from the upper echelons of society in terms of education, occupation, income, and socio-economic status.

The principal exceptions are found in communist societies, where efforts were made to secure significant representation of workers and peasants and, to a lesser extent, women. Even here, however, the elite remains unrepresentative in other respects, especially in terms of career patterns. Clearly such phenomena need explaining, but so also does the fact that there are many more individuals who have similar socio-economic backgrounds, yet are neither members of the elite in positional terms nor have sought elite positions. However, this is a question which will be explored further in Chapter 7. Of more immediate relevance is the nature of this type of evidence for the existence of an elite.

It is essentially inferential and deductive, in that it assumes that those holding particular positions in society actually exercise power and that all decisions are taken by them. A variation of this elite test is to examine particular decisions and ask whether those apparently involved have a common socio-economic background, but this, too, suffers from similar deficiencies; both methods are intrinsically circumstantial.

The second type of question addresses itself more to the concerns expressed by Michels about the ability of the elite to perpetuate itself in positions of power and influence. It therefore examines the recruitment process itself by asking who does the choosing and how is it done? Of course, many political positions or offices are elective and therefore involve a much larger group than the elite, however the latter may be defined. Although in some cases the choice is limited to a single candidate, many more cases offer a genuine choice to the electorate of two or more candidates, but studies in a number of countries show that in socio-economic terms the differences between successful and unsuccessful candidates are not great and that the selection of candidates is often in the hands of a small group of party leaders and activists, clearly lending support to Michels' oligarchical ideas. The evidence cannot and should not be ignored, but amounts to only a limited examination of the recruitment process, which, as already noted, will be explored further in Chapter 7.

A further type of test is known as the reputational approach, of which a typical and important example is Floyd Hunter's *Community Power Structure: A study of decision-makers* (1953). Hunter asked a representative panel of local citizens who *they* thought made decisions in Atlanta. They were asked to choose from lists supplied by local organisations and 'notables', such as the chamber of commerce, newspaper editors, and civic leaders. The panel's responses led Hunter to conclude that Atlanta was controlled by a business elite. Perception is a very important factor in social life in general and politics in particular, but the perceptual or reputational approach leaves the problem of matching impression or appearance with reality and distinguishing between potential and actual power. Again, it is not a case of dismissing the evidence, but asking whether it is sufficient.

The strongest challenge to elite theory, however, comes from what is known as the decision-making approach, an approach particularly identified with Robert A. Dahl, one of the leading proponents of *pluralist* theory.

PLURALISM

Dahl (1958, p. 466) sought to test elite theory by examining particular policy decisions and asking whether an identifiable elite was responsible for the outcome in each case. To do this he applied his elite test, arguing that for an elite to exist and dominate the decision-making process the following three criteria had to be met:

1. The hypothetical elite is a well-defined group.
2. There is a fair sample of cases involving key political decisions to which the preferences of the hypothetical ruling elite run counter to those of any other likely group that might be suggested.
3. In such cases, the preferences of the elite regularly prevail.

In *Who Governs?* (1961), which is based on decision-making in the town of New Haven, Dahl (as noted in the earlier discussion of power in Chapter 3) examined particular issues in three policy areas – urban renewal, public education, and the making of local party nominations. He concluded that the outcomes of the decisions on the three issues were determined by three mutually exclusive groups and therefore that no single elite existed, but there was a plurality of interests. However, far from suggesting that this plurality of interests competed on equal terms, Dahl argues that the various interests are unequal, particularly in the availability of resources, and therefore in their ability to influence decisions. Dahl also drew a distinction between what he termed 'social notables', 'economic notables', and the holders of political office. Effectively he was suggesting a system of competing elites.

Dahl describes such a system as a *polyarchy* – the rule of the many, in which the state and its political structures provide an arena in which interests can bargain and compete over policy proposals. Implicit in the polyarchical view of society is that a basic consensus exists about the form of society and its political structures, so that no one, except possibly a tiny minority, is seeking fundamental change in those structures or in the policies pursued through them. No one group in society constitutes a majority interest, and society therefore consists of competing, though not necessarily equal, minority interests. By definition no particular interest can perforce expect to prevail, even where its interests are directly and significantly affected, but, as another leading pluralist Nelson Polsby (1963) argues, in a polyarchy virtually all views or interests will be listened to by those charged with decision-making.

The pluralist view developed out of the concept of pressure or interest groups – organisations which seek to influence policy decisions affecting their views or interests. Interest group theory argues that society consists of a great variety of interests, many of which organise themselves to press the government to respond to their demands. As far back as 1908 A. F. Bentley put forward such a view in *The Process of Government*, but studies of pressure politics flourished in the 1950s and later, especially after the publication of David Truman's *The Governmental Process* in 1951. Pluralists took interest group theory a step further by arguing that if an interest existed it would develop organisational representation, since this was the only means of making its presence felt. The stress on organisation provides a linkage with the organisational elite theorists, especially Michels, though this was not the intent.

It was no accident that pluralist views came hard on the heels of increased academic interest in pressure politics, nor that it fitted in well with what was called 'the end of ideology thesis' (see Chapter 10), the view that there was, in liberal-democratic societies, a basic agreement on ends, and only disagreement over means. The common denominator was the American political system which, particularly in the late 1950s and early 1960s, best fitted interest group theory, pluralism, and the end of ideology thesis. How applicable these ideas were and are to other political systems is a different matter. Even so, it is the pluralists who have provided the principal non-Marxist challenge to elite theorists.

A critique of pluralist theory

The most obvious criticism that could be made of Dahl's study of New Haven, as it was of Hunter's study of Atlanta, was that it was atypical – that there was no reason to doubt the findings, but that they were not necessarily valid for other cities, let alone American politics generally. Certainly, American local government is not uniform in that significantly different systems operate from state to state, and case studies, such as Robert Presthus' (1964) *Men at the Top*, found greater evidence of elitism in other places in the United States than Dahl found at New Haven.

However, the most serious criticism of pluralism relates to what Steven Lukes has called the second and third dimensions of power. These were discussed in Chapter 3, but they are worth examining again in the context of pluralist theory. Bachrach and Baratz (1962, 1970) point out that pluralists deal only with observable decisions, issues that actually get onto the political agenda, and therefore ignore those that are kept off the agenda. This was tested by Crenson (1971) in a study of US Steel's ability to control the political agenda in the the steel town of Gary, Indiana. This is the second dimension of power. Lukes (1974) suggests that there is a third dimension, that of latent conflicts arising from the real interests of members of society. This relates to the Marxist concept of ideology as 'false consciousness', in which individuals are unaware of their real interests because the prevailing values in society lead them to misconstrue reality. Thus the perceptions of individuals will affect their political behaviour, leading in some cases to inaction rather than action.

The second dimension is a serious criticism of the pluralist view and it is not difficult to find evidence to support it, but the third dimension, while logically impeccable, is difficult to prove, since truth, like beauty is ultimately in the eye of the beholder. Nevertheless, it too is a serious criticism and in particular questions the consensual notions of pluralist theory. Clearly there are competing interests in any society, but even in American politics it is also clear that those who are active in politics are a minority; that those who hold and wield political power are a minority; that those who exercise influence are a minority; and, while it is possible to agree with pluralists that they are not all part of the same minority, it is an assumption that the majority of the members of society are represented in the political process and that they necessarily accept the political system and the policies it produces in their name. If this is the case for the United States, then it is even more the case for other political systems, some of which appear to fit elite theory more closely than they do pluralist theory. For instance, before the Communist Party gave up its 'leading role' in 1990, the Soviet Union appears to accord with elite theory. The Leninist theory of the Party as the 'vanguard of the proletariat' is explicitly elitist and the ability of its leaders to maintain control over it seems a clear example of Michels' 'iron law of oligarchy'. On the other hand, some writers claimed to have detected signs of pluralism in the USSR, arguing that interests were institutionalised through the Party, which responded to demands from below, as well as issued instructions from above (see Skilling and Griffiths 1971; Solomon 1983).

Much of the evidence for pluralism, like that for elites, is circumstantial, and pluralist theory can be seen as a form of elite theory, but one of competing elites, rather than a single elite. Additional light is thrown on both elite and pluralist theories by examining political socialisation, participation and recruitment in Part IV, but it is also helpful to look at totalitarian and democratic theories of the distribution of power.

TOTALITARIANISM

Totalitarianism and democracy are often understandably seen as diametrically opposed concepts, but they have in common concern with mass political participation in contrast with elite theory, which tends largely to dismiss the masses as subordinate and subject to manipulation by the elite, and pluralism, which sees the masses as a multiplicity of competing interests. Furthermore, both totalitarianism and democracy can usefully be seen us ideal types which in practice are tendencies rather than absolutes.

History is replete with regimes in which considerable power has been concentrated in the hands of an individual or small group of individuals, largely unrestrained, often arbitrary in its use, and in which failure to obey risks severe punishment, not infrequently death. Aristotle called such rule tyranny and both Greek and Roman history produced their quotas of tyrants; much of the history of medieval England is concerned with attempts to impose restraints upon monarchs; eighteenth-century Europe is sometimes described as 'the age of absolutism'; and the period between the First and Second World Wars has been called 'the age of dictators'. These regimes were variously described as tyrannical, absolutist, dictatorial, and, more recently, authoritarian. A number of justifications have been advanced for absolute rule, ranging from Plato's philosopher-kings to the divine right of kings, and Hobbes' Leviathan to Marx's dictatorship of the proletariat. In the first two, absolute rule was tempered by wisdom and God's law respectively; in the latter two, the end justifies the means, order being vastly preferable to violent chaos and a classless, communist society to anything that preceded it. Totalitarianism could therefore be said to be in the absolutist tradition, taking absolutism to its logical extreme by seeking to control everything in society, but this is also its distinguishing feature. Tyranny, absolutism and dictatorship demand obedience, but do not seek to be all-pervasive, to re-shape society in its entirety: totalitarianism demands not only obedience but belief.

Defining totalitarianism

Two types of definitions have been advanced, the phenomenological and the essentialist. Carl J. Friedrich (1954, 1969, p. 126) provided the most well-known phenomenological definition, according to which a totalitarian state has the following six characteristics:

1. A totalist or all-embracing ideology.
2. A single party committed to that ideology, usually led by one man.
3. Police power based on terror.
4. A monopoly of communication.
5. A monopoly of weaponry.
6. A centralised economy and control of all organisations.

Zbigniew Brzezinski, who collaborated with Friedrich in a study of totalitarianism, produced a definition to which he added the purpose of totalitarian regimes:

> Totalitarianism is a system in which technologically advanced instruments of political power are wielded without

> restraint by a centralised leadership of an elite movement, for the purpose of effecting a total social revolution, including the conditioning of man on the basis of certain arbitrary ideological assumptions proclaimed by the leadership, in an atmosphere of coerced unanimity of the entire population. (Brzezinski 1967, pp. 19–20)

Both Friedrich and Brzezinski emphasise the extent to which society is penetrated and controlled by those holding political power, to which Brzezinski makes the important addition that totalitarian regimes through that control and penetration seek to transform society from the present or perceived reality to an idealised form reflected in an all-pervasive ideology.

The second type of definition, the essentialist, seeks to isolate the *essences* or key attributes which explain the sort of characteristics delineated by Friedrich and Brzezinski. Hannah Arendt (1951, p. 466), in *The Origins of Totalitarianism*, states that 'total terror [is] the essence of totalitarian government'; J. L. Talmon (1952, pp. 1–2) argues that totalitarianism politicises the whole of life and 'is based on the assumption of a sole and exclusive truth in politics. It may be called political Messianism'; similarly, Harry Eckstein and David Apter (1963, p. 434) say that 'the essence of totalitarianism ... is that it annihilates all boundaries between the state and the groupings of society, even the state and the individual personality'.

Both types of definition stress the relationship between politics and society and a reasonable short definition of totalitarianism would be: a social system involving the political control of and intervention in all aspects of public and private life.

The origins of totalitarianism

Hannah Arendt (1951) explains the origins of totalitarianism in socio-historical terms, basing her conclusions on an analysis of the rise of Nazi Germany, but also applying them to the Soviet Union. She argues that totalitarianism in Germany developed as a consequence of four factors: first, a breakdown of community resulting from rapid industrialisation before and military defeat in the First World War, combined with the introduction both before and after the war of liberal ideas; second, the rapid enfranchisement of the masses in the absence of an appropriate liberal political culture, leaving them open to manipulation by demogogic leaders; third, the creation in the form of the National Socialist Party of a mass movement with which individuals could identify; and, finally, a population sufficiently large and widespread against whom considerable prejudice already existed – the Jews, who could be cast in the role of scapegoat for the ills of society. Similar, though not identical, features could be listed for the Soviet Union.

Talmon (1952) offers an ideological explanation, tracing totalitarianism back to eighteenth-century messianic beliefs, Rousseau's concept of the General Will, and Jacobin ideas in revolutionary France, all of which, he argues, are based on the belief that there is 'a sole exclusive truth in politics'. Talmon further argues that totalitarianism can take ideologically left and right forms, with Fascist Italy and Nazi Germany representing the totalitarian right and communist regimes in the USSR, the People's Republic of China (PRC), and Eastern Europe representing the totalitarian left. The latter he describes as 'democratic totalitarianism' because the regimes claim to know the true interests of the people and thus be able to realise their democratic will. Support for this view can be found in the Leninist doctrine of democratic centralism in which free discussion was centred within the Communist Party, but the party remained the custodian of the truth and the guide to action.

A third explanation of the origins of totalitarianism has been put forward by a number of psychologists who argue that some individuals exhibit particular psychological tendencies, such as aggression, intolerance towards groups in society other than their own, and deference to authority, attracting them to highly disciplined organisations, which, in certain social conditions, may secure or seize political power. The best known of the psychological explanations is that advanced by Theodor Adorno *et al.* (1950) in *The Authoritarian Personality*. They sought to measure various personality traits which, for example, rendered individuals receptive to taking orders, intolerant of opposition, and having a highly structured view of the world. In particular, they developed a number of scales, the best known of which was the Fascism or F-Scale. Erich Fromm (1941) in *Escape from Freedom* suggested that individuals who were alienated from the modern world sought refuge in authoritarian or highly structured societies, while Milgram (1974) conducted a series of laboratory experiments to test the extent to which individuals accepted orders from those they perceived to be in authority over them.

It is important to note that much of the research into totalitarianism was conducted in the late 1940s and early 1950s, in the immediate aftermath of the Second World War. It tended, therefore, to concentrate far more on what Talmon called totalitarianism of the right and on Nazi Germany in particular. Relatively speaking, far less attention was paid to communist systems. Studies of the 'authoritarian personality' in particular were directed largely at the Nazi experience, seeking explanations of how Hitler had 'subjugated' the German people, secured their 'unquestioning obedience', and 'persuaded' a significant number of them to perform what others regarded as atrocities. Thus one of the major criticisms made of Adorno and his colleagues is that they do not deal adequately with 'left-wing authoritarianism'. Later studies, like Milgram's, are criticised for the artificial nature of their experiments, but also because they concentrate on the concept of obedience to the neglect of the more subtle concept of acceptance. On the other hand, although Arendt's study (especially the first edition published in 1951) documents more fully totalitarianism in Nazi Germany than in the Soviet Union, the latter is far from ignored, while Talmon concentrates almost entirely on totalitarianism of the left, to which he regards communists as the natural heirs. It is worth noting that even when the earliest of these studies was published the Soviet Union had already existed nearly three times longer than Nazi Germany, though not, of course, Fascist Italy, and that since then the communist regimes of Eastern Europe had a life of some forty years and the People's Republic of China continues to survive.

None of the explanations offered alone seems to provide complete explanation of the origins of totalitarianism, but each emphasises a credible part of what is probably a wider whole. The rapid societal changes and the military defeats which preceded the Soviet and Nazi regimes may well have provided fertile ground for messianic answers to the uncertainties, dislocation and hardship that faced many people in Russia and Germany at the time, and it would be surprising if some individuals were not better psychologically suited to and disposed towards authoritarian regimes, but account also needs to be taken of the particular circumstances in which Lenin's Bolsheviks and Hitler's Nazis came to power.

The Tsar had been overthrown in Russia in February 1917 and, until the return of Lenin, his fellow Bolsheviks proposed to cooperate with the provisional government of Alexander Kerensky, but Lenin immediately abandoned the policy and single-mindedly set in train the Bolshevik seizure of power, which took place in October 1917.

In Germany Hitler's Nazi Party rose from winning less than 3 per cent of the national vote in 1928 and electing a mere twelve members to the Reichstag to winning 37 per cent of the vote in July 1932 and being the largest party, with 230 out of 608 seats, still short of an absolute majority, however. At a further election in November 1932 the Nazi vote dropped by two million and its number of seats fell to 196, but the NSDAP remained the largest party. However, the extreme fragmentation of the parties in the Reichstag made forming a government extremely difficult and, as leader of the largest party, Hitler was invited to take office as Chancellor at the end of January 1933. As it was the Nazis held only three of the eleven Cabinet posts, but Hitler used his power as Chancellor very skilfully, called another election in March, at which the Nazi vote increased to 44 per cent and the number of seats to 288, again short of a majority. But the election of fifty-two Nationalists gave Hitler a majority in the Reichstag and the means to consolidate the Nazi grip on power.

In both cases the role of the leader was crucial, but so also was what they did with power once it was in their grasp. The Bolsheviks and the Nazis not only moved swiftly to strengthen their grip, but used the power they had to impose a totalitarian regime, placing their supporters in key positions in the police and enforcing their will by the systematic use of terror. Once in power it became extremely difficult to loosen that grip: opponents were quickly eliminated, the media brought under strict party control, and the ideological penetration of society set in train.

A similar pattern can be delineated for the countries of Eastern Europe which came under Soviet hegemony at the end of the Second World War. For the most part totalitarian regimes were imposed from outside and depended ultimately, as the events of 1989 illustrated, on Soviet backing, but once installed the communist regimes rapidly made themselves virtually invulnerable internally. Much the same is true of the PRC: once Mao Zedong had militarily defeated the Nationalist forces of Chiang Kai-shek the way was open to extending his totalitarian regime to the whole of mainland China. The question remains, however, whether these regimes should properly be described as totalitarian.

Totalitarianism in practice

It is common to describe Fascist Italy, Nazi Germany, the USSR, the PRC, the various communist regimes of Eastern Europe, and one or two other countries like North Korea, Cuba, and Vietnam (North Vietnam before the American withdrawal from South Vietnam in 1972) as totalitarian. To a considerable extent these societies do fit Friedrich's six characteristics and Brzezinski's definition.

All are characterised by a single ideology, which claims to be all-encompassing in its applicability. There is an ideological view on all aspects of life, not simply the 'political' in a narrow sense. Thus arts are not merely harnessed for propaganda purposes, but must reflect the ideology; history assumes ideological truth and is rewritten and, if necessary, rewritten again and again to reflect that 'truth'; sport and other leisure activities are seen as a reflection of the ideology; and all expression of thought must be couched in ideological terms.

Each of the societies was or remains dominated by a single party. In a limited number of cases, such as Poland and the PRC, other parties were permitted to exist, but subject to strict control. Moreover, the single or dominant party is committed to the official ideology and the state apparatus is penetrated by or subject to party control. The dominance of a single individual obviously characterised the Soviet Union under Stalin, Germany under Hitler, Italy under Mussolini, and the PRC under Mao, but other dominant leaders emerged elsewhere – Tito in Yugoslavia, Enver Hoxha in Albania, Kim Il-sung in North Korea, Ho Chi Minh in Vietnam, and Fidel Castro in Cuba, although the position is less clear in other cases. However, after the demise of their leaders Fascist Italy and Nazi Germany collapsed in military defeat and the successors of Stalin, Mao, Hoxha, and Ho Chi Minh were and are less secure. Similarly, although clear leaders emerged in all the Soviet satellite states of Eastern Europe and Deng Xiao Ping became the dominant figure in the PRC, none was as secure as Stalin, Hitler and Mao. The Italian Fascist and the Nazi regimes were heavily dependent on their respective leaders and it is doubtful whether they would have survived the peaceful demise of Mussolini and Hitler. In the Soviet Union Khrushchev successfully resisted attempts to overthrow him from within the Communist party, before eventually succumbing to a party coup in 1964. His successor Leonid Brehznev secured a firm grip on the party, but it never assumed Stalinist proportions and none of Stalin's successors achieved his dominance. Indeed, in all communist regimes the party has been the vehicle of leader dominance.

The use of terror, backed by a widespread network of informers, encouraging informing (even from within the family), and generating an atmosphere of suspicion and fear, is also common to these societies. Police powers were enormous, often used arbitrarily, so that no one felt safe, and ultimately justice was conceived in terms of loyalty to the ideology, the party and, often above all, to the leader. Periodic purges reinforced the system, and fear of the concentration camp and the gulag, or worse, was ever present.

Control of all means of communication, especially the media, was crucial. Indoctrination, particularly through the education system, was widespread and the dissemination of information strictly controlled, not simply by preventing the 'wrong' information from reaching individuals, but in ensuring the provision of 'correct' information in appropriate ideological form. In Ceaucescu's Romania, for instance, all typewriters had to be registered and contacts with foreign tourists reported to the police within twenty-four hours.

Both the police and the armed forces were subject to strict control and the principal means of force were firmly in the hands of the state. The police, particularly the secret police, were a crucial means of societal control and the military clearly subordinate to the political leaders. Armed resistance was not necessarily impossible, but highly unlikely. The military was not only subject to indoctrination, but heavily penetrated by politically reliable individuals. In the case of communist regimes this was formally so through a network of political commissars.

In order to meet the policy objectives of the single or dominant party the economy was subject to central direction. Communist regimes especially had elaborate economic plans, usually covering five-year periods, with detailed production targets. Other societal organisations were subject to state control and there was widespread ideological penetration of all aspects of society.

The term 'totalitarian' clearly implies an absolute rather than a relative state of affairs, but for analytical purposes this is a disadvantage, since not only can it be argued that no society has ever been totalitarian in the absolute sense, but it means that a given society must be classified as totalitarian or not. Contradictory as it may appear, therefore, there is much to be said for using totalitarianism as an ideal type against which particular cases can be measured. This allows more fruitful comparisons between cases and of particular cases over time. In this sense, for example, Nazi Germany may be said to have been more totalitarian than Fascist Italy and the Stalinist Soviet Union more totalitarian than the post-Stalinist Soviet Union. This also makes sense in considering various aspects of political behaviour, especially socialisation. In the absolute sense socialisation in a totalitarian society must be totally successful, yet the experience of Eastern Europe under communism should serve as a reminder that the reality is more complex.

Applied therefore as a tendency rather than an absolute, totalitarianism is a more useful analytical tool. Least of all should it be used pejoratively, even though regimes normally associated with it are widely regarded as abhorrent. As an analytical tool it could, possibly usefully, be applied to fundamentalist Islamic regimes, such as Iran after the fall of the Shah. Muslims do not, of course, accept that their religion is an ideology, but Iran (and to a lesser extent some other Islamic states) share many of the characteristics associated with totalitarian states – an all-pervasive 'ideology', a single party or its equivalent, something close to a monopoly of communications, and extensive control over the operation of society.

Totalitarianism also focuses attention on the role of ideology and values and it should be acknowledged that all societies are pervaded by definable sets of values, but that key characteristic of totalitarian societies is that no conflict is permitted between rival or alternative sets of values. It is therefore misguided to see totalitarianism itself as an ideology; it is the relationship between ideology and society that characterises totalitarianism.

DEMOCRACY

'Democracy' and its adjectival antonym, 'undemocratic', are among the most widely used words in the political vocabulary, and possibly among the most disputed. With the exception of a small handful, such as Fascist Italy and Nazi Germany, all modern regimes have claimed or claim to be democratic. Is it therefore a meaningless term? What is almost certainly the most famous definition of democracy illustrates the problem. In his Gettysburg address Abraham Lincoln spoke of 'government of the people, by the people, and for the people'.

It may be assumed that 'government of the people' presents no problem, but beyond that difficulties arise which allow for widespread variations in interpretation. If it is conceded that in populous and complex modern societies not all the people may regularly or frequently be engaged in government (though not all would concede it), then 'government by the people' may be interpreted to mean governing in the name of the people or through their representatives, but how are such claims to be substantiated? Similarly, 'government for the people' may be no more than sheer altruism, but it may also mean claiming to know better that the people, knowing where their true interests lie. It is such claims that allow so many disparate regimes and societies to assume the epithet 'democratic'.

Historically democracy can be traced back to the Greeks, but neither Plato nor Aristotle looked favourably upon it. Plato feared the demagoguery that he associated with democracy and Aristotle regarded it as the perverted form of the rule of the many, although Aristotle's ideal of the polity or responsible citizenry has much in common with modern ideas of democracy. Similarly, in the eighteenth century democracy was widely equated with the rule of the mob and the Founding Fathers of the United States were not believers in democracy; they too feared the mob, regarding it as ignorant and therefore strongly inclined to irresponsibility. Individuals had, they believed, rights – freedom of speech and association, freedom from arbitrary arrest and imprisonment, and freedom of religion – but these were the rights of free men and citizens, and citizens had responsibilities as well as rights. Those rights, now normally seen as an essential part of democracy, in fact preceded modern ideas about democracy, as does the right to vote. In many of the New England townships direct democracy was indeed practised (and continues to be practised) through town meetings that decided particular issues and elected office-holders, but the right to participate was not universal. The right to vote in various elections, now regarded as absolutely fundamental to democracy, not only excluded women, but was linked to the ownership of property or subject to other limitations. Democracy was therefore treated with, at worst, outright hostility and, at best, fear and suspicion, so that its positive image is historically relatively recent.

Clearly democracy involves the consent of the governed and of the implementation of the popular will. Contract theorists like Locke (1924 [1690]) certainly favoured the idea of an elected government, but effectively introduced the other side of the democratic coin, that of popular control. Rousseau's ideal (1913 [1762]) was the Greek city-state in which all citizens (only a minority of the population in reality) could participate directly in making decisions, but he regarded this ideal as impractical in the Europe of his day, seeing only the island of Corsica as being a possible location for its fulfilment. In particular, Rousseau did not regard the idea of representative democracy as an adequate substitute for direct democracy. None the less, this is the principal form that democracy has taken in the modern world.

In practice, democracy is best seen as a principle involving popular consent and control on the part of the governed which may find expression in various political practices and forms of government. Like totalitarianism, it is more fruitful to see democracy in relative rather than absolute terms, so that it is possible to conceive degrees of democracy. This raises two fundamental questions. How is popular consent to be elicited? And how is popular control or accountability to be achieved?

The most obvious answer is by means of elections, but elections generate a whole series of further questions: Who should be allowed to vote? What is to be decided by elections? If it is to choose representatives, what should be the basis of representation – territory, population, interests, or what? How frequently should elections be held? What type of electoral system should be used? Should the will of a simple or relative majority (the largest number) prevail, or should an absolute majority of more than 50 per cent be necessary for certain decisions? Who should be able to decide when elections are held or should elections be held at fixed intervals? All these questions raise issues to which there are a multiplicity of answers, some of which are shown in Figure 4.3.

The democratic mechanisms available may be direct in the sense that the people (usually those who constitute the electorate) participate directly in deciding something, such as choosing a leader or determining a policy issue through a referendum. The device of recall allows a specified proportion of the electorate to demand that an elected representative or office-holder present himself or herself for re-election before the normal term of office has expired, and the initiative is a similar variation on the referendum, allowing the electorate to demand that an issue be decided by a direct vote. Both devices are used in a number of American states and both may be

Consent		Control	
Elections Referenda Initiatives Recalls	direct	Elections Referenda Initiatives Recalls	direct
Legislative representation Pressure politics	indirect	Rule of law Judicial review Legislative scrutiny Ombudsman systems	indirect

Figure 4.3 Democracy: consent and control mechanisms.

used to elicit consent and exert control. There are also indirect means of consent and control in that they may operate through intermediaries, in the form of organisations (such as the legislature or the judicial system), individuals (such as legislative representatives or an ombudsman), principles (such as the rule of law), or devices (such as judicial review.

It is therefore misleading to define modern democracy simply in terms of majority rule. The American Founding Fathers, precisely because they were not democrats, deliberately built a number of anti-majoritarian devices into the United States Constitution by incorporating a separation of powers to prevent any one individual or group of individuals from dominating all three branches of government – the executive, the legislature, and the judiciary – and various checks and balances, such as Senate approval of presidential appointments and the President's legislative veto. A particular problem arises when a permanent or quasi-permanent majority exists based, for instance, on religion or ethnicity, leading to significant discrimination by the majority against one or more minorities. This was the situation which prevailed in Northern Ireland between 1920 and 1972 with a Protestant/Unionist majority using its numerical advantage to discriminate against the Catholic/Nationalist minority. Using de Tocqueville's famous phrase, John Stuart Mill wrote of his fear of the 'tyranny of the majority' (de Tocqueville 1966 [1835–40], pp. 231–4), especially that of the 'ignorant' or less well-informed majority prevailing over an enlightened or better-informed minority (Mill 1887 [1840]).

Public opinion will be discussed in Chapter 9, but at this point it should be noted that in practice democracy is complicated by the very nature of public opinion, which can vary in intensity and in the extent to which it affects various individuals or sections of the public, as well as in relation to levels of information and socio-economic characteristics. Modern democracy therefore demands tolerance of others' opinions and in particular of the existence and opinions of minorities.

Furthermore, it is widely argued that various rights, including the right to vote and freedom of speech and association, are of little use if individuals or groups of individuals are suffering from high levels of social or economic inequality. Such individuals may care little about democracy or their rights and be far more concerned about survival and their material needs. Lipset (1960, 1983), for example, has argued strongly that there is a causal relationship between economic development and democracy. Using levels of income, industrialisation, urbanisation and education, he sought to demonstrate that democratic regimes developed and were sustained in those societies which had essentially met the material needs of their members. Linking the legitimacy of regimes with their material efficiency, Lipset and Rokkan (1967) suggested that a major factor in the political stability of such societies was solving what they termed 'non-bargainable' issues, such as those relating to language, religion and culture before basic economic matters are addressed. An important criticism of this view is that it is really theorising about the conditions conducive to stability rather that democracy and that it is therefore stability which is the key variable. Stability, however, is historically and contemporaneously more widespread than democracy and it is therefore more logical to suggest that stability is a necessary but not sufficient condition for democracy.

The same applies to the political, social and economic rights widely associated with democracy: even where various rights are widely available in practice, they are a necessary but not a sufficient condition for the existence of democracy (see Benn and Peters 1959; Finer 1970; Held 1987). Nor is it a matter of appropriate mechanisms, necessary as they are: ultimately democracy relates to values and attitudes and is therefore a matter of judgement not objective fact. As Edmund Burke (1883, vol. II, p. 29) wrote in the eighteenth century: 'If any ask what free government is, I answer, that for any practical purpose, it is what people think so.'

THE DISTRIBUTION OF POWER: AN OVERVIEW

Only elite theory and Marxist theory purport to offer a universal description and explanation of the distribution of power. Totalitarianism and democracy offer descriptions and explanations only for particular societies. Both elite and Marxist theories have something to say about totalitarianism and democracy. Mosca lent support to Mussolini's Fascist regime and the ideas of both Mosca and Pareto have been associated with the concept of the totalitarian state. Some Marxists not only readily identified Mussolini's Italy and Hitler's Germany as totalitarian, but also similarly regarded the USSR under Stalin. Elite theorists are often contemptuous of democracy, but some see it as a means of rejuvenating the elite and making it responsive to the needs of the non-elite. Schumpeter (1943, p. 269) adopts the position of a democratic elitist by defining democracy as an 'institutional arrangement for arriving at political decisions in which individuals acquire the power to decide by means of a competitive struggle for the people's vote'.

Marxists also tend to be contemptuous of democracy, at least of what is termed 'bourgeois democracy'. Marx himself did not believe that democracy was compatible with a capitalist society and envisaged a Rousseau-like direct democracy, using the example of the Paris Commune of 1871 to expound his vision of a communist society which would, by definition, be democratic. In a communist society the state would be replaced by direct popular control, involving elected officials (who would be paid proletarian wages and be subject to recall) and the abolition of the police, a standing army and a distinct judiciary (all of which would be replaced by citizens who would enforce law, order and justice). Private property would be abolished, the social division of labour would end, the market and monetary economies would disappear, and a classless society would emerge. The ideal of the communist society was 'from each according to his ability, to each according to his needs' (Marx 1989 [1875], pp. 24–87). Marx never spelled out how a communist society would come about, other than through an ill-defined 'dictatorship of the proletariat', nor how it would be sustained. However, he did acknowledge that there would be a lower or earlier phase of communism, and a later or higher stage. Subsequently, Lenin in *The State and Revolution* argued that these two stages were socialism and communism.

Lenin's view of democracy stemmed directly from his experience of practising politics: he stressed the dictatorship of the proletariat, essentially in the form of domination by the Communist Party as the 'vanguard of the proletariat'. A crucial Leninist doctrine was that of 'democratic centralism', based on the principles of 'freedom of discussion, unity of action', so that once the Party had decided on a course of action, all should work unequivocally to realise it. In practice, democratic centralism meant the overwhelming dominance of the Party leadership, epitomised by the Stalinist period, but still applicable to the post-Stalinist communist parties of the USSR and Eastern Europe until their position was undermined by *perestroika* in the Soviet Union and the collapse of communist regimes in Eastern Europe. Democratic centralism could be said to continue to prevail in the People's Republic of China, but not without noting that the dominance of the Chinese Communist Party was severely disrupted by the chaos of the Cultural Revolution between 1966 and 1969, the experience of which still reverberated well after Mao Zedong's death in 1976.

Elite theorists regard the practice of communist parties in power as indisputable evidence of a ruling class or elite in the 'socialist' societies in the USSR, the PRC and Eastern Europe. Certainly the oligarchical nature of these parties and the material privileges accorded to party *apparatchiks* and senior officials gives much credence to the claim. Although Marxists agree that the inherent contradictions of capitalist societies will inevitably cause a redistribution of power, some theorists argue that only a democratically organised but revolutionary mass movement can bring about a shift in power from the dominant capitalist class to the proletariat, others that a transformation to communism can be brought about by working within the liberal-democratic state.

The pluralist view of the distribution of power has been the subject of much criticism, but some of its leading proponents have sought to respond positively to that criticism, especially by acknowledging that the state develops its own interests and should not be seen as a neutral arbiter between competing interests. It is also accepted that the distribution of resources between competing interests is far from equal and that social and economic inequalities may restrict political equality and therefore the operation of democracy (see Lindblom 1977 and Dahl 1985). In addition, it can be argued that the pluralist contribution has been further enriched by the recognition of what have become known as new social movements (NSMs). These are pressure or interest groups concerned with issues such as feminism and the environment, cutting across traditional socio-economic cleavages, less formally organised, and emphasising protest rather than operating through traditional political machinery. NSMs will be discussed further in the context of political participation in Chapter 6.

One attempt to link all four sets of ideas about the distribution of power was made by Kornhauser (1959). He posited four Weberian ideal types of society, each depending on the relationship between elites and non-elites. Kornhauser argued that the form of society depended, on the one hand, on the extent to which elites were accessible, that is, open to ideas and influence from the non-elite, and, on the other, the extent to which non-elites were available for manipulation by the elite. From this relationship four types of society emerged. The first was a communal society – a traditional society with a closed elite and non-elites bound together by ties of kinship and community and therefore not available for manipulation. The second was pluralist society, characterised by competing elites, open to ideas and influence, and non-elites with diverse commitments and therefore unavailable for manipulation. The third was totalitarian society, which Kornhauser called 'a state of total mobilisation' of the non-elite by the elite, but in which the elite is not open to ideas and influence by the non-elites. The fourth type was mass society, characterised by a lack of communal or societal ties, enabling the elite to manipulate non-elites and the non-elites to manipulate elites. Kornhauser gives as examples of societies showing tendencies towards the mass society the United States during various populist movements in the latter part of the nineteenth century, the depression years after 1929, and the McCarthy period in the 1950s, and the Poujadists in France in the 1950s, but his classic example is the Weimar Republic, which, he argues, shows all the characteristics of the mass society.

Kornhauser's analysis provides one particular way of looking broadly at the distribution of power under different conditions. In general, he argues that most societies exhibit a mixture of two or more of his ideal types. What he demonstrates principally, however, is the value of an eclectic view rather than attempting to take a single, uniform view of how power is distributed in societies in general. There is thus a need to recognise that different models of the distribution of power fit different societies, that more than one model may be applicable, and that the applicability of a particular model is likely to vary significantly over time. This last point is vividly illustrated by the events in Eastern Europe and the Soviet Union in 1989 and since: what often seemed immutable changed so rapidly that few foresaw it and only the bold feel able to predict with any certainty what new distribution of power will emerge. Nor should it be assumed that a pluralist or a democratic model will become the norm, nor that the capitalist societies of the West will be the economic role models for Eastern Europe and the Soviet Union. Those capitalist societies themselves face significant change, especially from the growing economic, social and political influences of the EC and the consequences of the free-trade agreement between the United States and Canada, quite apart from the potential impact of relations with the Third World and environmental factors, such as global warming and the exploitation of the earth's natural resources. Power and its distribution are not static but dynamic concepts and any analysis of political behaviour within societies, which is the subject of Part III, must take account of that.

PART III

POLITICAL BEHAVIOUR AND SOCIETY

INTRODUCTION

To understand power and its distribution further it is necessary to examine political behaviour within societies, in particular to explore who takes part in politics and why. There are, of course, problems in defining what constitutes political activity, but there are even greater problems in exploring *why* individuals engage in political activity. Some explanations are or appear to be self-evident, especially those of an instrumental nature in that politics serves as a means to a clearly defined end, such as preventing the construction of a proposed road or securing the payment of previously denied welfare benefits. Such explanations may be clearly articulated by those involved, but other explanations may be less apparent to actors and observers alike.

One explanation for political involvement or lack of it which is not necessarily evident to the participant or non-participant is that of socialisation, defined by White (1977, p. 1) as a 'long and complicated process of learning to live in society'. Beneath that deceptively simple definition, however, lies a major conflict between socialisation conceived as a deterministic process, on the one hand, and as an adaptive process on the other. The deterministic view has been criticised in two major respects: first, it is obvious that individuals are not behavioural clones of parents, teachers or others in society and that they are, to varying and often significant degrees, capable of innovation and change; and second, that, while socialisation may well be a major factor in explaining the persistence of a given society, societies can and do change for endogenous as well as exogenous reasons. As Wrong (1961, p. 192) has argued: 'All men are socialised . . . but this does not mean that they have been *completely moulded* by the particular norms and values of their culture' (emphasis added).

Socialisation, then, is seen as important in determining an individual's knowledge, values and attitudes and therefore their behaviour, but offers only a partial explanation. Other factors and variables need to be taken into account. In this context knowledge is defined basically, though not exclusively, as factual information about society, about individuals and groups of individuals, and about the world beyond, in all cases both past and present. It may not always be factual information because individuals may be misinformed, but treat such information as though it were true. Values are defined as basic beliefs about the nature of society, about individuals and groups of individuals, and about the world beyond. They may be moral, religious, social or political beliefs, for example, simple or complex, well founded or less well founded, positive or negative, but to varying degrees will underpin and inform an individual's attitudes or opinions on specific matters, individuals, issues and events. Similarly, an individual's knowledge will underpin and inform both values and attitudes, but not necessarily sequentially in that knowledge, rather than preceding the formation of particular value or attitude, may be used to support it after its formation. Socialisation therefore needs to be seen in dynamic rather than static terms, as a process which continues throughout life.

A key variable is the individual's personality. Although the question of personality is subject to much discussion as to how far it is the product of inherited traits rather than environmental influences – the nature versus nurture argument – that in no way diminishes its importance. That different personality traits and types exist is well established and the relationship between personality and an individual's knowledge, values and attitudes is likely to be an important factor in influencing their political behaviour.

A second key variable in this process is the individual's experience, which may reinforce existing knowledge, values and attitudes or change them. Experience consists of events and issues, in some of which there will be direct involvement by the individual, but in many simply an interest or awareness of their occurrence or existence.

How far socialisation accounts for political participation is an important question, but other explanations need to be explored, particularly the motivational and psychological dimensions of participation. With the important exception of voting, politics in all societies is a minority activity and the most active – the holders of political, administrative and other offices in the state – are very few in number. How typical they are of society generally, how they are recruited, and what motivates them are major questions for political sociology. Part III is therefore concerned with examining and developing models of political socialisation, participation and recruitment, using the variables already discussed – those of knowledge, values and attitudes, experience and personality.

Chapter 5

POLITICAL SOCIALISATION

INTRODUCTION

Political socialisation may be defined as the process by which individuals in a given society become acquainted with the political system and which to a significant degree determines their perceptions of politics and their reactions to political phenomena. Academically it was the subject of much attention in the 1960s and 1970s, but subsequently became a matter of dispute and criticism as attempts to give it a firmer empirical foundation ran into a variety of difficulties. This has led to its relative neglect in the sense that there is a tendency either to take political socialisation for granted or to minimise its role as its empirical shortcomings have become evident. This is unfortunate in that in social behaviour generally the concept of socialisation is widely accepted and that alone establishes a *prime facie* case for its relevance to political behaviour.

Herbert Hyman's (1959) *Political Socialisation* was the first systematic treatment of political socialisation by a political scientist. Hyman drew upon work already done in anthropology and psychology, but in due course two types of definitions emerged, one narrow, the other broad. These are well-summarised by Fred Greenstein (1968, p. 551): 'the deliberate inculcation of political information, values and practices by institutional agents who have been formally charged with this responsibility' and 'all political learning, formal and informal, deliberate and unplanned, at every stage of the life cycle, including not only explicitly political learning but also nominally non-political learning of politically relevant characteristics'. This latter definition is sometimes criticised as being unduly broad, but it illustrates the distinction between conscious and deliberate socialisation, on the one hand, and unconscious and environmental socialisation, on the other.

The narrow definition of political socialisation is well-illustrated by the overt attempts in totalitarian societies to inculcate particular values through the educational system, as quotations from Lenin and Hitler demonstrate:

> Only by radically remoulding the teaching, organisation and training of the young shall we be able to ensure that the results of the efforts of the younger generation will be the creation of a society that will be unlike the old society, that is a Communist Society. (Speech by Lenin to Young Communist League, 2 October 1920)

> When an opponent declares, 'I will not come over to your side', I calmly say, 'Your child belongs to us already ... What are you? You will pass on. Your descendants, however, now stand in the new camp. In a short time they will know nothing else but this new community'. (Speech by Hitler, 6 November 1933)

> [W]e have set ourselves the task of inoculating our youth with the spirit of this community of the people at a very early age ... And this new Reich will give its youth to no one, but itself take youth and give to youth its own education and its own upbringing. (Speech by Hitler, 1 May 1937)

In Nazi Germany children were taught that their first loyalty was to the state as personified in the Führer, Adolf Hitler. All textbooks were required to conform with Nazi ideology and even in mathematics textbooks 'appropriate' examples were used. These included calculating the areas and populations of the colonies which Germany lost as a result of the First World War, the capacity and performance of military aircraft, and questions relating to the 'Jewish problem', such as the number and proportion of Jews in Germany. Outside the school socialisation operated extensively through the *Jungvolk*, for children between the ages of ten and fourteen, and over the age of fourteen the *Hitler-Jugend* for boys and the *Bund Deutscher*

Mädel for girls. Incidentally, military examples were still used for mathematical problems under the communist regime in East Germany.

A similar pattern existed in the Soviet Union: all textbooks and teaching had to conform to the official line, a process extending from nursery school through to higher education. Mathematical problems were also used overtly for socialisation purposes, as the examples cited by a former *New York Times* Moscow correspondent illustrate:

> The first cosmonaut was a citizen of the Soviet Union, Comrade Yuri Gagarin. He made a flight round the earth in 108 minutes. How many hours and how many minutes did the first flight around the earth last?
>
> In our country the world's first atomic icebreaker, *Lenin*, was built. What is the length and width of this icebreaker if it is known that 1/8 of its length consists of 16 metres 75 centimetres, and 1/5 of its width is equal to 5 metres 52 centimetres?
>
> A brigade of oil workers must drill 6 kilometres 650 metres per year. In the first half year it drilled 4 kilometres 900 metres, and in the second 1 kilometre 50 metres less. Did the brigade fulfil its annual plan? If it overfulfilled it, by how much?
>
> A *sovkhoz* [state farm] pledged itself to give the state 3,350 tons of cotton. But it gave 4,500 tons, then added another 1/10 of this quantity. By how many tons did the *sovkhoz* overfulfil its obligation? (Shipler 1985, p. 104)

Socialisation in the Soviet Union was further reinforced through the Young Pioneers, to which almost all children between the ages of nine and fourteen belonged, but membership of the principal youth organisation, the *Komsomol*, was much more selective, the recommendation of a Communist Party member or two *Komsomol* members being necessary. The *Komsomol* was an important channel of recruitment into the Communist Party itself and *Komsomol* members received direct political instruction and other training. All males in the USSR were also subject to socialisation through serving as military conscripts. The parallels with socialisation in Nazi Germany are marked.

Ivan Volgyes (1975) in *Political Socialisation in Eastern Europe* points out that problems in mathematics often related to matters such as hours of work and the socialist work ethic and that in all communist states there were separate courses on ideology. Volgyes found that the emphasis varied from one country to another, but that a number of common themes emerged. These included the building of socialism, anti-imperialism, socialist morality and patriotism. In 1990 newspapers reported that students returning to North Korea from Eastern European countries that had seen the collapse of communist regimes and the abandonment of communist ideology were required to undergo 're-education' in order to ensure their ideological reliability and loyalty to the regime of Kim Il-sung.

The broad definition of political sociology involves both deliberate or overt socialisation and unconscious or covert socialisation. It is therefore strongly related to, though not synonymous with, the concept of political culture. This was defined by Almond and Verba (1963, p. 14) in *The Civic Cultures* as 'the political system as internalised in the cognitions, feelings and evaluations of its population', and later by Almond and Powell (1966, p. 50) as 'the pattern of individual attitudes and orientations towards politics among the members of a political system'. In *The Civic Culture* Almond and Verba posited three types of political culture: the parochial, the subject, and the participant. Parochial political culture is characterised by a low awareness of government, low expectations of government, and a low level of political participation; a subject political culture by higher levels of awareness and expectation, but a low level of participation; and a participant culture by high levels of awareness, expectation, and participation. They were intended as Weberian ideal types, but of the five countries covered by Almond and Verba's survey, Mexico approximated to a parochial culture, Italy and West Germany to a subject culture, and Britain and the United States to a participant culture, although they acknowledged that all forms of political culture are in practice mixed.

Almond and Verba have been criticised for applying and assuming that similar values are applicable to all five countries, but the concept of political culture remains important, not least because the criticism itself implies that values differ from one society to another and that failure to take account of those values risks failing to understand that society. It has also been suggested that Almond and Verba assume a uniform political culture within a given society. However, while there are tendencies in that direction, they acknowledge that a society's political culture may be fragmented to the extent that not only are there conflicts within a political culture, but alternative political cultures may exist. What needs to be acknowledged is that in most societies one or more alternative political cultures will exist.

It is probably not sensible to regard political socialisation as synonymous with political culture, but to see political culture as the product of political socialisation. This leaves political socialisation to be defined more broadly as the means by which individuals acquire political knowledge or information, political values or basic beliefs, and political attitudes or opinions on specific matters. Exploring political socialisation further then becomes a matter of seeking answers to four related questions:

1. What is learned?
2. When is it learned?
3. How is it learned?
4. What is the relationship between political socialisation and political behaviour?

A good deal of research has been done on the second and third questions, and a fair amount on the first (see Langton, 1969 and Dawson, Prewitt and Dawson, 1977), but the key question, and the most difficult to answer, is the last. Moreover, most of the research on political socialisation has been done in and on the United States, and although quite a lot has been done on other countries it tends to be fragmented.

A THEORY OF POLITICAL SOCIALISATION

Figure 5.1 puts in the form of a model the variables and processes that contribute to political socialisation. It begins by suggesting a number of agencies of socialisation, such as the family, peer groups, and the mass media through whom the process operates. These in turn operate through three major mechanisms – imitation, instruction, and motivation throughout the individual's life. At no point, however, is it suggested that each of these variables is of equal importance; on the contrary, it is likely that their importance will vary from society to society, from one individual or group of individuals to another, and, not least, over time. An individual's knowledge, values and attitudes are, it is suggested, to a significant degree

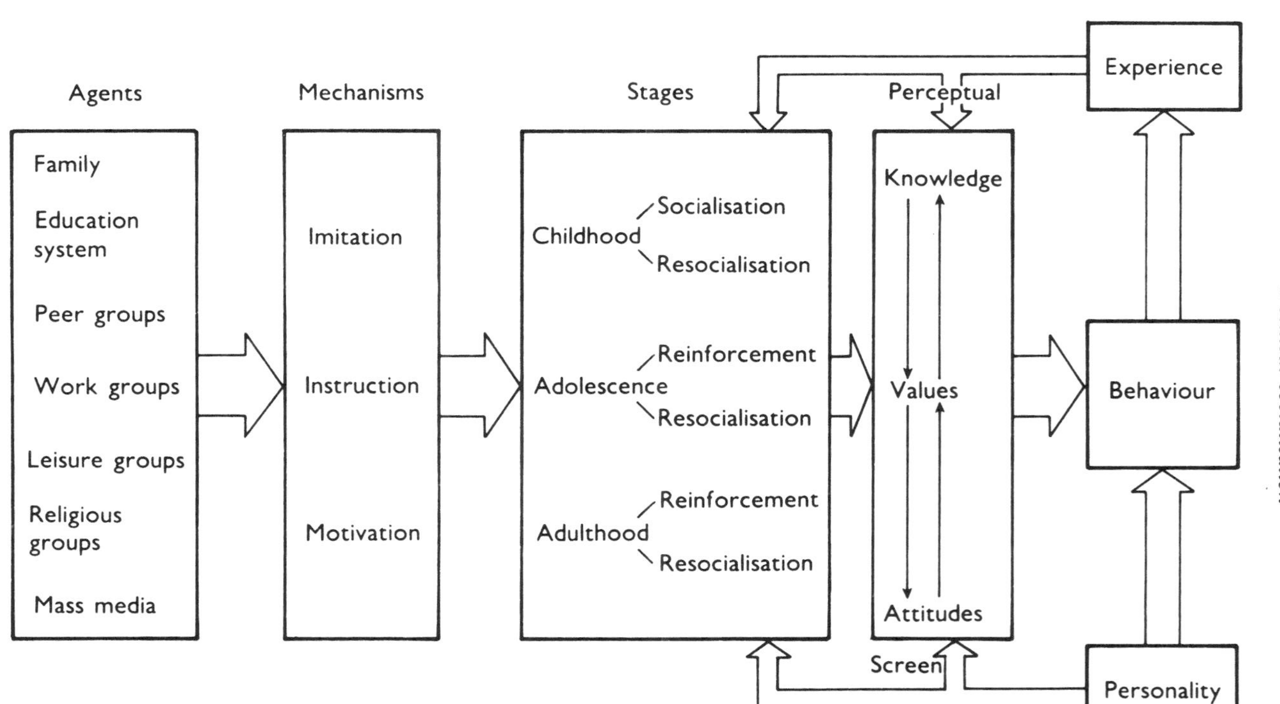

Figure 5.1 **A model of political socialisation.**

the product of the socialisation process. However, the model also seeks to define socialisation as a dynamic, continuing (though not necessarily continuous) process which may contribute to the persistence of particular values and attitudes, but also to their being modified and changed. Socialisation may therefore involve resocialisation, as well as the reinforcement of values and attitudes.

Closely linked to the socialisation process are the two independent variables of the individual's experience and personality and these interact with the other variables to produce a perceptual screen through which the individual reacts to external political phenomena and stimuli, and where appropriate, engage in political activity. In this context, of course, appropriate behaviour may be a decision not to engage in political activity. Political participation, however, is the subject of Chapter 6.

What is learned

There is a strong presumption in socialisation research that the basis of much behaviour, political no less than social, is acquired in the early stages of life. In a major study of childhood political socialisation Easton and Dennis (1969) suggest four stages in the socialisation process (see Figure 5.2). Easton and Dennis' research, which was conducted in the United States, found that initially children came to recognise the existence of authority – someone who had the right to issue orders or give instructions, such as parents, policemen, teachers, and politically, the President. In due course, however, they became aware of a distinction between the internal or private authority of parents and teachers and the external or public authority of policemen and the President. There then followed a realisation that impersonal political institutions, such us Congress, the state

1. Recognition of individual authority.
2. Recognition of a distinction between internal and external authority.
3. Recognition of impersonal political authority.
4. Recognition of a distinction between institutions and the individuals associated with them.

Figure 5.2 The stages of childhood political socialisation (Source: Easton and Dennis (1969)).

legislature, and the Supreme Court, and processes, such as voting, existed. Finally, there came an awareness that there was a distinction between such institutions and processes and the persons who operated or were involved in them – that ultimately the institutions outlived and transcended the individuals – so that idealised images of particular individuals, such as the President or a senator, are transferred to the presidency or Congress.

Similar stages of development have been found in studies elsewhere, but within both the United States and other countries differences emerge in relation to age, socio-economic status (SES), gender, IQ, and religion. The most significant of these differences is found in the levels of *political efficacy*, that is, the extent to which individuals feel they are able to exert influence over politics, which varies principally in relation to SES and IQ (Milbrath and Goel 1977, p. 60).

In general, the picture that emerges of what is learned is one of a progression from the simple to the complex, from a limited to a broad conception of politics and political institutions, from identity with a particular country and the recognition of visible symbols of political authority to more abstract concepts, such as voting, democracy, and ideology. Individuals acquire varying degrees of knowledge about politics. This knowledge, however, is the basis for and is interpreted by various values held about political ideas and phenomena, which in turn form the basis for particular attitudes or opinions.

When it is learned

The short answer to when political socialisation occurs is throughout life, but in practice, as the above discussion suggests, childhood and to a lesser extent adolescence are generally regarded as more important than adulthood. Nevertheless, increasing attention has been paid to adult socialisation and to the idea that socialisation is a lifelong process rather than one confined to the first twenty or so years of life, important as those early years may be for most people in most societies. Volgyes (1975, p. 1–3), in his study of Eastern Europe, refers to 'generational socialisation', that is, the conscious or sub-conscious socialisation of children by adults, and to 'resocialisation', which he sub-divides into a 'revolutionary phase' and a 'continuum phase'. When a new regime with significantly different ideological values comes to power, he argues, it will seek not only to socialise the younger generation, but resocialise the older generation and convert their values from the old ideology to the new. Beyond that, however, the regime will seek to reinforce its ideological control by a continuing process of socialisation, especially through the workplace and the media. In such circumstances all societal activities are in principle, and to a significant extent in practice, subject to ideological evaluation, and behaviour is therefore expected to conform actually or ostensibly to explicit ideological norms. Socialisation is, therefore, largely conscious and overt, as in the case of the North Korean students cited earlier.

Such a picture is recognisable in totalitarian societies, but how far is adult socialisation applicable to other societies? The tendency to regard socialisation as an exclusively childhood and adolescent phenomenon has been challenged explicitly by a number of sociologists and implicitly by Marxist theorists. The former see socialisation as a lifelong process which helps the individual adapt to changing circumstances and situations. This view is widely, though not exclusively, associated with what is known as the 'symbolic interactionist' view, summarised by White (1977, pp. 5–6) in his study of socialisation: 'Lifelong socialisation becomes a cumulative process whereby the individual is able to adapt existing knowledge and behaviour to new situations. A bank of social values, attitudes and actions is built up and the social actor can draw on them in combination to suit the needs of changing role situations.'

Thus it is argued that within the family, peer group, work group, and leisure groups there is interaction between individuals, leading to the adjustment of behaviour in anticipation of and as a result of experience. For example, within marriage there will be socialisation between partners, not necessarily on an equal basis, and similarly, within the family between parent and child and child and parent. Other interaction occurs between employers and employees, between employees, between friends and acquaintances, within voluntary associations, such as trade unions and social and sports organisations, and so on. The difficulty for political socialisation is that much is implicit rather than explicit, but, more particularly, that identifying what is specifically political can be even more difficult. That, however, focuses attention on an important aspect of socialisation, that for the individual it is an inclusive rather than a discrete process, part of the individual's experience. This is not to say that certain aspects of socialisation, political or otherwise, are not explicit, still less that they are not specifically related to the family or peer group, work situation or politics, or whatever, but that they do not occur in isolation.

For instance, someone joining a political party and becoming an active participant will become acquainted with various behaviour patterns and norms which reflect the way in which the party operates. In some cases these patterns and norms will be formalised into rules and therefore be largely explicit, but much will be informal, such as the use of appropriate language illustrated by modes of address – 'comrades', 'brothers and sisters', 'colleagues', 'ladies and gentlemen', or 'friends', or references to opponents as 'Tories' or 'socialists'. An example of resocialisation can be found in the two Houses of Parliament. The House of Commons has more extensive and elaborate standing orders than the House of Lords. To a significant extent this is because the party battle is fiercer in the lower house, whereas the upper house is able to rely more on informal restraints. It is reflected in the fact that the Speaker of the Commons has considerable authority and clearly designated powers to enforce it, whereas the Lord Chancellor, who is Speaker of the Lords, has no such authority and debates are largely self-regulating. Thus former Members of Parliament, used to the rough and tumble of the Commons, who are awarded peerages and become members of the upper house, normally rapidly learn different norms of behaviour; they are, in short, socialised or, more accurately, resocialised into appropriate behaviour.

The Marxist view is not dissimilar in that it argues, implicitly rather than explicitly, that socialisation is a continuing process and necessarily so, since the ruling class must ensure that its ideas prevail in society. Thus, sometimes consciously and overtly, but often subconsciously and covertly, the dominant ideology is sustained in part through the continuing socialisation of society, initially through the education system and subsequently through the prevailing mode of production. Essentially, Gramsci's concept of hegemony and Althusser's concept of ideological state apparatuses are effectively forms of socialisation theory through which the dominant ideology is able to prevail. There is, in fact, a curious parallel between the Marxist view of political socialisation and the functionalist view of it, in that both see socialisation as the means by which a society perpetuates itself. However, for the functionalist, socialisation is part of the explanation of societal stability or equilibrium and therefore to be seen in a positive light, whereas for the Marxist, socialisation is a block to societal change, something to be broken not welcomed. To that extent the Marxist view of political socialisation is instrumental and deterministic, but only to the point that once the exploited class becomes aware of its exploitation the old socialisation process begins to break down and a new one begins.

The interactionist view, in contrast, not only admits the possibility of change, but sees it as a natural though not inevitable consequence of socialisation through experience. Individuals adapt and modify their behaviour according to experience and society may change as a consequence. As far as political socialisation is concerned, research suggests that individuals may change their values and attitudes through social and geographical mobility. For example, moving from one neighbourhood to another, particularly where it reflects a change in SES, is likely to affect an individual's political perceptions and behaviour. Thus research in the United States has shown a tendency for party identification to change among Democrats who go to live in Republican areas, though not the reverse.

It seems distinctly perverse not to allow for socialisation continuing into adulthood and operating throughout life. Much of that socialisation is likely to be reinforcing earlier experience, rather than fundamentally changing values and attitudes, but it is no less important for that.

How it is learned

Much of the research into socialisation in general and political socialisation in particular, as already noted, has concentrated on childhood, placing, as might be expected, considerable stress on the role of the family and the school as agents of socialisation; but the broader view of socialisation argues that, important as family and school may be, other agents exist – peer groups, work groups, leisure groups, religious groups, and the media. If it is the case that the basic parameters of behaviour are laid down during childhood and, to a lesser extent, adolescence, then the family and the school are likely to be the most important agents of socialisation in most modern societies.

The relative importance of different agents, however, needs to be approached with care. For example, in a highly religious society or section of society the church or the mosque, or other religious groupings, may play a major socialising role from an early stage in an individual's life. That this may be reinforcing family or societal religiosity is beside the point, especially if it does so forcefully. Nor should it be assumed, whatever the later impact of other agents may be, that family and school are necessarily congruent; they may well conflict, as was certainly the case for some religious families in Nazi Germany and for many Poles and Czechs under communist regimes. Religious sects in particular frequently find that their values conflict with those of the wider society to the extent that they seek to isolate themselves from that society and effectively retain control over the socialisation process. Such conflicts were important in the founding of some of the American colonies, in the history of groups like the Huguenots and the Mormons, in the development of and continued existence of Amish and Hutterite colonies or communities in the United States and Canada, and, perhaps above all, in the history of the Jews and the founding of the state of Israel.

Furthermore, important as the family and school may be in the earlier stages of socialisation, other agents are likely to assume greater prominence later. The role of peer groups in many primitive societies has been well established by anthropological research, but peer groups also operate in a socio-economic setting, particularly in relation to status, and often operating through, but not synonymous with, work, leisure and religious groups. Different occupations are associated with particular life-styles and often reflected in status symbols.

The mass media are widely regarded as an important agent of socialisation in general and of political socialisation in particular. In modern societies the media are the major source of the population's information about what is happening in their society and in the world at large. Governments of all types and complexions are not only mindful of this, but to varying degrees use the media to impart their points of view. All governments seek to influence the media and not a few to control them. There can be no doubt that in totalitarian societies the control of the media is seen as crucial to the continued dominance of the regime and, moreover, as a major agent of political socialisation. It is not merely a negative matter of censorship, but a positive one of continued inculcation and reinforcement of the regime's ideology. All information disseminated by the media must conform to the prevailing ideology. Information which cannot be made to conform is suppressed, and the relationship between fact and reportage is loosened to the point that, if necessary, fiction becomes fact and a new reality is created. It was no wonder that, as a reporter in Nazi Germany in the 1930s, William Shirer (1960), author of *The Rise and Fall of the Third Reich*, sometimes found himself unable to determine what was true and what was not.

The role of the media in political socialisation in other societies is less clear, largely because it is more complex. In some societies media censorship is widespread, but in many others governments lack the control of the media found in dictatorial and totalitarian societies. There are often competing media, representing conflicting views or providing alternative sources of information. Yet any case for adult socialisation must include a place for the media. Information is not a neutral commodity, untainted by its source or by the medium by which it reaches its audience. It has to be selected, packaged and, above all, interpreted. The newspapers people read, the television programmes they watch, the radio programmes they listen to will reflect to a significant degree the values and attitudes they acquired earlier, in part through the socialisation process. The media will, in turn, reinforce or modify those values and attitudes, continuing the process of socialisation and resocialisation.

The mechanisms through which socialisation takes place fall under three heads: imitation, instruction, and motivation. Imitation is the copying of the behaviour of other individuals or groups of individuals and is generally most important in childhood. Instruction is the more or less intended learning of appropriate behaviour through formal education and less formally through discussion groups and other activities, such as vocational training. Motivation is the learning of appropriate behaviour by experience, by a process of trial and error. Instruction is clearly most important in childhood and adolescence, but is also likely to be periodically important in adult life, while motivation is common to the whole life cycle.

The relationship between political socialisation and political behaviour

The relationship between socialisation and behaviour is much the most difficult aspect of socialisation theory to explore. Much of the research on it is based on inferential data, principally matching socio-economic data with actual behaviour. This is especially common in studies of electoral behaviour, in which correlations between socio-economic characteristics, such as occupation and education and voting behaviour are used to support the argument that the latter is to a significant extent the product of political socialisation.

Studies of British electoral behaviour, for example, have found strong and persistent correlations between party preferences and social class. Indeed, in the late 1960s Peter Pulzer (1967, p. 88) went so far as to suggest, 'Class is the basis of British party politics; all else is embellishment'. More specifically, Butler and Stokes (1969) in their study *Political Change in Britain* of electoral behaviour found extremely high correlations between the party their respondents supported when they first voted and the party preferences of their parents. However, other, more recent studies have suggested a marked decline in class voting (Franklin 1985; Rose and McAllister 1986). This decline has been attributed in part to significant changes in the social composition of the electorate – in particular, a decline in the size of the working class – and in part to what has been called 'partisan de-alignment' – a partial uncoupling of the association between party preference and class (Crewe *et al.* 1977; Crewe 1984). Franklin and Rose and McAllister suggest that a major reason for partisan de-alignment has been a greater willingness on the part of voters to base their electoral choice on policy issues rather than parties. Certainly, between 1964 and 1987 there was a significant decline in the proportion of voters who identified strongly with their parties and in the proportion of the electorate supporting the two major parties, Conservative and Labour. There is widespread agreement on the impact of changes in the social composition of the electorate: 'it is now more middle class, less religious, more educated, and more equal' (Heath *et al.* 1991, p. 200); and that those changes have benefited the Conservatives and Liberal Democrats (and their predecessors) more than the Labour Party. But there is less agreement over changes in class voting beyond this.

All these studies, however, provide evidence to support the view that political socialisation is an important factor in electoral behaviour in Britain and, by inference, in political behaviour more generally, but they also provide evidence for the view that other factors are important too – especially short-term factors, such as particular issues and attitudes towards the government's competence and handling of affairs. Indeed, Heath *et al.* (1991) provide specific evidence of a decline in the association between electoral choice and parents' party preferences and an increase in the importance of voters' attitudes in determining electoral behaviour (see also Denver 1989).

Correlations of varying strengths between socio-economic characteristics and electoral behaviour are common and by no means limited to industrial societies or liberal-democracies. For instance, elections in many Third World societies are notable for high levels of tribal or ethnic voting. Other studies have found correlations between socio-economic characteristics and feelings of apathy, alienation and similar concepts, which will be discussed further in Chapter 6. There remains, however, a major empirical problem of establishing that the relationship between particular socio-economic characteristics and political behaviour is in general causal and that it is to a significant degree the product of political socialisation. There is also a serious empirical gap between psychological studies, which tend to concentrate on the individual, and sociological studies, which tend to concentrate on groups. Nevertheless, it is doubtful whether the vast majority of such relationships, especially where they are statistically strong, are spurious, and they therefore require explanation. Political socialisation offers at least a partial explanation.

Political socialisation is also widely seen as a major explanation of legitimacy, by Marxists as well as non-Marxists. The question of societal persistence is of crucial importance to socialisation theory, since it is arguably the transference of knowledge, values and attitudes from one generation to another that explains the ability of a political system to survive through its widespread acceptance in society, and to acquire and maintain legitimacy. There is, however, a danger that a link between political socialisation and legitimacy is seen in unduly deterministic terms, with no allowance for, let alone an explanation of, societal change. One answer, of course, is to argue that fundamental changes in society are the result of a breakdown in political socialisation, which may well be true in some societies, most notably those with totalitarian tendencies. An alternative approach is to argue that in most societies political socialisation is not monolithic, but will reflect whatever conflicts are found in a particular society to the point that alternative or rival socialisation processes will exist. Furthermore, by arguing that socialisation is a lifelong process and that personality and experience are key variables in that process, it is possible to argue that political socialisation may play a role in changing society as well as preserving it.

Two examples illustrate such a view. The first arises from studies carried out during the 1950s of refugees from the Soviet Union. One of these studies found that younger respondents who had grown up under the Soviet regime normally accepted the Soviet system initially and had seldom always been opposed to the regime. Moreover, they generally retained important ideological commitments, such as support for the welfare state and for state ownership of various industries, and tended to blame the Soviet *leadership* rather than the *political system* for their disillusionment (Bauer, 1955).

The second example concerns the changing attitudes towards the Federal Republic of Germany in the years after its founding in 1949. In 1951 opinion polls found that only 32 per cent of respondents agreed with the view that Germany was to blame for the Second World War, but by 1962 the proportion had risen to 62 per cent. Similarly, of Roosevelt's famous 'Four Freedoms' – of religion, of speech, from fear, and from want – there were significant shifts in all except religion between 1949 and 1965 when respondents were asked which they thought the most important; in 1949 the rank order was 'from want' (35 per cent), 'of speech' (26 per cent), 'from fear' (17 per cent), and 'of religion' (12 per cent), whereas in 1965 it was 'of speech' (54 per cent), 'from want' (19 per cent), 'of religion' (14 per cent), and 'from fear' (10 per cent) (EMNID 1967).

In the first case it could be argued that the Soviet system and some of its important ideological values retained a significant degree of legitimacy, despite disillusionment in other respects; and in the second that over a period of a decade and a half West Germany gradually acquired substantially increased legitimacy, marked by a much greater stress on idealistic liberal-democratic values and a marked decline in materialistic concern with survival. The logic of this argument is that by definition political socialisation is a relatively slow process, but a process that can be associated with change, at least in relation to legitimacy. In some cases, however, the 'old' socialisation process may be too strong and a new regime may never acquire more than limited legitimacy, or may rapidly lose legitimacy under stress. The Weimar Republic of Germany (1919–33) could be cited as an example of the former and the Fourth French Republic (1946–58) of the latter.

What this in turn suggests is that if the gap between the socialisation process and reality is never bridged or becomes too great, the political system comes under increasing strain and is likely to collapse or at least undergo important change. This, it could be argued, is part of the explanation of what happened in Eastern Europe in 1989 and what is continuing to happen in the former Soviet Union. Indeed, there were reports from East Germany in 1990, prior to unification, that the education system was having to undergo massive adjustments to cope with the abandonment of the 'old' picture of the West and its replacement by the 'new'. Younger children were having difficulty in accepting the changes that have taken place, since these changes contradicted much that they had been taught. In particular, the psychological adjustment required to shift the picture of the Communist Party and its leaders from one of virtuousness to one of wickedness was considerable.

A CRITIQUE OF POLITICAL SOCIALISATION THEORY

A major criticism of political socialisation is that much of the research into it is heavily concentrated on American experience and is therefore ethnocentric. There is some force in such a criticism, not least when it is associated with functionalist interpretation, which tends to imply an inherent superiority in the American political system; but ultimately it amounts to not much more than a warning not to assume that American experience is universal. It does, however, lead to a more important criticism, which is that because a great deal of the American experience suggests a broad homogeneity, there is insufficient allowance for variable or fragmented political socialisation producing a conflicting rather than a homogeneous political culture. Even more important, as already discussed, it presents particular difficulties in relating political socialisation to societal change.

Far harsher criticisms have been made by David Marsh (1971), who points out that most political socialisation research has concentrated on the process rather than the outcome. In other words, the effect on political behaviour and on the political system is taken for granted. He goes on to argue that it tends to assume that the values and attitudes of adults are primarily the product of childhood socialisation and that individual opinion has a collective impact on the operation of politics. He also says that little or no account is taken of personal or situational factors operating at the time. Finally, Marsh rightly deplores the general absence of longitudinal or panel studies which examine the values, attitudes and behaviour of the same individuals at regular intervals over a fairly lengthy period of time.

The criticisms by Marsh and others are both reasonable and telling, but there is danger of the theoretical baby being thrown out with the empirical bathwater. What is required is more and better research, especially longitudinal studies. Certainly, much of the early theorising was inadequate and concentrated too much on childhood socialisation. Like much research into political behaviour it relied and continues to rely on inferential data and stressed prediction at the expense of explanation. However, neither the criticism nor the inadequacy of the research precludes the development of a theory of political socialisation which incorporates change, especially a theory which takes account of experience and personality. Such a theory would need to emphasise the role of reinforcing and conflicting variables and of the individual's long-term and short-term environment. In short, what is needed is a theory of political socialisation which is related to other aspects of political behaviour, especially participation and recruitment, the subjects of the next two chapters.

Chapter 6

POLITICAL PARTICIPATION

INTRODUCTION

Political participation is the involvement of the individual at various levels of activity in the political system, ranging from non-involvement to the holding of political office. Inevitably political participation is closely linked to political socialisation, but it should not be seen solely as either an extension or the product of socialisation. Moreover, it is relevant to a number of theories important in political sociology. For instance, it is essential to both elite and pluralist theories, though its role in each is profoundly different. Elite theory confines significant political participation to the elite, leaving the masses as largely inactive or to be manipulated by the elite. For pluralism, however, political participation is the key to political behaviour in that it constitutes a major factor in explaining the distribution of power and the deciding of policy. Political participation is just as crucial to Marxist theory: class consciousness leads to action or participation, ultimately in the form of revolution, while neo-Marxists, such as Gramsci and Althusser, explain the survival of capitalism by its ability to control participation through hegemony. Leninist theory stresses the participatory role of the Communist Party as the 'vanguard of the proletariat'. Indeed, unless it is defined narrowly as a synonym for democracy, political participation may be said to be a universal phenomenon, not in the sense that all individuals necessarily engage in political activity, nor that it is equally common in form or extent in all societies, but that it is found in all societies.

Geraint Parry (1972) suggests that it is neces
aspects of political participation – the mode
intensity, and its quality. By mode he means w
whether it is formal or informal, and argues that t
according to the opportunity, levels of interest (t
specific), the resources available to the individual,
attitudes towards participation in the society conce ...y
whether it is encouraged or discouraged. Intensity seek ... measure how many individuals participate in particular political activities and how often they do so, which again is likely to vary according to opportunities and resources. Quality is concerned with the degree of effectiveness achieved by participation, seeking to measure its impact on those wielding power and on policy-making. This too will vary from society to society, according to opportunities and resources, and from case to case.

FORMS OF POLITICAL PARTICIPATION

In his book *Political Participation* Lester Milbrath (1965) posited a hierarchy of participation, ranging from non-involvement to holding public office, with the lowest level of actual participation being voting in an election. He divided the American public into three groups: 'gladiators' – those frequently active in politics (between 5 and 7 per cent); 'spectators' – those minimally involved in politics (about 60 per cent); and 'apathetics' – those uninvolved in politics (about 33 per cent). In the second edition (Milbrath and Goel 1977) a more complex hierarchy was adopted which sought to accommodate different types of 'gladiators', especially those who engaged in various forms of protest, rather than suggesting a unidimensional hierarchy. Implicit in the earlier, unidimensional version was the suggestion that those higher up the hierarchy had engaged in or continued to engage in activities lower down the hierarchy. However, in another study of participation in the United States Verba and Nie (1972; see also Verba, Nie and Kim 1978) found a more complex picture and divided their respondents into six groups. These were the totally passive (22 per cent); those whose only political activity was voting (21 per cent); 'localists' (20 per cent), whose only political activity was confined to local politics and issues; 'parochials' (4 per cent), whose only concern was what affected them personally;

…mpaigners' (15 per cent), who were involved in politics only in relation to particular issues on which they campaigned; leaving 'total activists', those involved over the whole range of politics, to number 18 per cent. Parry and Moyser (1990) found a similar pattern in Britain, which will be examined more closely later in the chapter.

The concept of a hierarchy of political participation, therefore, need not involve activity at one level as a precondition of activity at another, nor need protest be singled out as a particular form of activity in a hierarchical sense. Essentially the purpose of a hierarchy need be no more than a delineation of different types of political participation linked to the proposition that the higher the level of activity, the lower the level of participation, as measured by the numbers engaged in a particular activity. Figure 6.1 is a hierarchy of political participation in that sense. This hierarchy is intended to cover the whole range of political participation and to be applicable to all types of political systems. The significance of the various levels is, of course, likely to vary from one political system to another, and particular levels may be of greater consequence in one system and little or no consequence in another.

At the top of the hierarchy are those who hold various types of office within the political system, including both holders of political office and members of the bureaucracy at various levels. They are distinguished from other political participants in that, to varying degrees, they are concerned with the exercise of formal political power. This does not exclude the actual exercise of power, nor the exercise of influence, by other individuals or groups in society.

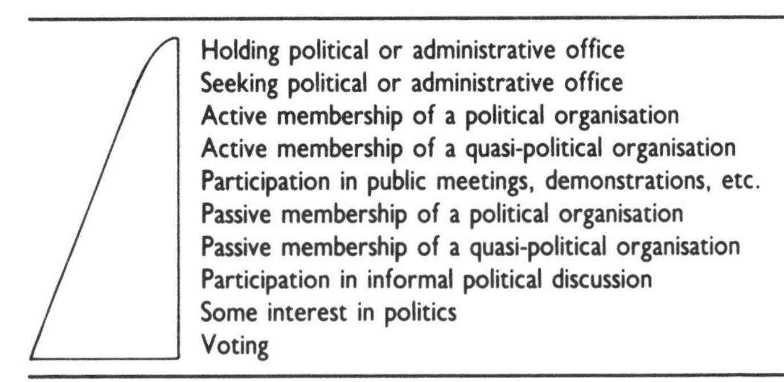

Figure 6.1 **A hierarchy of political participation.**

Power may not reside among the office-holders, but they remain important because they are normally the formal repositories of power. Any consideration of office-holders must also include some consideration of those who aspire to and seek the offices concerned. The roles of office-holders and potential office-holders, however, will be dealt with in Chapter 7, where political recruitment is considered.

Below those who hold or seek office in the political system are those who are active members of various types of political or quasi-political organisations. These include all types of political parties and pressure (or interest) groups. From the point of view of the political system, political parties and pressure groups may be defined as *agents of political mobilisation*. They are organisations through which individual members of society may participate in certain types of political activity involving the defence or promotion of particular ideas, positions, situations, persons or groups through the political system.

The basic distinction between parties and pressure groups lies in their range of attitudes. Pressure groups are organisations which seek to promote, defend or represent limited or specific attitudes, whereas parties seek to promote, defend or represent a broader spectrum of attitudes. The support that pressure groups and parties receive, however, may be specific or diffuse, stemming, that is, from only a few individuals or groups in society, or from a diverse and large number of individuals or groups. Thus a pressure group has limited objectives, such as the introduction, repeal or modification of certain laws or regulations, the protection of the interests of a particular group in society, or the promotion of particular ideologies, beliefs, principles or ideas. In some cases the objective is especially limited – the abolition of capital punishment or opposition to the siting of an airport, for instance – and the pressure group ceases to operate once its objective has been achieved (or defeated). In other cases the objective is of a continuing nature – the protection or extension of civil rights and liberties or the defence of various economic interests, for example – in which case the pressure group concerned has an indefinite existence.

The range of matters which may give rise to pressure groups is obviously legion, but it is clear that some of these groups will attract only limited, others widespread, support. Trade unions, for instance, may fall into either category according to the size and nature of the industry or occupation in which they operate. Similarly, the extent to which groups are involved in *political* activity varies considerably, from the group operating entirely within the political sphere to the group which does so only occasionally, even rarely. A group like the Campaign for Nuclear Disarmament, for instance, operates for the most part as a specifically political pressure group, whereas groups like the Automobile Association are not concerned solely or even primarily with providing motorists with a political voice. In Figure 6.1, therefore, the term 'political organisation' is intended to cover both political parties and those pressure groups whose *raison d'être* is primarily political, and the term 'quasi-political organisation' to include those pressure groups and other organisations whose function is only partly or intermittently political.

Political parties, like pressure groups, may enjoy diffuse or specific support, but differ from pressure groups in that they have diffuse rather than specific attitudes. Their objectives range over the whole spectrum of problems with which society is faced, although a particular party may place greater emphasis on some problems or aspects of problems than others. Some parties however, have a broad support base, others a narrow support base. The pragmatic, bargaining mass parties of modern democracies and the totalitarian mass parties of Nazi Germany and various communist states are examples of broad-based parties, while the regional, religious, ethnic and elitist parties found in many parts of the world are examples of narrow-based parties.

Participation in parties or pressure groups may take an active or passive form, ranging from holding office in such an organisation to the provision of financial support through the payment of subscriptions or membership dues. No sharp distinction between active and passive membership is intended and the individual may move from one to the other as circumstances vary. There remains, nevertheless, a basic commitment to the organisation through membership, which may have some political significance, both for the organisation and the individual, by strengthening the bargaining position of the organisation and influencing the political behaviour of the individual.

For various reasons individuals may not belong to any political or quasi-political organisations, but they may be persuaded to participate in some form of public meeting or demonstration. This form of participation may be spontaneous, but it is often organised by political parties or pressure groups as part of their political activity.

Many, perhaps in some cases all, of the participants will be members of the organising bodies, but not necessarily, and non-members may be persuaded to support the objects of the meeting or demonstration. Such activity is, however, intermittent and does not have the continuous nature of even the minimal commitment of membership of a political or quasi-political organisation. None the less, in hierarchical terms it is a more active form of participation than passive membership of a party or pressure group and involves fewer individuals in society.

Another intermittent form of political participation is that of informal political discussion by individuals in their families, at work or among friends. Obviously, the incidence of such discussions varies both among individuals and in relation to events. More discussion is likely during election campaigns or at times of political crisis, while discussion may be inhibited or encouraged by the attitudes of the family, fellow workers or friends.

Some people may not discuss politics with anyone, however, but may still have some interest in political matters and maintain that interest through the mass media. They will be able to keep themselves informed about what is happening and form opinions about the course of events, but they will tend to limit their participation to this and, possibly, to voting.

The act of voting may be regarded as the least active form of political participation, since it requires a minimal commitment which may cease once the vote is cast. Furthermore, regardless of other restrictions which may exist, the act of voting is inevitably restricted by the frequency of elections.

In considering political participation, however limited it may be, some attention should be paid to those who do not participate at all in the political process. Whether this is by choice or because of factors beyond the control of the individual remains to be seen.

Two matters have been deliberately excluded from the hierarchy in Figure 6.1: alienation and violence. This is because neither can be properly considered in a hierarchical sense. It will later be argued that alienation may result in participation or non-participation: an individual who feels hostile towards society in general or the political system in particular may withdraw from all types of participation and join the ranks of the totally apathetic, or may become active at various levels of participation. Participation does not necessarily involve acceptance of the political system and alienation may be expressed by political activity as well as inactivity.

Similarly, violence may manifest itself at various levels in the hierarchy, most obviously in the form of violent demonstrations or riots, but also through various political and quasi-political organisations, some of which may regard violence as an effective means of achieving their ends.

THE EXTENT OF POLITICAL PARTICIPATION

The data shown in Table 6.1 relate, of course, specifically to Britain, but the basic picture that emerges is universal in that the higher levels of political participation involve only a tiny proportion of the population, the lowest levels a majority: in short, politics is essentially a minority activity. Although in countries like Britain and the United States opinion-poll evidence shows that more than 50 per cent of the population express *some* interest in politics and between 60 and 75 per cent say they sometimes discuss politics with other people, only 15–20 per cent say they are very interested. Of course, in many societies the highest level of participation is in elections, although electoral turnout varies considerably from one country to

Table 6.1 *A hierarchy of political participation in Britain, 1989.*

Question: Which of the things on this list have you done in the last two or three years? (percentage replies)	
Stood for public office	1[a]
Taken an active part in a political campaign	3
Written a letter to an editor	5
Urged someone outside my family to vote	10
Been elected an officer of an organisation or club	13
Made a speech before an organised group	13
Presented my views to a local councillor or MP	13
Urged someone to get in touch with a local councillor or MP	15
Helped on fund-raising drives	31
Voted in the last election	68

Source: Jacobs and Worcester (1990), Figure 16.3, Socio-political activism (based on a MORI Opinion Poll).
Note: [a] The 650 MPs and 26,000 local councillors in England, Scotland and Wales comprise 0.07 per cent of the adult population.

another. In the pre-Gorbachev Soviet Union and the former communist states of Eastern Europe turnouts of more than 99 per cent were the norm, and some Third World countries, such as Egypt, claim similarly high figures. A number of liberal-democracies, such as the Netherlands, Austria, Italy, Belgium and Australia regularly experience turnouts in excess of 90 per cent, although voting is compulsory in Australia and Belgium; average turnout in West Germany, Denmark, and Norway is 80 per cent, in the United Kingdom and Canada 70 per cent, and in Switzerland and the United States 60 per cent or lower. These figures relate to national elections (and sometimes referenda) and turnout in regional and local elections, by-elections, and primary elections for choosing party candidates are invariably lower, often as low as 30 per cent.

Most other forms of political participation attract a far smaller proportion of the adult population, particularly small if the passive membership of parties and pressure groups is excluded. Such data give prima-facie support to elite theories, but fall far short of proof, since only further investigation would reveal whether the politically active minority actually constitutes an elite – a matter pursued further in Chapter 7.

There is ample and widespread evidence that political participation at all levels varies according to SES, education, occupation, gender, age, religion, ethnicity, the area and place of residence, personality, and the political environment or setting in which participation takes place. The characteristics shown in Figure 6.2 reflect tendencies, not absolute behaviour patterns. These tendencies, however, are based on a large number of studies, and although studies of liberal-democracies in general and the United States in particular predominate, a growing number are based on other types of political systems and other countries (see Milbrath and Goel 1977). The characteristics are clearly not mutually exclusive: for instance, a working-class male may not have had a full-time education beyond the secondary level, but is likely to belong to a trade union; similarly, a middle-class female may have had post-secondary education, but not belong to a union. In both instances these are conflicting characteristics and it is difficult to construct a matrix which demonstrates the relative importance of each. Nevertheless there is clear evidence that individuals subject to a number of reinforcing characteristics or pressures are more likely to participate in politics than individuals subject to cross-pressures.

Higher levels of participation	Lower levels of participation
More education, especially higher education	Less education, especially only secondary or primary
Middle class	Working or lower class
Men	Women
Older, especially middle-aged	Younger and elderly
Married	Single
Urban residents	Rural residents
Longer residence	Shorter residence
Social involvement and membership of groups or organisations	Less social involvement and/or conflicting group membership
White	Non-white
Ethnic majorities	Ethnic minorities

Figure 6.2 Socio-economic characteristics and political participation (Source: Milbrath and Goel (1977), pp. 86–122).

The association between socio-economic characteristics and participation needs to be looked at with some care, partly because there are important exceptions to the tendencies suggested in Figure 6.2 and partly because changes can and do occur over time. Two examples will suffice to illustrate the first point. For instance, rural residents in Japan are an important exception to the generalisation that participation is greater among urban dwellers. In the same way, in many Third World countries people living in rural communities have a much stronger sense of identity than those living in rapidly expanding urban areas and participation is often higher in rural areas. The second example reflects the existence of strong trade union movements in a number of European countries and in Australia and these are associated with increased levels of manual or working-class participation where unions are closely associated with one political party.

Much the best and most important example of a changing tendency is the participatory gap between men and women in countries like Britain. Thus Parry and Moyser, citing Milbrath and Goel, comment:

> A standard finding has been that there is a gender gap in citizen participation in favour of men. The evidence of the present survey is that this view must be revised, since the

> participatory gap in favour of men is now very slight indeed in Britain. ... [Indeed if] we then control for resources along with other personal factors, such as age, the gender gap actually reverses itself for overall participation and women are seen to be more active, relatively, than men in party campaigning and collective action as well as voting. (Parry and Moyser 1990, p. 159)

This finding is confirmed by Pippa Norris (1991, p. 74) who, using data from the 1987 British Election Study and the 1986 British Social Attitudes Survey, concludes that 'the conventional view is no longer valid ... as men and women are remarkably similar in their mass behaviour and attitudes across all modes of participation', with the important exceptions of seeking and holding political and administrative office. How far such findings are applicable to women in other, similar political systems is not clear, but evidence of the involvement of women in what Parry and Moyser call 'collective action' – operating through formal or informal groups – can be found in other countries and may be particularly associated with the growth and impact of the feminist movement. As Parry and Moyser (1990; p. 160) found, within a particular category significant differences may emerge: 'the single woman is more active than the single man and the most active, in relative terms, are female single parents ... one small group of women ... are intensely participatory – members of feminist groups ... they were in the top 6 per cent of participants and were particularly involved in collective and direct action rather than voting or contacting.'

There is also evidence that political activity has increased among some black and Asian groups in industrial societies. The growth of the civil rights movement in the United States, following the Supreme Court ruling in *Brown* v. *Topeka Board of Education* in 1954 that separate schooling for blacks was unconstitutional, is a case in point. Black demands for political action to enhance social and political equality intensified under the leadership of Martin Luther King. Violent protests also developed, especially in the later 1960s, but black political participation undoubtedly increased generally and became especially intensive among small groups in the black population. Similarly, the growth of the black and Asian population in Britain from the 1950s onwards eventually led to greater political activity in particular parts of the country, notably in urban areas and parliamentary constituencies in which there were significant concentrations of blacks and Asians. In the case of Asians the impact of the Moslem religion added a further dimension, vividly illustrated by the bitterness aroused by Salman Rushdie's novel, *The Satanic Verses*. In the Labour Party, Black Sections were formed in the 1980s and in the general election of 1987 one Asian and three black candidates were elected Labour MPs. The picture that emerges in both the United States and Britain is one of generally lower levels of participation among non-whites compared with whites, but also of increasing non-white participation and a growing number of political activists among non-whites.

EXPLAINING POLITICAL PARTICIPATION

Milbrath and Goel suggest that participation varies in relation to four major factors: political stimuli, social position, personal characteristics, and political environment. To these need to be added skills and resources and commitment. The more the individual is exposed to political stimuli in the form, for example, of discussing politics, belonging to an organisation engaged in some form of political activity, or having access to relevant information, the more likely is political participation. The latter, however, also varies according to the individual's personal characteristics: the more sociable, dominant and extrovert personalities are more likely to be politically active. As already suggested in Figure 6.2, social position, as measured by education, place of residence, class and ethnicity, affects participation considerably. The political environment or setting is also important in that the political culture may encourage or discourage participation and the form or forms of participation regarded as most appropriate. Thus the 'rules of the game', such as the electoral franchise, the frequency of elections, the number of offices to be filled by election, attitudes towards meetings and demonstrations, the extent and nature of parties and pressure groups, and so on, are all significant variables.

It is also important, however, to take account of the skills possessed by and the resources available to the individual. Social skills, analytical skills, organisational ability, oratorical skills are all likely to increase participation, but activity also requires resources, notably time and, not infrequently, money, either directly in the form of subscriptions or donations or indirectly in the form of affording time off or assistance in kind. Resources may also take the form of contacts and relations with other individuals and the influence and power that may result from such contacts and relations. In most cases the individual also needs commitment, commitment to an ideal or a cause, a leader or an organisation, although this more than anything raises questions concerning the explanation of political participation.

Figure 6.3 suggests the way in which the variables influencing political participation interact, starting with the individual's perceptual screen of knowledge, values and attitudes through which the individual initially considers actual or potential political situations. The individual may be subject to various political stimuli, including motivation, but account must also be taken of the skills and resources available and the individual's personality. This produces a decision on whether to participate or not, for action or inaction, which feeds back to the perceptual screen in the form of experience.

It is also clear from the work of Verba and Nie (1972) cited earlier and from Parry and Moyser (1990) that political participants constitute a number of more or less self-contained clusters, as shown in Table 6.2 which demonstrates that 'voting apart, political participation in Britain is sustained by slightly less than a quarter (23.2 per cent) of the population' (Parry and Moyser 1990, p. 150) and, more interestingly, the more active participants concentrate their efforts largely within particular modes. The largest category (8.7 per cent)

Table 6.2 *Types of political participation in Britain, 1984–85.*

Type	%	
Almost inactive	25.8	
Just voters	51.0	
Collective activists	8.7	Total activists = 23.2%
Contacting activists	7.7	
Direct activists	3.1	
Party campaign activists	2.2	
Complete activists	1.5	
Total	100.0	

Source: Parry & Moyser (1990) p. 150.

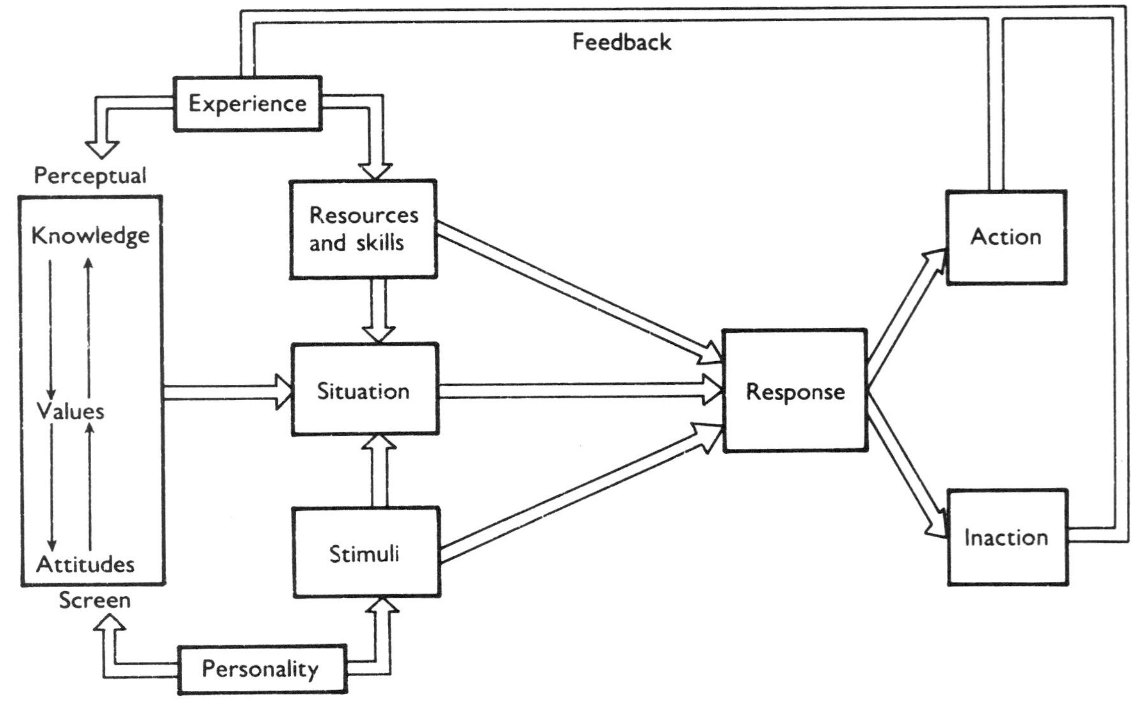

Figure 6.3 **A model of political participation.**

engaged in collective action and operated through formal and informal groups; the second largest (7.7 per cent) engaged in contacting MPs, civil servants, local councillors, and the media; the third largest but much smaller group (3.1 per cent) engaged in direct action, such as blocking traffic and protest marches, political strikes and boycotts; the fourth largest (2.2 per cent) were almost exclusively involved in campaigning for a political party, especially fund-raising and canvassing for support; and only the fifth group (1.5 per cent) engaged in political activity across the range of modes. A tiny proportion (0.2 per cent) 'had used physical force against political opponents' (Parry and Moyser 1990, p. 149) and were excluded from further analysis because they were so few in number.

The study also showed that resources 'constituted a major basis for activism' (1990, p. 163), but that values, as measured on a left–right spectrum played on even more important part, with 'high involvement at the extremes of the spectrum but with a left-ward bias' (1990, p. 162). Most important of all, however, was the finding that participation does have an impact by getting issues onto or higher up the political agenda and actually influencing policy. Parry and Moyser anticipate that levels of participation are likely to increase, especially with the spread of educational qualifications and a growing willingness to use less conventional methods to influence those holding political power.

An important part of that willingness to use less conventional methods to influence public policy has manifested itself in the form of what have been called 'new social movements' (NSMs). These are essentially a species of pressure or interest group expressing different concerns and operating in ways different from those traditionally associated with pressure groups. Offe (1985) identifies four criteria which distinguish NSMs from traditional pressure groups: issues, values, modes of action, and actors. On issues, NSMs are concerned with matters such as: 'the body, health and sexual identity; the neighbourhood, city, and physical environment; the cultural, ethnic, national, and linguistic heritage and identity; the physical conditions of life, and survival of humankind in general' (Offe 1985, p. 829). Their values tend to be universalistic rather than specifically socio-economic, with a stress on 'autonomy (with their organisational correlates of decentralisation, self-government, and self-help) and opposition to manipulation, control, dependence, bureaucratisation, regulation, etc.' (1985, p. 829). The internal operation of

NSMs is characterised by informal organisation, a blurring of the distinction between members and leaders, and an emphasis on widespread voluntary activity and fund-raising. Externally, NSMs often adopt non-negotiable positions, find compromise difficult, and have no concessions to offer in negotiation. Those active in NSMs do not fall into traditional left–right, liberal–conservative, or socio-economic groupings, but into categories based, for example, on age, gender, a locality, or a concern for the whole human race. Socio-economically their members tend to be drawn from the new middle class of what Offe calls 'the human service professions' and white-collar, public-sector workers, some elements of the traditional middle class, especially those with more extensive education, and socially and politically peripheral groups, such as the unemployed, students, housewives and the retired. The development of NSMs is particularly associated with the growth of state interests and with the concomitant expectations that governments can and should provide solutions to an increasingly wide range of societal problems.

The development of NSMs also focuses attention on the question of motivation, which needs further discussion, not least because a variety of motivational theories have been put forward, ranging from the instrumental to the psychological. Parry (1977) divides explanations of political participation into two types, the instrumental and the developmental.

Instrumental theories regard participation as a means to an end, that is for the defence or advancement of an individual or group of individuals and as a bulwark against tyranny and despotism. Thus the instrumentalist argues that individuals are the best judge of their own interests, that government involving the governed is more effective, that those affected by decisions have a right to participate in the making of decisions, and that the legitimacy of the government rests on participation. The ultimate inheritors of instrumental theory are therefore utilitarians and pluralists.

Developmental theory argues that the ideal citizen is the participant citizen and participation is therefore seen as the exercise of societal responsibility. Participation is a learning experience which develops or produces a citizen conscious not only of rights but of duties and responsibilities. Such a view can be found in the writings of Aristotle, J. S. Mill, de Tocqueville, and Rousseau, and is also an important part of both conservative and socialist ideas. For the conservative, however, the stress is on the responsible individual citizen and therefore on individual action; for the socialist it is on society's responsibility for the individual and therefore on collective action.

A different type of motivation is essentially economic. The leading advocate is Anthony Downs in *An Economic Theory of Democracy*. Downs (1957, p. 300) offers a rigorous theory of participation which, although intentionally limited to voting behaviour, can be applied to other levels and types of participation. He posits a rational, calculating individual who seeks to minimise costs and maximise gains operating in a system in which 'parties act to maximise votes, and . . . that citizens act rationally'. It is a theory which, while easy enough to understand, is less easy to prove or disprove. None the less, it is possible to illustrate its likely operation by examining electoral turnout. A large electorate, frequent elections, and long ballots involving many decisions by the voter, commonly produce a lower turnout and the Downsian explanation is that individuals find it more difficult to perceive their best interests in such circumstances because the outcome is more difficult to predict. On the other hand, closely fought elections, important elections, and those where the issues are clearly defined, commonly produce a higher turnout. The Downsian explanation is that important elections affect individuals' interests, that individuals are more likely to be able to affect the outcome of a closely fought election, and that clearly defined issues enable individuals to perceive their interests more easily. It is, however, important to note the considerable stress laid on perception, and perceptions may or may not be accurate though they may still form the basis of rational behaviour.

Olson (1965) argues that rational self-interest leads the individual to weigh the costs of participating in group or collective action against the benefits of being a member of the group, pointing out that gains made by group action are not necessarily available only to members of the group. It is also questionable whether individuals necessarily approach social or political matters in such a calculating fashion: participation may meet other needs, most obviously psychological needs. At the same time, writers like Downs and Olson argue powerfully for rationality being a significant factor in explaining political participation.

There are strong statistical correlations between levels of political participation and levels of what is known as *political efficacy*, that is the individual's sense of political effectiveness, the feeling that it is possible to influence politics and policy (see Milbrath and Goel 1977, pp. 57–61). Higher levels of political efficacy correlate with other variables, such as higher SES and higher levels of education. It is also argued that political participation may meet individual psychological needs (Milbrath and Goel 1977, pp. 46–9 and 74–85).

Such views have long been associated with the concept of the authoritarian personality, but also more widely with ego-satisfaction, self-esteem, and social recognition. Weber suggested four ideal-type explanations of social and therefore political action and behaviour, such as participation. Two are rational – the 'purposively rational' and the 'value-rational' – and two non-rational (but not irrational) – the 'affective action' and the 'traditional action' (1947, pp. 115–18. See also Giddens 1971, pp. 152–4). Purposive-rational behaviour is that in which the individual evaluates a possible action in terms of the cost and benefits of means and ends, whereas value-rational behaviour does not question ends but evaluates the costs and benefits of particular means. Rational economic behaviour of maximising benefits and minimising costs to achieve a considered goal is an example of purposively rational action. Accepting a religious or ideological ideal as a goal and seeking the most effective means of achieving it, subject, of course, to any constraints imposed by the ideal, is an example of value-rational action. Affectual action is governed by the emotions and traditional action by custom and habit. Although Weber's ideal-type explanation of social actions and behaviour can be criticised for failing to explain how changes in behaviour occur, that is, moving from one type of action to another, it explicitly recognises the importance of values and of meeting individual needs.

Robert Lane (1959) has usefully summarised the role that political participation may fulfil for the individual: as a means of pursuing economic needs, as a means of satisfying a need for social adjustment, as a means of pursuing particular values, and as a means of meeting subconscious and psychological needs. In this context it is important to consider not only those who participate politically but those who do not. Non-involvement in politics has been variously ascribed to apathy, cynicism, alienation, and anomie, but some distinction between these states of mind needs to be drawn (see Milbrath and Goel 1977, pp. 61–74). Defined simply, apathy is a lack of interest, cynicism is an attitude of distaste and disenchantment, while alienation and anomie both involve a feeling of estrangement or divorce from society, but where alienation is characterised by hostility, anomie is characterised by bewilderment. The available evidence suggests that the totally apathethic are, at the very least, cynical, and more often alienated or anomic. Apathy, cynicism, alienation and anomie, however, are all matters of degree and may therefore affect not only those who shun all forms of participation, but also those who are involved in political activity. Relative degrees of apathy, cynicism, alienation and anomie may account for non-participation at the higher levels of political participation while not precluding activity at the lower levels of the hierarchy. Alienation, far from taking a passive form, may also result in considerable political activity, particularly that involving violent political action and revolution. Non-involvement or low levels of participation may be the result of factors largely beyond the individual's control, most obviously where particular groups of individuals are denied the formal or legal right to participate or are forcibly prevented from exercising their rights or their desire to engage in some political activity.

CONCLUSION

There is every reason for agreeing with Dowse and Hughes (1986, p. 288) that 'there is little systematic theory relating social, psychological and political variables to participation in politics', but that participation is related to social and psychological variables and to the individual's skills and resources cannot be doubted. Furthermore, it is important to see political participation as part of wider social behaviour, not isolated from it. This makes it all the more difficult to research. Motivation is especially difficult to investigate, since not even the individual may be aware of that motivation, or may seek to conceal it, while for observers the difficulties are, if anything, greater. The reliance on essentially inferential data is understandable, but leaves a crucial gap in the research, which, like that into political socialisation, needs to be linked more closely with psychological studies and with the wider use of longitudinal research. Nowhere is this more important than in the more active forms of political participation, not least in that study of those who seek and hold political and administrative office – the field of political recruitment.

Chapter 7

POLITICAL RECRUITMENT

INTRODUCTION

Political recruitment is the process by which individuals secure or are enlisted in the roles of office-holders in the political system, mainly political and administrative office, but in some cases including other office-holders, such as members of the judiciary, the police and the military. Most studies of political recruitment tend to concentrate on political office-holders, such as presidents, prime ministers, ministers, members of legislatures, or local councillors. Indeed, there is a considerable though not exclusive stress on *elective* office. This is understandable, but unfortunate for two reasons. First, some of the most important offices mentioned above are not elective. For example, in most parliamentary systems the prime minister normally holds office by virtue of being leader of the largest single party represented in the legislature, whether that party has an absolute majority or is part of a coalition. It could be said that prime ministers are indirectly elected, since in certain countries like Britain the electorate effectively has a choice between the leaders of two major parties, but this ignores changes of leadership between elections, implies that electoral behaviour is solely or predominantly determined by a choice between leaders rather than parties or policies or other factors, and takes no account of post-election or inter-election coalition formation. In most systems, moreover, ministers or political heads of government departments are appointed, not elected.

A second and in many respects more important criticism is that, although political and administrative offices are invariably institutionally separate, the higher levels of administrative office are of crucial importance politically. The role of the bureaucracy in advising on policy and organising its implementation is at least as important as that of the politicians. Similarly, the efficiency of the lower echelons of the bureaucracy has a vital role in the survival of the state. Furthermore, in some political systems the bureaucracy is thoroughly politicised, most notably in the former communist states of Eastern Europe and the Soviet Union, and remains so in countries such as the People's Republic of China and North Vietnam, where party penetration and control of the bureaucracy remains extensive. In other cases, there exists a significant degree of politicisation, as evidenced by the American 'spoils system' whereby appointments to key posts in the federal public service are subject to direct political control. Nor should it be forgotten that, as Weber argued, bureaucracies develop a life of their own and therefore have a vested interest in their continuance: in the face of bureaucracy it is a considerable assumption that power lies solely in the hands of the politicians.

To a lesser but still significant degree, the same could be said of the holders of judicial office. The judiciary is also part of the apparatus of the modern state, enforcing its laws, giving its actions legitimacy, and sustaining its hegemony. In addition, the judiciary usually becomes more specifically involved in day-to-day politics through its rulings and its interpretation of the law – often, though not always, to the benefit of the state and those currently holding political office. In particular, the judicial review of cases allows the courts to pronounce on the legality or otherwise of the actions (or sometimes inactions) of politicians and officials, thereby affecting public policy and the course of politics. Judicial review is at its most potent where political action is subject to the test of constitutionality. Under most written constitutions – and most states have written constitutions – the laws passed by the legislature and the actions of the executive and its agencies may be challenged on the grounds that they are contrary to the constitution. Consequently, such legislation is invalid and such actions must, if possible, be reversed and may not lawfully be repeated.

The net of political recruitment can be spread further to include the police and the military for similar reasons, that they too may play important political roles. How important and how extensive those roles are varies from one political system to another, but in all modern states the police and the military, like the bureaucracy and the judiciary, are a crucial part of the state apparatus. Above all, in Weber's definition of the state, control of the police and the military is the state's ultimate claim to legitimacy. This remains true even in those systems where the police and the military are seen as, and see themselves as, professional bodies and constitutionally, morally, and ideologically subordinate to the government.

It therefore follows that if the relationship between the bureaucracy, the judiciary, the police, and the military, on the one hand, and the government, on the other, is an important question, then so is the way in which all office-holders – and not just the politicians – are recruited.

A MODEL OF POLITICAL RECRUITMENT

As already noted, many of the earlier studies of political recruitment tended to concentrate exclusively on elective offices (Seligman 1961, 1972; Barber 1965; Browning 1968; and Prewitt, 1970), but from these emerged a number of key variables which have wider applicability. Would-be office holders need to be 'eligible' for the offices to which they aspire, to meet not only formal requirements, such as citizenship, residence, or education, but informal ones, too. The latter are related to such factors as age, gender, and experience. Clearly, they need to be motivated and must have the necessary resources available, such as appropriate skills, time, and financial support. The political system itself is a key variable, providing the setting for the recruitment process and essentially laying down its ground rules. These combine with other variables to form what several writers refer to as 'an opportunity structure', a combination of circumstances and personal characteristics which increase or decrease the likelihood that a particular individual will, in the first place, seek and, in the second, secure office.

A number of studies also draw a distinction between what are termed 'self-starters' – those who seek office on their own initiative – and those who are persuaded to seek office by others. The latter are often referred to as being 'agency-recruited', that is enlisted by the efforts of various agents – most obviously political parties, in the case of elective office, but also pressure groups, fellow-workers or friends, or more formally by official bodies established for the purpose in the case of administrative and other offices.

The machinery of recruitment is also an important factor, but can take a variety of forms and combination of forms. Probably the most important historically is that of simple inheritance, particularly in the form of monarchies, but also through aristocracies and the ownership of property, and even today in the case of institutions like the House of Lords. Another ancient method, in this instance designed to militate against corruption and manipulation, or the domination of an office or position by a particular individual or group of individuals, is that of sortition or the drawing of lots. This was used in ancient Greece and remains the method by which elections in Britain are determined in the event of a tied vote. With large electorates its occurrence is extremely rare in parliamentary elections, but there was at least one case of an election being decided by lot in the local government elections of 1990. Rotation is a device with similar intentions – to prevent undue domination of an office – and is quite widely used. Since 1952, for example, American Presidents have been limited to two full elected terms; in a number of Latin American states an incumbent president may not be immediately re-elected, and in Mexico never re-elected. The American practice of political appointments to top posts in the federal civil service – the 'spoils system' – is a form of rotation, so also are the purges characteristic of totalitarian regimes, though they have other purposes as well.

Purges also illustrate the role that force may play in political recruitment: Hitler's 'night of the long knives' in 1934, when the leaders of the SA were murdered on his orders, Stalin's Great Purge of the 1930s, and the purging of the Chinese Communist Party in the Cultural Revolution of 1966–69 are the best-known examples. However, the most common use of force in political recruitment is in the form of internal military intervention, common, though by no means exclusively, in many Third World countries. Finer (1962) suggests four levels of intervention by the military: influence over and above professional advice; 'blackmail' – the threat of intervention to influence policy; displacement – removal of one civilian regime to make way for a more amenable one; and supplantment – the direct assumption of power by the military. The last two categories are clearly important forms of political recruitment. The use of force may also be involved in the ostensibly legitimate removal of someone from office by compelling their resignation under duress. Assassination, which is as old as politics itself, is another obvious example of force in political recruitment. However, removing someone from office, whether by coup d'état, forced resignation or abdication, or assassination, does not always produce a clearly designated successor and may therefore be seen as a negative form of political recruitment, but crucially important for all that. Force, of course, is the principal means by which Pareto's 'lions' gain power.

A more peaceful but no less ancient means of political recruitment, and historically extremely widespread, is that of patronage – the distribution of offices through existing office-holders or under the auspices of those with higher status in the society concerned. Historically, patronage has often involved bribery and corruption, as was the case with parliamentary elections in Britain, especially before 1832. Patronage was also the basis of recruitment to the British civil service before the Northcote–Trevelyan reforms in the nineteenth century introduced open, competitive examinations. The American 'spoils system' remains an important example of patronage, with as many as 3,000 posts in the gift of an incoming president.

What in some respects may be seen as a special form of patronage is what has been termed 'the emergence of natural leaders', usually the choice of a leader by selective consultation. Such a process is not uncommon in various social organisations in which posts are filled by election, but elections are not infrequently uncontested because a generally acceptable candidate has emerged. The most significant political example of 'emergence' is the means by which the leader of the Conservative Party in Britain was chosen before a system of election was introduced in 1965. A senior party figure with no personal ambitions to become leader would take soundings amongst other senior party figures and a candidate would emerge, as did Harold Macmillan in 1957 and Lord Home in 1963.

This process, however, could be seen as an informal version of the more widespread, formal practices of nomination, appointment, and co-option. Indeed, overlaps are inevitable. Members of British and American Cabinets, for instance, are appointed – the nominees of the Prime Minister and the President respectively. All civil servants are appointed, although on whose advice usually varies according to their rank. Judges in the United Kingdom are appointed on the advice of the Lord Chancellor, in his capacity as head of the judiciary, but Justices of the United States Supreme Court are only nominated, not appointed by the President – the Senate must approve their appointment. The co-option of individuals to committees is common in local government in Britain, including cases where the individual failed to secure election as a councillor, in order to draw upon their expertise and experience.

However, much the most common process associated with political recruitment is that of election, that is, choosing between two or more candidates for office by means of casting ballots or votes. Elections are used mostly to choose political office-holders, such as chief executives or members of legislatures, but may also be used to fill other offices, such as judicial and other legal posts in the United States. The Australian Labor Party decides who will be members of the Cabinet when the party wins power and, since 1981, the British Labour Party has been committed to including all members of the elected 'Shadow Cabinet' in a Labour Cabinet when first formed, although the distribution of portfolios remains a matter for the leader of the party as Prime Minister.

In examining the role of elections as a means of political recruitment it is necessary to take account of a number of factors affecting their nature and operation. Most elections are direct elections in that the votes cast specifically determine the outcome, but in a few cases elections are indirect in that the votes cast choose representatives who, allegedly wiser or more experienced than the full electorate, then make the final choice. For example, the Founding Fathers of the United States instituted an electoral college to choose the President and Vice-President rather than use a direct election. Constitutionally, the electoral college remains in place, but those elected to the college now represent the majority vote in each state and are bound by convention to support the majority party's candidates. A second factor is the nature of the electoral franchise – who has the right to vote – which may range from universal adult suffrage to a severely restricted electoral roll.

The electoral system is also of crucial importance and includes the method of counting votes, allocating seats, and apportioning districts. Whether or not a system of proportional representation is used is almost certain to be significant and the drawing of the boundaries of electoral districts or constituencies may have a marked impact, in both cases advantaging one or more parties at the expense of others (see Rae 1967). Indeed, particular electoral systems or devices may be introduced to achieve particular ends, such as the use of the second ballot in the Fifth French Republic to enable the Gaullists to exploit the division of the left between socialists and communists, or of an electoral threshold in West Germany, which laid down that a party must win at least 5 per cent of the votes cast before it can take up any seats in the legislature, to minimise the chances of a large number of parties winning seats. A particular electoral system may also be retained precisely because it favours one or more parties, as is the case with the 'first past the post' system in Britain, which favours the two major parties at the expense of smaller parties. Public elections may also be used within parties to choose candidates in the form of primary elections, used, for instance, in the United States and Belgium. Many parties also use elections for internal candidate selection and for choosing their party leaders, the latter sometimes through leadership conventions.

The final method widely used in political recruitment is that of selection, a regular and systematic process for choosing candidates within parties through selection committees or choosing bureaucrats by examination and various other achievement criteria. In practice, political recruitment often operates using a mixture of methods. For example, choosing party candidates may involve an initial nominating procedure by different groups within the party, followed by a selection process in which a small committee draws up a shortlist of candidates, from which the final choice is made by election by a much larger representative body.

In a study of the selection of British candidates for the first elections to the European Parliament in 1979, Martin Holland (1986) developed a model which distinguished first between the potential pool of candidates – the 'eligibles' – and those who actively sought candidatures – the 'aspirants'; then between those aspirants who were selected as candidates by the political parties and those who were not; and finally between those who won election to the European Parliament and those who did not. Such a model can be widely applied to the selection of party candidates for election, generally requiring modification only in relation to variations in the machinery of selection. However, a more generalised recruitment model can be developed, using the concepts of 'eligibles' – all those who meet the basic requirements or broadest criteria for the office concerned – and 'aspirants' – those who are eligible and who actively seek office. The term 'eligibles' is meant to apply not just to formal qualifications, such as citizenship or residence, but to those socio-economic characteristics which are commonly found among those who are successful in securing office, such as higher levels of education, certain occupations, and men rather than women. Most studies of political recruitment point out, first, that those recruited to whatever office are generally unrepresentative of the population as a whole and, second, that in terms of socio-economic characteristics those recruited constitute only a small proportion of those who may be described as 'eligibles'.

It is quite clear from these studies that *demand* factors are of vital importance – that is, the criteria which are applied by those responsible for choosing office-holders – but it is also clear, implicitly rather than explicitly, that *supply* factors play at least as important a part. Thus seeking an answer to the question of why many are called but few are chosen is crucial to the study of political recruitment, but so is answering the question why so few make themselves available to be called. A supply–demand model is, therefore, a useful way of looking at political recruitment, especially if this is combined with the idea of a succession of 'opportunity structures' that become increasingly stringent as demand factors come to predominate, as shown in Figure 7.1.

The model in Figure 7.1 posits a process in which ostensibly the whole adult population is available to be recruited to a given office, but this pool of potential office-holders is reduced to a much smaller group by a primary opportunity structure effectively involving the application of socio-economic criteria, the socialisation process, and the formal requirements of particular offices. Ultimately, most of the adult population have no wish, no ambition, no motivation, and no psychological disposition to seek office, and the 'eligibles' are reduced to a relatively small number. At this stage criteria tend to predominate over control, which is weak, largely because supply is more important than demand.

To progress from being 'eligibles' to 'aspirants' individuals must penetrate and take advantage of a secondary opportunity structure. They need to be psychologically disposed towards seeking office, they require motivation and ambition. The application of socio-economic criteria becomes more stringent – some individuals are considerably better placed than others in terms of age, education, and occupation, and women and ethnic minorities are invariably disadvantaged. Resources in the form of knowledge, different types of

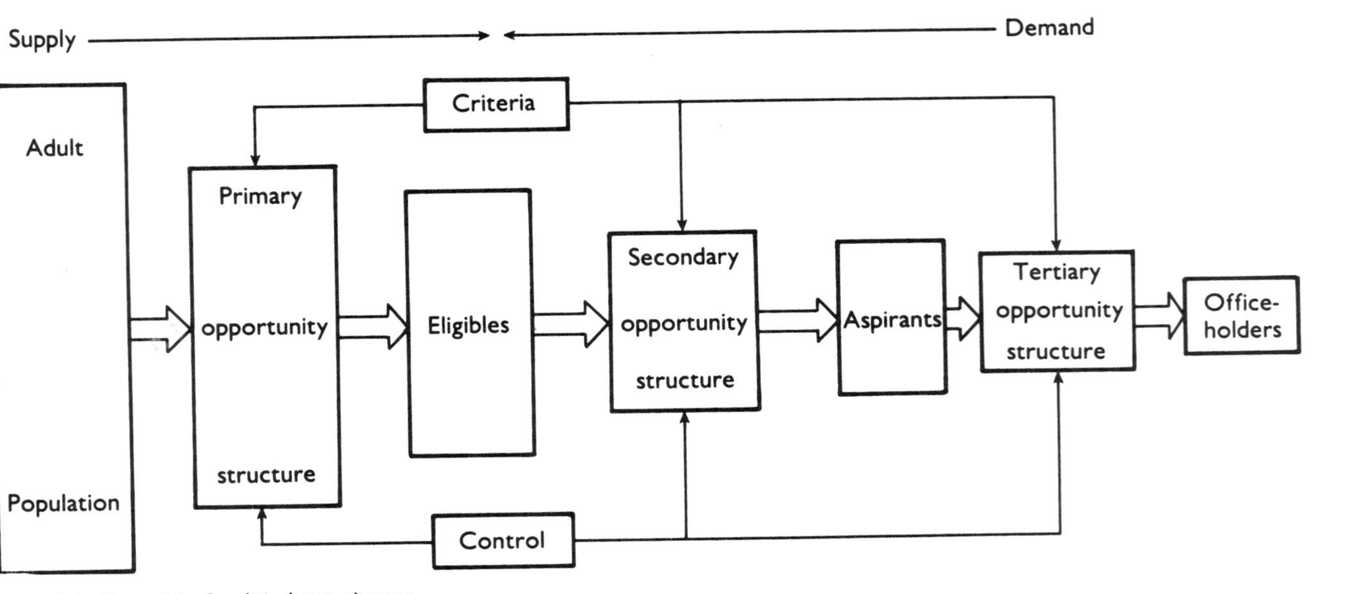

Figure 7.1 **A model of political recruitment.**

experience, various skills, such as public-speaking ability and administrative or organisational skills, the availability of time, and often of money, all become important. The individual's values and attitudes, particularly as reflected in their ideological position, are likely to be significant, especially for specifically political offices. And finally, the individual's social milieu, their SES, membership of various organisations in society, friendships and personal contacts, provide the setting. Just as criteria become more specific and therefore stringent, so control becomes stronger through the application of the earlier stages of the machinery of recruitment. Control, however, becomes crucial and is at its greatest at the stage of the tertiary opportunity structure, which translates a proportion of aspirants into office-holders.

The tertiary opportunity structure operates through the same factors, but applies with much greater specificity and stringency. Motivation and ambition must be especially strong, experience particularly appropriate, skills well developed, values and attitudes clearly held, and the social milieu strongly supportive. The factors affecting each stage of the opportunity structure are shown in Figure 7.2.

Recruitment to political office

The two principal types of political office are members of the executive – presidents, prime ministers, cabinet and other ministers and members of legislatures – representatives, congressmen, senators, Members of Parliament, and so on. Both have their equivalents at local level and, in some political systems, notably federal systems, at regional level. However, in some political systems there may be a significant overlap between the two. This is most commonly the case in parliamentary systems, in which members of the government or executive are also normally members of the legislature. In fact, it may be a constitutional requirement in order to render them directly accountable to the legislature and their continuance in office will normally depend on retaining the support of a majority in the legislature. This contrasts with the American separation of powers, in which the Constitution expressly forbids membership of more than one branch of government. Another variation is found in France, where, since the founding of the Fifth Republic in 1958, there has been a partial separation of powers: the President and members of

Primary	Secondary	Tertiary
Socio-economic characteristics	Socio-economic characteristics	Socio-economic characteristics
Age	Age	Age
Gender	Gender	Gender
Ethnicity	Ethnicity	Ethnicity
Education	Education	Education
Occupation	Occupation	Occupation
Residence	Residence	Residence
Socialisation	Psychological disposition	Psychological disposition
Formal requirements		
	Personality	Personality
	Socialisation	Socialisation
	Motivation	Motivation
	Ambition	Ambition
	Resources	Resources
	Knowledge	Knowledge
	Skills	Skills
	Experience	Experience
	Time	Time
	Money	Money
	Ideological disposition	Ideological disposition
	Values	Values
	Attitudes	Attitudes
	Socialisation	Socialisation

Figure 7.2 The primary, secondary and tertiary opportunity structures.

the National Assembly (the lower house of the French Parliament) are elected separately; the President appoints a Prime Minister, who forms a government dependent upon securing and retaining majority support in the National Assembly, but the Prime Minister and his ministerial colleagues may not be members of the Assembly, although they may take part in its debates. France is thus a hybrid, with a combination of the fusion and the separation of powers.

Recruitment to political office is most commonly by election, especially in the case of legislative office, but even here other forms of recruitment are found. The British House of Lords has a combination of an hereditary and nominated membership, the latter in the form of life peers; the French Senate is indirectly elected by means of an electoral college; the Canadian Senate is wholly nominated on the advice of the Prime Minister of the day. Many heads of government are also directly elected, such as the American and French Presidents, but many are chosen by other means, most commonly by being the leader of a political party. Even elected heads of government usually stand in the name of a party, as do the overwhelming majority of those who hold legislative office. Political parties are therefore much the most important agencies of recruitment to political office. The first crucial step in most political careers, therefore, is to secure the support of a party, usually as its candidate for a particular office.

The means by which parties choose candidates and the criteria they apply in doing so varies considerably, however. In the United States virtually all candidates are chosen by means of primary elections in which registered electors of the party concerned (in a few instances all registered electors) are given the opportunity to choose the party's candidate in a public election, conducted in exactly the same way as the election for the office itself. The principal and crucial exception is the choice of presidential candidates, in which the final choice is made at national party conventions consisting of delegates representing each of the states. However, an increasing proportion of these delegates is chosen by primary election, so that primaries now effectively determine the choice of presidential candidates as well. In most other countries the choice of candidate is an internal matter for the party, unregulated by law (unlike primaries) and conducted largely in private rather than public. The means used mostly consist of a mixture of selection by small groups and election by a larger body within the party. What differs is the extent to which the national party leadership has control over the process.

In the American case the national party leadership has little or no control, since continuing party organisation exists almost entirely at state or lower levels. Also, the extremely widespread use of primary elections to choose candidates weakens what little control exists. Would-be candidates can and do use state and local party machines as opportunity structures – the initial recruitment process frequently begins at the state or local level with individuals being encouraged to think of themselves as possible candidates either in the immediate or not too distant future. Presidential candidatures are obviously more complicated, since aspirants must conduct a prolonged campaign through a large number of state opportunity structures, including an increasingly large number of primaries, culminating in the national party conventions. Such control as exists is therefore found almost entirely at state or lower levels and is diffused rather than concentrated.

The situation in Britain is in some respects similar in that there is widespread local autonomy in the way in which parties choose candidates for local and parliamentary elections (see Rush 1969 and 1986). Effectively, the national parties hold a watching brief over procedures and a loose form of 'quality control', so that the national leadership can, if it feels sufficiently strongly, prevent a particular individual from being chosen, but cannot ensure the selection of a particular individual it favours. There is therefore procedural uniformity within each party, and an acceptance that the national party has a veto, but that the latter will be used sparingly. A partial exception to this is that the Labour Party has a constitutional provision that allows the national leadership to impose a candidate on a local party where the candidate is being chosen to fight a by-election. Under Neil Kinnock's leadership this power of imposition has been used on two occasions, but it remains the exception to the general rule.

In some political systems, including several Western European countries, what is known as the party list system operates and control is largely concentrated at the national level. Under the party list system the national party leadership decides who should be placed on a list of party nominees and in what order, leaving the voters to decide only which party they support. Control is at its greatest, however, in totalitarian systems, in which the party leadership has more or less absolute control. It is possible to argue that control is inversely related to the importance of the office, that is, the greater the degree of control the less important the office in terms of the exercise of power. Certainly, members of representative or legislative bodies in communist systems were singularly lacking in power or influence and were there largely to give legitimacy to the decisions of the government, effectively, of course, the Communist Party. Conversely, American Congressmen and Senators, especially the latter, are important actors on the political stage. Party discipline is lax and party cohesion low and neither their party colleagues in Congress nor the President can take their support for granted. British MPs lie somewhere between the two, with strong party discipline and high cohesion, but with the capacity not to be taken for granted and therefore from time to time actually to be influential.

The criteria that may be applied in recruitment to political office inevitably vary in type and intensity. Some are formal, most obviously and commonly citizenship, but there may be residence requirements (would-be US Senators must reside in the state they seek to represent, for example), even age limits beyond the age of majority (US Senators must be at least 30, the President 35), but ultimately it is informal criteria which determine the outcome of the recruitment process. In the primary opportunity structure it is likely to be factors such as gender, ethnicity, education, and occupation, both as supply and demand factors. Women may feel, rightly or wrongly, that there is prejudice against them seeking political office, or that they lack appropriate qualifications or experience; similar feelings may be held by particular ethnic groups. These are supply factors, but they may also be negative demand factors if such feelings are in any way a reflection of reality. Particular occupations lend themselves more readily to developing a political career in terms of skills, time, and money. The oratorical, debating and probing skills of the lawyer are perhaps the most obvious example and may go a long way to accounting for the disproportionately large number of lawyers found in most legislatures. A legal career, along with others such journalism and teaching, also provides flexibility of time, often vital in nurturing a political career. Various occupations provide sufficient money not only to create time, but to 'invest' in a political career by the payment of donations, entertainment, secretarial and other similar expenses, and even in some cases bribery and corruption.

Those engaged in recruiting political office-holders are usually willing to apply criteria related to the aspirant's psychological disposition (e.g. how strongly motivated they are), to the extent of their relevant resources (e.g. how well-informed they are), and, especially where parties are involved, to their ideological disposition (e.g. how radical or moderate their views are). As each successive stage in the recruitment process is reached, so the application of these criteria becomes more stringent and an increasing premium is likely to be placed on experience, both generally and specifically. Depending on the post to be filled, various types of experience become relevant. A successful career in whatever occupation the individual has pursued to date is seen as an advantage, but specific types of experience such as previous executive, legislative or administrative experience may be especially useful.

For example, in the United States, excluding those presidents who succeeded to office from the vice-presidency through the death (and in one case resignation) of the incumbent and who served only the expiry of that term, twenty-three of the thirty-five presidents elected from 1789 to 1988 had had executive and legislative experience prior to election, while nine had had executive experience only, and three legislative experience only. It should be noted, however, that although experience includes having held a Cabinet post or having been a state governor, it also includes having held high military command or having been vice-president. If these last two categories are excluded on the grounds that military command is not strictly political experience, and that experience as vice-president varies considerably from one administration to another and is sometimes almost a sinecure, then the number of presidents who have had executive and legislative experience is reduced to fourteen (less than half the total), and those with executive experience to only four. Presidential candidates may be drawn from a wide field, and although often active in politics prior to nomination, their political experience may be strictly limited or negligible. This is even more likely with members of the Cabinet, who may be drawn from a variety of spheres and whose political experience may be non-existent.

In contrast, most British Cabinet ministers will have served a parliamentary and ministerial apprenticeship before first entering the Cabinet. Thus the average number of years served in Parliament before entering the Cabinet by Labour ministers between 1964 and 1970 and 1974 and 1979 was 14.8 years, and by Conservative ministers between 1970 and 1974 and in Margaret Thatcher's first Cabinet in 1979 was 13.2 years. Likewise, more than 90 per cent of the Cabinet ministers appointed to newly formed governments between 1970 and 1979 had had previous ministerial experience, including in many cases previous membership of the Cabinet. For Prime Ministers parliamentary and ministerial apprenticeships tend to be even longer: for the eight individuals who held the premiership for the first time between 1945 and 1979, the average length of parliamentary service was 25.4 years and the average number of years as a minister 10.8. John Major, who succeeded Margaret Thatcher as Prime Minister in 1990, has been an MP for 11.5 years and served as a minister for seven years, including three in the Cabinet, and was thus relatively less experienced than average. Neil Kinnock would be the first Prime Minister since Ramsay MacDonald in 1924 never to have held ministerial office before becoming Prime Minister, although he has considerable parliamentary experience, having been first elected in 1970.

Members of legislatures have frequently had experience of contesting elections unsuccessfully before first being elected to the legislature. They may also have had experience in local government, which may in turn form the most tangible political basis for local connections with the areas they represent. Members of the French National Assembly, for instance, commonly have particularly strong local government bases and often retain local office after securing national office.

In communist systems the route to political office is very clearly marked through the Party, both within the Party itself and in the governmental machine. Here loyal party service, ideological rectitude and, not infrequently, being the protégé of a more senior figure are crucial criteria.

The routes to political office inevitably vary and the opportunity structures vary accordingly, but the key factors are the extent to which the process is subject to control and the nature of the criteria applied in determining which of the many become the few who secure political office.

Recruitment to administrative office

The filling of administrative posts in most modern states is largely systematised through the regular use of permanent bodies established specifically for recruitment purposes. Open competition, usually by examination, various practical tests (such as role-playing), psychological tests and interviews. Applications are invited at regular intervals from 'suitably qualified' individuals, the qualifications or criteria depending on the nature of the posts to be filled. These may be divided horizontally, in terms of the levels of ability and skills required, or vertically, in terms of the specialised tasks and skills required, and in practice, usually some combination of the two. Administrative positions are therefore subject to considerable control and, to a large extent, clearly defined criteria, especially in regard to formal qualifications. The British civil service, for example, has long recruited entrants at the graduate and lower levels of educational attainment for senior, middle and junior rank posts by defining the degree of initiative required and responsibility to be assumed, while recruiting separately those needed to fill specialised tasks, such as legal, scientific, or medical work.

Some important variations between political systems are found relating to the machinery of administrative recruitment. France, for instance, has a specific training programme and recruitment agency for administrators in the form of the École Nationale d'Adminstration (ENA), but the most important difference is the extent to which appointments to the bureaucracy are subject to political control. Mention has already been made of the American 'spoils system' – the filling of senior administrative posts with political appointees. In contrast, Britain and France have politically neutral civil services in that, although governments come and go and different political parties hold power, the bureaucrats remain in office and are expected to serve the politicians of whatever party equally faithfully. In the British case this process is carried to the extent of departments making contingency plans in the period shortly before an expected general election to deal with the possibility of the government being defeated and the main opposition party coming to power. In communist, and not a few Third World countries, loyalty to the incumbent regime is paramount and the whole process of administrative recruitment (and subsequent advancement) is subject to rigid political control.

The recruitment of judicial, police and military personnel

In most modern states the judiciary, the police and the military are clearly subordinate to the politicians. Judges, police and military personnel are normally recruited on the basis of appropriate professional qualifications or training, usually on a systematised basis in respect of criteria and control. For these reasons judicial, police and military offices are not widely seen as 'political', but from a Marxist point of view all three are as political as conventional political offices. For a Marxist, judges are part of the state apparatus, part of the means by which the ruling class is able to maintain itself in power. The police and the judiciary enforce the ruling class's laws and the military are the ultimate enforcers of the state's claim to authority and legitimacy. Such a view does not have to be conceded in its entirety to admit the significance of judges, the police and the military. Their roles understandably vary from one political system to another and over time. What is important is to acknowledge that within the context of the state and its relationship with society their recruitment can and should be examined within the parameters of political recruitment, not excluded from it.

Patterns of recruitment

Different political systems are characterised by different patterns of recruitment, especially in the extent to which recruitment is subject to control. Liberal-democratic systems tend to be more open, others, notably totalitarian systems, more closed, while developing societies often have fragmented systems of recruitment involving a mixture of the traditional and the modern. Other differences emerge according to the types of offices to be filled, especially in the case of political and administrative positions, in which different methods of selecting office-holders are used, different degrees of control exerted, and different criteria applied. However, there are also strong similarities in the results of political recruitment, in who is chosen: office-holders generally tend to be drawn from similar groups in terms of their socio-economic characteristics, from higher rather than lower status groups, from the better-educated and more skilled occupations, and from men rather than women. This is readily apparent in the socio-economic backgrounds of British MPs, as Table 7.1 shows. The data in Table 7.1 speak largely for themselves, but it is worth noting that only 5 per cent of the adult population are graduates and a similar proportion have attended public school, but much the most striking feature is the overwhelming male dominance of membership of the House of Commons.

Similar patterns emerge in virtually all studies in that office-holders are socio-economically unrepresentative of the population at large. The pattern may vary from one system to another – workers and women were far better represented socio-economically in bodies like the Supreme Soviet of the USSR than in most representative assemblies, largely as a result of conscious efforts to achieve better representation, but the basic pattern follows that already found in political participation. The correlation, however, between office-holding and socio-economic characteristics is much stronger than that between these same characteristics and lower levels of

Table 7.1 *The socio-economic background of British MPs, 1987.*

Characteristics	Conservative %	Labour %	All %
Education			
Graduates	73.1	57.6	66.0
'Oxbridge' graduates	46.1	15.7	33.1
Public-school education	62.7	12.7	42.1
Occupation			
Professions	33.3	41.0	37.5
Business	51.5	4.8	33.5
Miscellaneous	14.4	24.5	17.7
Workers	0.8	29.7	11.2
Hall-Jones Occ. Scale			
Classes 1–2	85.0	55.9	74.3
Classes 3–7	15.0	44.1	25.7
Gender			
Male	95.4	90.8	93.7
Female	4.5	9.2	6.3

Source: Rush (1988), pp. 22–3, 24, 25 and 26.

participation and as such forms a major basis for claiming the existence of a political elite. Political recruitment thus lends prima-facie support to elite theories, but the evidence remains largely inferential, as the discussion of elite theory in Chapter 4 showed. There is also another serious gap in both elite theory and recruitment theory – the relationship, if any, between the socio-economic characteristics of those who hold office and their behaviour as office-holders.

There are a limited number of studies which explore the relationship between the behaviour of office-holders with their socio-economic characteristics, seeking to answer the question of whether it makes any difference who is recruited to what office. Studies of British MPs' support for various policies and ideological positions in the period 1945 to 1959 by Finer *et al.* (1961) and Berrington (1973) found statistical correlations between socio-economic characteristics and legislative behaviour, but any causal link still had to be inferred. Similarly, recruitment studies consistently show that right-of-centre and left-of-centre parties attract or recruit would-be and actual office-holders from different backgrounds, though not exclusively so, as Table 7.1 illustrates. Such correlations should not be dismissed because a clear causal relationship remains unestablished, but should be used as a starting point for more research. Socio-economic characteristics are a crude but useful predictor of behaviour, but their causal significance remains to be researched in much greater depth, not least in seeking an answer to what distinguishes those who secure office from the many others of essentially similar background. Ultimately, political recruitment needs to be seen in the wider context of political participation and the politics of particular societies, if meaningful generalisations are to be made.

PROBLEMS OF POLITICAL RECRUITMENT THEORY

Studies of political recruitment suffer from many of the same problems as wider studies of political behaviour, complicated by the necessity to take account of the characteristics of particular political systems. Thus the tendency, common in studies of political behaviour, for research to be heavily concentrated on American experience has led to accusations of ethnocentricity, but these are probably exaggerated and less important than taking account of system-specific factors. Almost inevitably, American studies concentrate heavily on elective offices to the neglect of offices filled by nomination or appointment. More generally, recruitment theory tends to neglect other types of office, especially administrative positions, yet especially the higher echelons of bureaucracies play a crucial role in the operation of politics, and the recruitment of administrators should not be ignored. Nor should that of the judiciary, the police and the military, insofar as they too are a part of the political system in general and the state apparatus in particular.

There is also, again as in other aspects of political behaviour research, a heavy reliance on inferential data, mostly in the form of socio-economic characteristics. Such data are easily gathered and lend themselves to statistical analysis, but there remains a serious problem of establishing a causal link between characteristics and behaviour. Further research should see socio-economic data as its starting point, not its culmination, requiring exploration and explanation, not assumptions. In particular, such data needs to be linked with the psychological dimension of recruitment, which has hardly been explored at all: motivation is assumed, but little investigated.

Much is also known about the machinery of recruitment and about the demand side of the supply–demand equation. Again, such matters are relatively easy to research: recruitment machinery is largely institutionalised and many of the criteria applied by those individuals involved in the choosing of office-holders are not difficult to elicit. It is far more difficult, however, to investigate the supply side of would-be office-holders. The relatively exclusive socio-economic background of those who secure office is well documented, but there is little or no research on the many more of similar backgrounds who do *not* seek office. Once again the psychological dimension needs to be explored, but there may be other factors related to the primary opportunity structure.

It is possible, however, to construct a generalised model involving supply and demand, recruitment agencies, criteria, control, and what have been termed 'opportunity structures'. And, while significant differences in the machinery of recruitment should not be ignored, the overall similarities that exist are more important than the detailed differences in recruitment patterns. For political recruitment theory to proceed further requires the development of links with career patterns. Too many studies stop at recruitment, rather than going on to examine what office-holders do once they are in office. This in turn needs to be taken to it logical conclusion, to what may be termed 'de-recruitment' – how careers end, in particular whether they end voluntarily or involuntarily. Such an approach would lead to assessments of the nature of the office to be filled and the role to be performed, and whether certain types of individuals are more suited to such offices and roles.

PART IV

POLITICAL COMMUNICATION, PUBLIC OPINION AND IDEOLOGY

INTRODUCTION

Public opinion and ideology cannot exist without communication, but then neither can society. Yet communication has received little attention from political sociologists. Public opinion is to some extent an exception, but here far more work has been done by researchers and writers in other fields. Indeed, communication studies have expanded enormously since the 1950s and the mass media, especially television, have been the subject of much research. In particular, there has been a great deal of interest and speculation about the relationship between the mass media and public opinion. Earlier interest in public opinion had centred largely on the role of propaganda, especially on its use in the totalitarian societies of Nazi Germany and the Soviet Union under Stalin.

It is, however, self-evident that communication is concerned with far more than public opinion, let alone propaganda. Communication is a vital part of the processes of political socialisation, participation and recruitment, although its role is usually and understandably taken for granted. The interplay between an individual's knowledge, values, attitudes, experience and personality discussed in Part III is the product of communication. Political behaviour cannot therefore be fully understood without a knowledge of the communication process.

Public opinion might be regarded as the most obvious product of political communication, but it should not be seen in the narrow context of democracy. The fact that by definition public opinion is seen as the motivating force of democracy should not be allowed to obscure the wider relationship between the members of society and those who exercise power in society, whatever its norms or values may be. As noted in Chapter 4, Kornhauser (1960) based his theory of the mass society on the relationship between elites and non-elites, between the openness of elites to influence by non-elites and the extent to which non-elites could be manipulated by elites. Public opinion was therefore seen as a source of information or as something to be shaped.

Whatever its role, however, public opinion is the expression of values and attitudes, and it can be argued that the values and attitudes held by an individual or group of individuals are clustered in such a way as to provide a coherent view of the world or, in short, an ideology. It is a moot point whether everyone can be said to have an ideology and, even if it is conceded that they do, whether they necessarily think in ideological terms. Even so, it can hardly be denied that ideology has loomed large in the history of the twentieth century. Marxists and non-Marxists have developed different concepts of ideology and the role it plays in society, but in doing so they have emphasised its significance. Its importance in defining totalitarian regimes was noted in Chapter 4, but ideology was no less important in the clash between the superpowers after 1945, especially when the Cold War was at its height.

Ideology also emphasises the importance of values in understanding society, both socially and politically. Societies do not operate in value-free vacuums but are themselves the product of values. The development in the 1950s and 1960s of the concept of political culture is an explicit recognition of the importance of values. Whether the study of society can be value-free or objective remains open to question, but what is no longer in question is the importance of acknowledging and taking account of a society's values.

Chapter 8

POLITICAL COMMUNICATION

INTRODUCTION

Political communication is the transmitting of politically relevant information from one part of the political system to another, and between the social and political systems. Relevant information refers not just to factual matters about, for example, what has happened, but also to the transmitting of ideas, values, and attitudes. By definition communication is vital to all political and social behaviour; without communication there can be no politics and no society. Political communication is the dynamic element of the political system. Karl Deutsch (1963) in his classic study *The Nerves of Government* places communication at the very heart of an understanding of politics.

Analytically, it is perfectly acceptable to speak of political communication, rather than communication in general. Clearly, there are specifically political messages that can be identified, such as the speeches of politicians, election manifestos, governmental decisions, policy discussions, and as on, and similarly there are channels of communication which are largely or exclusively political, such as legislative debates, party conferences or conventions, policy meetings, and current affairs programmes on radio and television. However, political communication is not structurally part of the political system, but is an integral part of society's communication system. Particular communication patterns may, to a greater or lesser extent, be identified as political in the sense that politics is their main concern – meetings of the British Cabinet or between an American President and his advisers are obvious examples of political communication, but the communication processes they use are not peculiarly political. The circulation of documents before a meeting and interpersonal discussion at a meeting are common phenomena outside the political sphere. The mass media may be subject to very considerable political control in some societies, but they are not exclusively political. In seeking to understand the role and operation of political communication it is therefore necessary to examine communication theory generally, rather than from a solely political point of view.

THEORIES OF COMMUNICATION

In what has become a well-known adaptation of his definition of politics, Harold Lasswell (1948b) described communication as seeking an answer to the question: who says what, in which channel, to whom, with what effect? Lasswell's formula is simple and straightforward; it identifies four of the five elements to be found in any communication model: the source of a message, the message itself, the channel by which the message is transmitted, and the receiver of the message. For the communication process to be dynamic, however, to proceed beyond the transmission of a single message, it is necessary to introduce a fifth element – feedback, or the reaction or response of the recipient of the message.

In such a model the source could be an election candidate, whose message might be a number of specific policy proposals. The channel might be a television interview and the receiver or audience the members of the electorate watching the broadcast. The response or feedback would be the approval or disapproval of the proposals or the candidate or both. The channel used for feedback could take a variety of forms: the most likely would be the voting behaviour of those who watched the broadcast, but a few might contact the candidate to express their views (even offer to help in the candidate's campaign), some might write to a newspaper, the proposals might provoke some form of demonstration, and so on.

This example, however, illustrates a number of problems with such a simple and basic model. No distinction is drawn between interpersonal and mass communication and there is no doubt that some models lend themselves more to one form of communication than the other. Lasswell, not unreasonably given his particular interest in political communication in general and propaganda, assumes communication is a persuasive process, that the communicator intends to influence the audience. By definition this is the intent of propaganda, although Lasswell acknowledges that it may not achieve its purpose. However, without conceding for a moment that all political messages are propaganda, it is not unreasonable to accept that many are intended to influence their audiences, but this tends to limit communication to the conscious and manifest, when much communication is sub-conscious and latent. No account, moreover, is taken of messages which fail, for whatever reason, to reach the receiver or audience.

A further problem is that, as in most areas of social science, there are no agreed definitions of many of the terms commonly used. For instance, some theorists use the terms 'channel' and 'medium' as interchangeable, others insist that there is clear distinction between the two, using 'channel' to refer to 'the physical means of carrying the signal' and 'medium' as an agency 'capable of transmitting codes along a channel' (O'Sullivan *et al.* 1983; pp. 31–2 and 134), a less than satisfactory distinction. For the purposes of examining political communication it is probably better to regard the two as synonymous and to concentrate on the different forms they can take and their significance for communication.

Clearly, communication can take place in a variety of ways. John Fiske (1982) divides media into three categories: presentational, representational and mechanical. Presentational media include the individual's voice, face and body using the spoken word and gesture, in which the communicator is the medium; representational medias include all written and printed matter, photographs and paintings, banners and graffiti, all of which establish an existence independent of the communicator; and mechanical media include the telephone, radio, television, film, telex and fax machines, and the like. The communication process involves choosing a channel or medium and putting the message in a form suitable for that choice. In practice, of course, various constraints will limit, even determine, the choice of medium, such as the availability of various mechanical means, time, cost, and personal inclination.

Two early theorists, Shannon and Weaver (1949), also pointed out that the communication process is subject to what they called 'noise', or interference in the process which affects or distorts the message. They distinguished between 'engineering or mechanical noise' and 'semantic noise'. Mechanical noise is normally physical in origin and is not intended by the source to affect the message. Examples of such noise are poor reception on radio or television, crossed telephone lines, and speech impediments. Semantic noise is related to problems of language, accent, the use of jargon, and socio-cultural differences. In either case the message is not received precisely in the form that it was sent and may therefore be misunderstood.

The possibility of a message being misunderstood focuses attention on two other important variables in communication – coding and decoding, and perception. All messages have to be put in an appropriate form or code to suit the channel or medium used. Furthermore, if the message is to be understood, the code needs to be one that is understood by both the sender and the receiver of the message. The most common form of code is, of course, language, but there are many others, such as gesture, use of the eyes, facial expressions, tone of voice, the use of colour, expected behaviour, and the use of symbols. Just as messages have to be put in code, so they have to be decoded and much depends on the ability of the individual or individuals receiving the message to understand the original code (see Schramm 1954). This in turn introduces the question of perception, already noted as important in political socialisation, participation and recruitment. The perceptions of both the sender and the receiver of a message are likely to affect the coding and decoding, in that the sender will interpret information before composing a message about it and the receiver will interpret the information contained in the message on receiving it. Beauty, as the saying goes, is in the eye of the beholder (see Gerbner 1956).

Only a brief reference has been made to the distinction between interpersonal communication and mass communication, but it is an important distinction, partly because some communication theorists have concentrated more or less exclusively on one or the other, and, more importantly, because theories which encompass both types have proved difficult to develop. For obvious reasons different, though not mutually exclusive, channels are more common in one than the other. Non-verbal communication – the use of gesture, facial expressions, and body language – is extremely common in interpersonal communication, whereas the printed word and pictures, still and moving, are the most common form of mass communication. The spoken word is widely used in both and the crucial difference between the two is that interpersonal communication usually takes place between a small number of individuals, either face to face or at a distance by telephone or some form of written communication. In contrast, mass communication takes place between one individual or small number of individuals or organisation and a much larger number of individuals, to the point that the size of the audience may not be known and, to the sender of the message, may also be largely undifferentiated.

Given appropriate resources and facilities interpersonal communication is easier to research, not least in ascertaining whether the message has been received and understood as intended. It is a considerable assumption, however, that everyone in a mass audience has received, let alone understood a message. Market research techniques have done much to demonstrate that mass audiences are in reality significantly differentiated, that certain types of product are more popular with some types of consumer than others, that different types of advertising will attract some would-be consumers and repel others, and that different media or different parts of the same medium may be used to target particular audiences.

In the context of political communication Katz and Lazarsfeld (1955, 1957) put forward the 'two-step' flow theory, which they developed from an earlier study of the 1944 presidential election in the United States (Lazarsfeld *et al.* 1944). They argued that messages sent via the mass media did not, in most cases, make their impact directly, but through 'opinion leaders', whose judgement individuals trusted because they belonged to similar socio-economic groups, thus providing a link between mass and interpersonal communication. A logical development of the two-step flow theory is the multistep flow model, which suggests a more complex interrelationship between the media and individuals and groups of individuals. The importance of both models is that they stress the social context of communication and do not see audiences as passive and undifferentiated recipients of media messages.

Finally, account also needs to be taken of the role of what White (1950) calls the 'gatekeeper' function, in which stress is laid on points in the communication process at which decisions on the handling of information or the message are made. These may be mechanistic, as in the case of deadlines for the submission of copy for a newspaper, or personal, as in the case of editors or sub-editors of a newspaper. McNelly (1959) elaborated on the gatekeeper function in an examination of the factors affecting the flow of international news. The gatekeepers for the reporting of an international event include the correspondent personally deciding to file a story, the telephone, telex, fax, or satellite system for transmitting copy, the possibility of censorship at source, the existence of time zones and deadlines, and editorial and sub-editorial decisions. Much will depend on what are called 'news values', the professional criteria applied in the selection of news. These not only vary from one type of medium to another, but from one medium to another within the same type. Television news, for example, has to be more selective than newspapers and has a natural preference for film and action, rather than still photographs or 'talking heads'. The television audience is also relatively undifferentiated, whereas newspapers have more clearly defined audiences and can give 'our readers what they want'. For the popular press this tends to be stories with a 'human interest', usually presented in highly personalised terms; for the 'quality' press 'in depth' coverage and the less personal approach are the norms.

These variables can be usefully summarised in the form of a basic communication model somewhat more sophisticated than that discussed earlier, as shown in Figure 8.1. In considering the model it is important to stress that it is not meant to be specifically political, but is a generalised model. Yet more complex and elaborate models can be and have been developed for general purposes, but also to apply to communication in particular circumstances. Deutsch (1963), for instance, developed a model specifically to analyse foreign policy-making and it is possible to develop appropriate models to apply to the operation, say, of the British Cabinet system or communication within bureaucracies or political parties. As was the case with political recruitment, such models need to take account of the machinery and arrangements peculiar to particular cases.

The model also needs to be seen in the context of political socialisation and participation, especially in the application of the concepts of coding and decoding, which are intended to encompass the perceptual screen suggested in the socialisation and participation models found in Chapters 5 and 6. Moreover, the model is not meant to imply that all messages are necessarily received, nor is the diagrammatic equality given to feedback intended to imply that

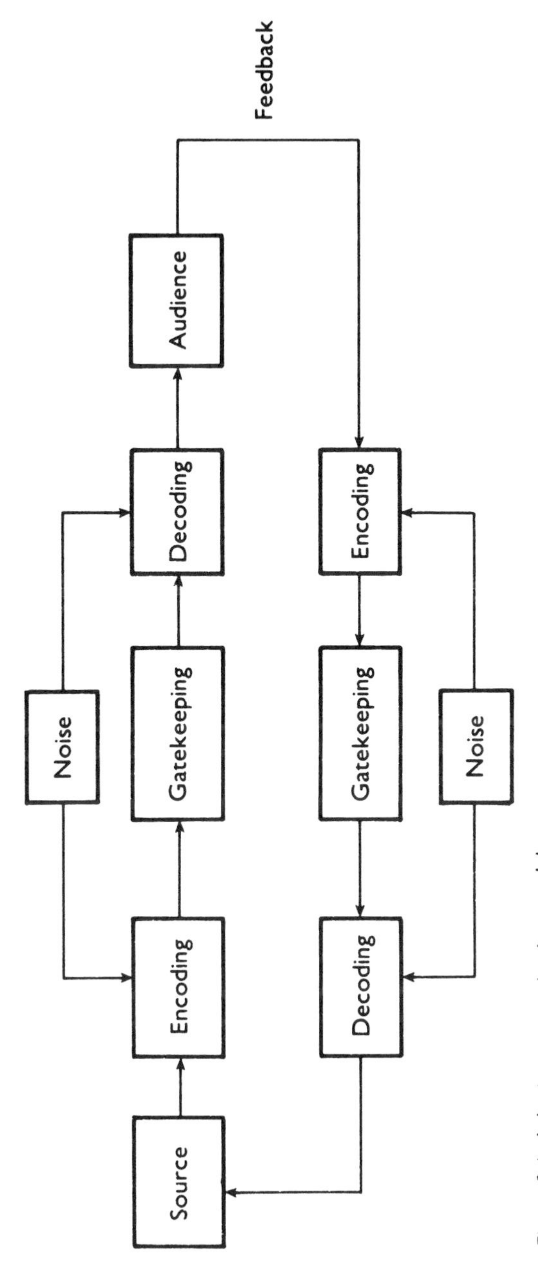

Figure 8.1 **A basic communication model.**

feedback always occurs or that it is always of equal importance to the original process. There may be circumstances in which feedback is more important, in others, perhaps most, less important. Even so, silence may be as eloquent a form of feedback as a specific message and will usually be noted.

THE CHARACTERISTICS OF POLITICAL COMMUNICATION

It was suggested earlier that political communication operates through a society's communication system and, although there are specifically political messages and specifically political channels of communication, most obviously within the political system itself, much political communication is conducted through societal channels, and political messages are not always differentiated from other messages, especially in the minds of the receivers. For example, only a limited amount of the output of the mass media is specifically political, particularly in the case of radio and television, although, of course, hegemonic theorists, such as Gramsci, and structuralists, such as Althusser, would use a much wider definition of what is political. In addition, much that is political or has political significance is not necessarily recognised as such by many members of society. The increased prominence of environmental issues, for instance, has raised the political profile of some of them and made others, not previously perceived as having a political significance, be seen as political. Crime, for instance, is not necessarily seen as political unless or until it takes a form or reaches proportions that lead members of the public to feel that the government should take some action to deal with it.

Political communication, as in the case of communication in other contexts, operates both vertically and horizontally, that is, in elitist terminology, hierarchically between rulers and ruled, invariably in a two-way flow, and laterally between individuals and groups of individuals. It follows that different individuals and groups will have discernible and differing communication networks and patterns of communication. Political office-holders, for example, will count among both sources and audiences their fellow office-holders, members of the bureaucracy, their political supporters and opponents, leaders of pressure groups, the mass media, and the general public.

The channels which they use are likely to include formal and informal face-to-face contacts at the interpersonal level, direct and indirect contacts with the mass media, pressure groups, and members of the public. In short, office-holders are likely to have extensive communication networks, highly sensitive to political phenomena. In contrast, members of the general public will mostly have much more limited networks as far as political communication is concerned, far more dependent on the mass media, and operating in an intermittent and fragmented way.

Political communication uses three principal channels: the mass media; pressure groups and political parties; and informal contacts between individuals and groups of individuals. The mass media are particularly important for the widespread dissemination of political information and in most societies are the most important source of such information, with television being the most significant. The media also play a part in the formation of public opinion by publicising the views of individuals and groups. This can lead to the media playing a significant part in the process of agenda-setting – effectively contributing to what issues will be regarded as important and which more important than others, a matter to be discussed further in Chapter 9.

Pressure groups and political parties are especially important in two-way contacts between politicians and bureaucrats, various types of political activists, and between these and specialised or particular sections of public opinion in society. Informal contacts between individuals and groups of individuals are also important, especially through the two-step flow theory in which opinion leaders act as channels of information, as sources of social pressure to adhere to various norms, and as sources of support for group cohesion in social and political behaviour. However, as is the case with political participation, political communication should not be seen in isolation, even though analytically this is possible, but as part of wider communication patterns in society at large.

THE FACTORS INFLUENCING POLITICAL COMMUNICATION

Political communication, like communication generally, is inevitably affected by a variety of factors – physical, technological, economic, socio-cultural and political.

Physical barriers to communication have always been significant, whether in the form of mountains, seas, deserts or sheer distance. This was especially so historically in that poor roads and limited technology meant that geographical mobility was restricted and communities within a particular society were largely isolated from one another. This remains true in much of the Third World. Technological developments have reduced many of these physical problems, so much so that Marshall McLuhan, one of the foremost communication theorists, described the world as 'a global village'. Modern technology has facilitated the development of the mass media, so that information can be transmitted cheaply over vast distances at great speed to reach a wider and wider audience. For example, with high levels of illiteracy, many Third World countries were profoundly affected by the introduction of the transistor radio, simply because radios no longer required an on-line source of energy or cumbersome batteries. The development of communication satellites is bringing about yet further dramatic changes, not least with the peculiarly political impact that the dissemination of information via satellite is very difficult to control.

Even so, important physical factors remain: many communities, even in advanced capitalist societies, remain relatively isolated, but perhaps the best example is the impact of time zones. Countries like the United States, Canada, and the former Soviet Union, with four (excluding Alaska), five, and eleven time zones respectively, have fragmented communication networks, particularly affecting radio and television networks and the distribution of newspapers. For obvious practical reasons the simultaneous broadcasting of programmes throughout the country does not occur and this has resulted in fragmented radio and television networks in the United States and Canada, with a much greater stress on local stations. Furthermore, neither the United States nor Canada has a national newspaper in the European sense, even though one or two are nationally available such as the *New York Times*, the *Wall Street Journal*, and Toronto's *Globe and Mail*. The Soviet Union was a partial and significant exception to this rule in that there was a national radio and television network and two national newspapers, *Pravda* and *Izvestia*, the organs of the Communist Party and the Soviet government respectively. However, the USSR is also an example of the significance of political factors in determining the communication network, a question to be discussed below.

Patterns of communication can also be affected by economic development. Less developed societies tend to have fragmented and localised communication networks, but economic development leads to the more extensive development of the mass media and a greater reliance by politicians and people on the mass media. More people, therefore, are reached by the same channels and receive the same messages, resulting in a strong tendency towards greater uniformity in communication patterns. This may be partly offset by socio-cultural factors, such as literacy levels, and the extent to which a society has a common language or at least a lingua franca. In addition, particular channels are used by different groups according to socio-economic status, such as differing readerships for different newspapers and viewers for television channels and programmes. Variations also exist in informal contacts between individuals and groups of individuals, and where there are ethnic or religious differences they are likely to affect communication patterns considerably.

Last and by no means least, political communication is affected by various political factors, notably the extent to which the communication network is subject to political control by the government. The mass media in many societies is subject to various levels of censorship, most obviously in totalitarian or authoritarian systems. Nazi Germany and the communist systems of the Soviet Union and Eastern Europe, for instance, exerted close control over the mass media and, commonly, over the means of reproducing information – the printing press, photocopier, and, in Romania, even typewriters. Control of information, however, is relevant in all societies: censorship exists in some form in most, even if it is limited to what is regarded as obscene or pornographic, and few governments do not try to to retain control over information in some form or other, subscribing implicitly to the belief that information is power.

The characteristics and nature of political communication is, of course, crucial to the formation and expression of public opinion. That, however, is the subject of Chapter 9.

CONCLUSION

In spite of the great deal of research done on communication there is no generally accepted model of communication. The main reason for this is that the number of variables that normally comprise such

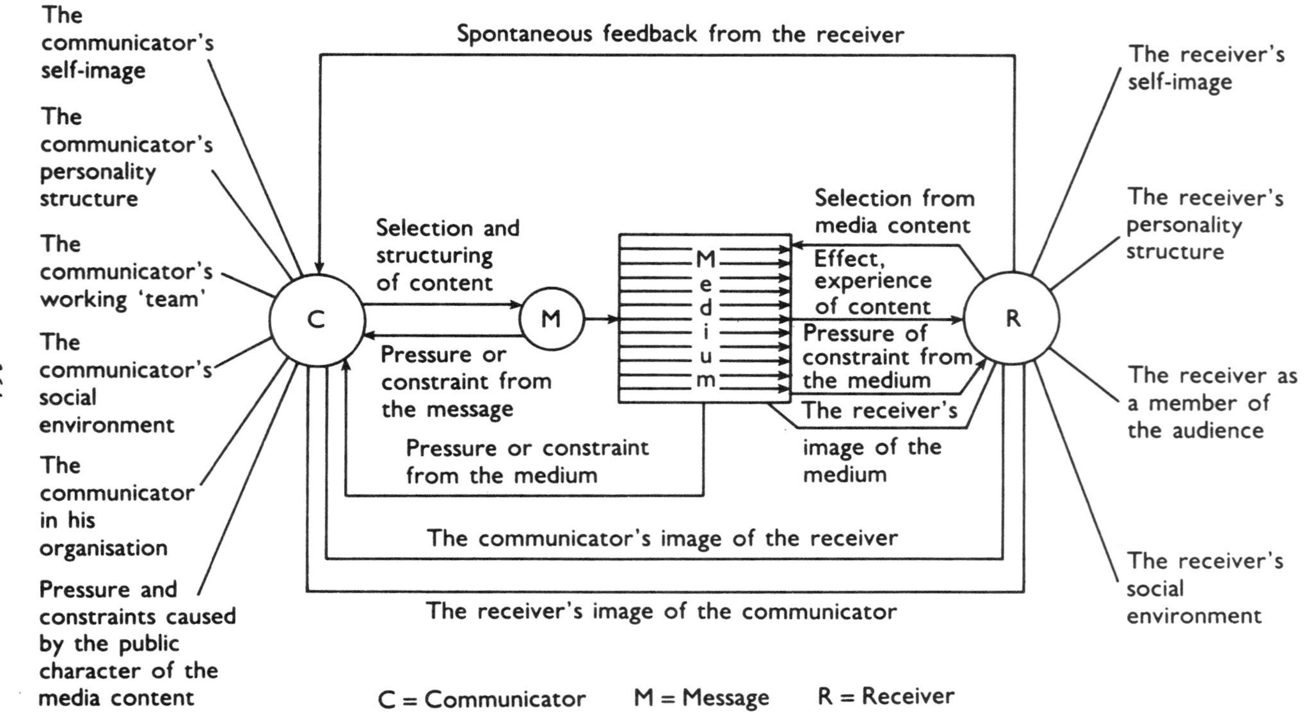

Figure 8.2 **Maletzke's communication model (Source: Maletzke (1963), as adapted by McQuail and Windahl (1981)).**

a model and the complexity of their interrelationship act as severe constraints. None the less, using a model to delineate the variables discussed earlier is helpful in that it provides a valuable and visible checklist. Much the most comprehensive model of this sort is that based on the work of Maletzke (1963), shown in Figure 8.2. Maletzke's model incorporates the personal and social characteristics of both the communicator and the receiver of the message, taking account of self-image and personality on the one hand, for instance, and the social and organisational environment on the other. The gatekeeping role and the constraints imposed by the medium are acknowledged. The mutual images of communicator and receiver are taken into account and there is provision for feedback from receiver to communicator. Above all, the model recognises the complexity of the communication process – a precondition for understanding public opinion and ideology.

Chapter 9

PUBLIC OPINION AND SOCIETY

DEFINING PUBLIC OPINION

> [Opinion] is the content of a person's consciousness, without any judgement as to its truth or untruth. (Pollock 1976, p. 228)

It is all too easy to assume that public opinion on particular matters is simply the sum of everyone's opinion in a given society. There is a tendency to treat public opinion as though it were a single entity, almost a single human being, but while opinion on a particular matter may be unanimous or near unanimous, in most cases it is divided. There is also a tendency to assume that everyone has an opinion about everything, but there is ample evidence to show that on many, probably most, issues some individuals will have no opinion. And it is not uncommon to find on some issues that these individuals constitute a majority.

Table 9.1 provides a good example of the extent to which people may hold no opinion, as expressed by the proportion of 'don't knows' in a 1976 poll on devolution proposals for Scotland. In a series of questions on the proposals the proportion of 'don't knows' was approximately four times higher in England and Wales than in Scotland, and the highest proportion in England and Wales was 45 per cent, compared to only 15 per cent in Scotland. These figures should come as no surprise: Scottish respondents would be expected to be more interested, and therefore more likely to have an opinion,

Table 9.1 *Proportion of 'don't knows' on devolution proposals for Scotland, 1976.*

	England and Wales %	Scotland %
Mean	34	9
Median	41	9
Range	7–45	0–15

Source: Social Surveys (Gallup), 1976.

than English and Welsh respondents. Furthermore, the latter would probably have been less well informed about the proposals and this may have increased the proportion of 'don't knows'. This view is reinforced when it is noted that the lowest proportion of 'don't knows' among English and Welsh respondents was in response to a question on various alternatives to devolution if Scotland remained part of the United Kingdom, and the second lowest proportion on whether Scotland should remain part of the United Kingdom, both questions which clearly affected England and Wales.

Similar data can be found in polls which regularly ask whether respondents are satisfied or dissatisfied with a range of government policies, relating to inflation, unemployment, the Health Service, education, defence, and so on. On economic questions such as inflation or taxation the proportions of 'don't knows' tend to be very low, but on other issues the proportions may be as high as 40 per cent. Proportions also vary over time. For example, in February 1975, soon after Margaret Thatcher was elected leader of the Conservative Party, as many as 41 per cent of respondents in a poll felt unable to say whether they were satisfied or dissatisfied with her as leader; by November 1975 the proportion had fallen to 19 per cent. Exactly the same phenomenon can be seen with Neil Kinnock: in November 1983, a month after becoming Labour leader, the corresponding proportion of 'don't knows' was 50 per cent; by September 1984 the proportion had dropped to 26 per cent (Social Surveys (Gallup) 1975 and 1983–4).

Pollock's assertion that opinion may or may not be true is also important. Relative ignorance or being misinformed are not necessarily a bar to holding an opinion about something, and opinion may be based on what someone believes to be the case, rather than what it actually is. There is also survey evidence that opinions change when respondents are given additional, usually accurate, information. Table 9.2 shows, for example, how opinion on the pay of British MPs shifted markedly when respondents were told how much MPs were paid. More than a third initially regarded MPs as overpaid and only 14 per cent as underpaid, but approximately a third of the respondents believed that MPs were paid more than £4,000 a year, when the true figure was £3,250. Once the latter was revealed, the proportion thinking MPs overpaid fell to 15 per cent and that thinking them underpaid rose to 33 per cent.

Opinion can also be divided into long-term and short-term aspects by drawing a distinction between values or broader opinions and attitudes or specific opinions, as was done in considering political socialisation and participation. Public opinion itself can be divided into the following four categories:

1. *Expert opinion* Those who are acknowledged specialists in the area of opinion concerned.
2. *Informed opinion* Those who have reasonable knowledge or acquaintance with the area of opinion concerned.
3. *Affected opinion* Those directly affected by the issue or matter concerned.
4. *Public opinion at large* Anyone not falling into any of the above categories.

Table 9.2 *Changes of opinion on MPs' pay in relation to respondents' information.*

Opinion	Before information given %	After information given %
Grossly overpaid	11	4
Rather overpaid	25	11
Paid about right amount	38	50
Rather underpaid	13	28
Grossly underpaid	1	5
Don't know/no answer	12	2
Total	100	100

Source: Review Body on Top Salaries: Ministers of the Crown and Members of Parliament, Cmnd. 4836, December 1971.

The importance of these categories is likely to vary according to the issue, those involved, general awareness of the issue, the extent to which opinion is organised through political parties and, more especially, pressure groups, and so on. Within these categories opinion may, of course, be divided.

THE CHARACTERISTICS OF PUBLIC OPINION

Lane and Sears (1964) argue that public opinion has four major characteristics: direction, intensity, salience, and consistency.

Direction means that, as already suggested, public opinion is normally divided into two or more views, quite apart from those who hold no opinion on some matter. Within a particular group or section of opinion it is possible that opinion on an issue is unanimous, but it is doubtful whether this is true of public opinion in general on any issue, although the proportion holding a particular view may be very large. It is also likely that in public opinion in general there will always be at least a few 'don't knows'.

Intensity refers to the fact that some individuals hold particular opinions more strongly than other individuals, which may make the former more likely to act on those opinions, clearly an important matter when considering political participation and recruitment. The data in Table 9.3 illustrate intensity of opinion in relation to party preferences. At the time the poll was taken the Labour Party had a substantial lead in the opinion polls, but fairly similar proportions of the supporters of the two major parties felt 'very' or 'fairly

Table 9.3 *Intensity of party preferences in Britain, 1990.*

Support party	Conservative %	Labour %	Liberal-Democrat %
Very strongly	6	12	–
Fairly strongly	13	17	2
Not very strongly	7	8	2
Not at all strongly	3	2	2
None of these	8	11	2
Total party support	37	50	8

Source: International Communication & Marketing Research, September 1990.

strongly' about their party preferences – 51 per cent of Conservative supporters and 58 per cent of Labour supporters, compared to 27 per cent and 20 per cent respectively who felt 'not very strongly' or 'not at all strongly'. In contrast, not only was support for the Liberal Democrats at the time only 8 per cent, but none of the party's supporters felt 'very strongly' and only 25 per cent 'fairly strongly'. The strength of commitment or intensity of feeling of supporters of the two major parties was thus markedly greater than that of Liberal Democrats. The same poll also asked respondents how strongly they felt about ten policy issues and again a clear pattern emerged regarding intensity: a mean proportion of 20.8 per cent 'agreed strongly' and of 22.9 per cent 'disagreed strongly' with particular propositions. However, the proportion varied considerably from issue to issue – from 6 to 49 per cent among those 'agreeing strongly' and from 5 to 50 per cent 'disagreeing strongly'. Although categories like 'very strongly' and 'not at all strongly' are crude and imprecise measures, they clearly demonstrate the existence of intensity and in no way diminish its importance.

Salience resembles intensity in that it also measures how strongly opinions are held, but relates to the relative importance of opinions held by an individual or group of individuals. Obviously, just as some individuals feel strongly about particular issues, so they will also feel more strongly about one issue compared with another. This is shown most commonly by opinion poll questions which ask respondents which of a range of problems they regard as the 'most important', as illustrated in Table 9.4. Inevitably which problem or problems are seen as the most important is likely to vary. For example, before the general election of 1979 the cost of living was seen as most important, followed by strikes and unemployment. This undoubtedly reflected public concern with rising inflation and the so-called winter of discontent, but in 1980 unemployment rose significantly, moved to the top of 'most important problems' and remained there until inflation again became a major cause of concern. Just as how strongly people feel about a particular issue is likely to effect their behaviour, so also is what priority they give to one issue over another.

Consistency also concerns the relationship between opinions, but focuses on the extent to which holding one opinion is consistent with holding another. Generally speaking, individuals are likely to hold opinions that are mutually consistent – hence the possibility of

Table 9.4 *Salience of problems facing Britain, February 1990.*

Most important problem	%
Cost of living	25
Housing	24
Unemployment	11
Health	8
Other economic	6
Environment	3
Law and order	2
Pensions	2
Strikes, unions	2
Other	12
Don't know	5
Total	100

Source: Social Surveys (Gallup), 1990.

ideology, but it also possible to hold contradictory views, though often as a result of ignorance or misinformation. As an example, in an opinion poll in 1968 respondents were asked whether they approved of the proposed Race Relations Bill, and then specifically whether they approved making it an offence to discriminate on racial grounds in areas such as employment, selling a house, and membership of a trade union, all specific provisions in the Bill. The results are shown in Table 9.5, and it is clear from the table that in spite of 42 per cent expressing approval of the Race Relations Bill in principle, equal or larger proportions actually disapproved of the Bill's main provisions. Of course, it is entirely reasonable of someone to disapprove of the specific provisions but still give general approval to the Bill. However, it is unlikely that the proportions ranging from two-fifths to half the respondents who disapproved of the Bill's main provisions and the two-fifths who approved of the Bill generally were mutually exclusive groups. Almost certainly much of the inconsistency is explained by respondents not knowing precisely what the Bill proposed and, as was noted earlier in the case of MPs' pay, opinion is likely to change if more or different information is provided.

It is important to note that where opinion is translated into action the possibility of inconsistency is bound to increase, since salience

Table 9.5 *Consistency of opinion on Race Relations Bill, 1968.*

A. Attitudes towards the Bill	%
Approve of the Bill	42
Disapprove of the Bill	29
Don't know	29
Total	100
B. Racial discrimination should be an offence in	**% disapproving**
Employment	47
Selling a house	49
Membership of a trade union	40

Source: Social Surveys (Gallup), 1968.

will come into play. Choosing between particular political parties or candidates in an election, for example, may mean making hard choices between general support for a party or candidate and the range of policies for which the party or candidate stands. Not all the policies of a party or candidate will necessarily be acceptable to the elector, but other parties and other candidates and their policies are perhaps less acceptable. In the 1950s and 1960s opinion polls regularly found a majority of Labour supporters against further nationalisation, in spite of the fact that the party was pledged to take more industries into public ownership. More recently, clear majorities of the electorate have not been in favour of the privatisation policies of the Thatcher government, nor of the abolition of the Greater London Council, but this did not prevent the Conservatives implementing these policies and winning the elections of 1983 and 1987.

Consistency may also be looked at over time, that is, whether individuals hold the same opinions or attitudes over shorter or longer periods of time. The evidence here is somewhat conflicting: using panel data, Butler and Stokes (1969) found that only 43 per cent of their respondents held consistent opinions on nationalisation between 1963 and 1970, but Alt (1979) and Crewe and Sarlvik (1980) found clusters of attitudes which would suggest a reasonable degree of consistency over time. Such findings are, of course, important in considering how far such clustering constitutes an ideological position, a matter to be pursued further in Chapter 10.

Opinion is therefore a complex phenomenon, complex enough when limited to the individual, but infinitely more so when considered collectively in the form of public opinion.

THE FORMATION OF PUBLIC OPINION

> Opinions are what they are because personal attitudes are what they are, and these attitudes stem from the nature of the personality, in turn the evolving result of the dynamic interaction of the person and his environment. (Childs 1965, p. 110)

In examining Childs' view that opinion is the product of the interaction between the individuals and their environment it is necessary to link opinion-formation to the concept of political socialisation and in particular with the interrelationship between three variables – knowledge, values, and attitudes, as suggested in Figure 9.1. As in political socialisation, knowledge is defined as information about various phenomena and is mainly factual, but also crucially includes knowledge of other opinions and matters believed to be fact. Thus, in considering an individual's knowledge, perception is a vital factor. As noted in the introduction to Part III, values are defined as basic beliefs or the individual's broad range of views on matters

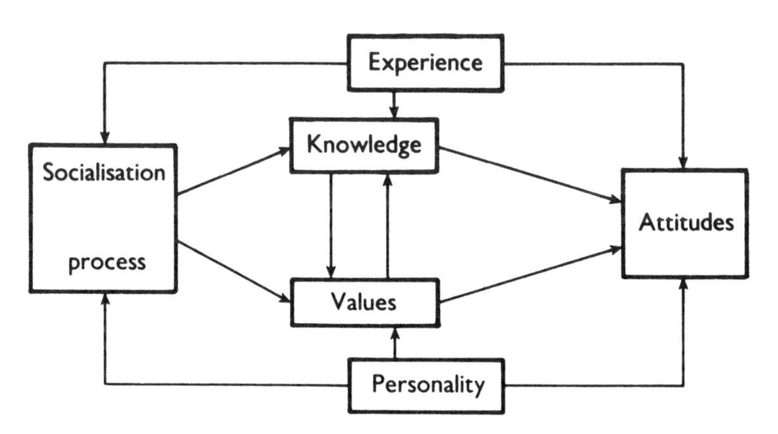

Figure 9.1 The formation of opinion: a model.

such as liberty, the free market, or on liberalism, socialism or communism, and may therefore be strongly related to ideology; and attitudes are defined as opinions on specific matters, such as a particular policy proposal or a candidate in an election. These three variables themselves need to linked, however, with two other key factors – the individual's personality and experience. The psychology of opinion-formation is an area in much need of further research, and, while considerable attention has been paid by authors like Adorno *et al.* (1950) and Eysenck (1954) to the role of personality in politics, more specific and systematic work is required to develop a clear view of the relationship between personality and opinion formation. Nevertheless, there is no reason to doubt that a relationship exists, especially in the shaping of values.

Similarly, much work needs to be done to explore the relationship between experience and opinion formation, not least because, as Lane and Sears (1964) suggest, experience provides the testing ground for values, leading individuals to evaluate the various elements in the communication process. Thus sources, channels and audiences are subject to scrutiny: are they to be trusted or regarded as reliable? This can be put in the form of a series of simple, but crucial questions. Does the individual believe a message received from a particular source? Does the individual believe a message transmitted through a particular channel? And is the message directed at a particular audience? Messages from, for example, politicians the individual supports are likely to be believed; those from politicians the individual does not support are more likely to be rejected or at least treated with scepticism. The media may be biased: certainly newspapers are commonly identified with particular ideologies and political views, television less so, but much depends on the perceptions of the individual and upon the extent to which the media is subject to political control. Politicians habitually direct their messages at particular audiences, most obviously to their supporters, but also to those they believe may be open to persuasion. Thus some messages may receive a hostile reception to the point of being rejected, but that may be because a particular audience is likely to be hostile anyway and the message is not directed at them. Messages may therefore be negative as well as positive and much communication is likely to have a reinforcing impact, rather than a proselytising one.

The model shown in Figure 9.1 suggests that particular attitudes or opinions are the product of the socialisation process and the individual's personality and experience on the one hand, and specific factors relating to particular issues on the other. Socialisation, personality and experience thus create on environment which enables the individual to react to particular issues and form attitudes or opinions. However, whether the individual reacts to a particular issue is likely to depend on three factors: whether the issue is brought to the individual's attention; whether the individual is interested in the issue; and how much information the individual has about the issue.

The first of these factors is commonly known as agenda-setting and the principal agenda-setters are political parties, most obviously through their election manifestos but, in practice, constantly bringing issues before the public and seeking to benefit from doing so. Parties also set broad agendas, combining a number and range of issues into a more or less coherent programme, but other agenda-setters, notably pressure groups, concentrate on specific matters, often a single policy, some on a continuing basis, others spasmodically. The media also play a major role in agenda-setting, partly by publicising the activities of parties and pressure groups, but also in their own right by taking up issues and forcing parties and pressure groups, individuals and groups of individuals, to respond or at least become aware of those issues. At the same time, it is important to remember the negative aspects of agenda-setting, noted especially in the discussion of power in Chapter 3. Issues can be kept off the political agenda or kept low down in its priorities, so that individuals are unaware or less aware that an issue exists.

It is at this point that the second factor comes into play – the extent to which the individual is interested in a particular issue. Awareness is not enough; the individual may have no opinion and where an opinion exists intensity and salience become crucial. It has already been noted that on many issues the proportion of 'don't knows' is very high, but where the individual is affected by or interested in an issue the likelihood of being in the 'don't know' category declines.

In the same way, the more individuals know (or think they know) about an issue, the more likely they are to have an opinion. There is ample evidence that the better informed and better educated are more likely to have an opinion than the less informed and less well educated. Not that ignorance – in the sense of not knowing – is a bar to holding an opinion and more may depend on the individual's perception of the 'facts' of the matter than the actual reality.

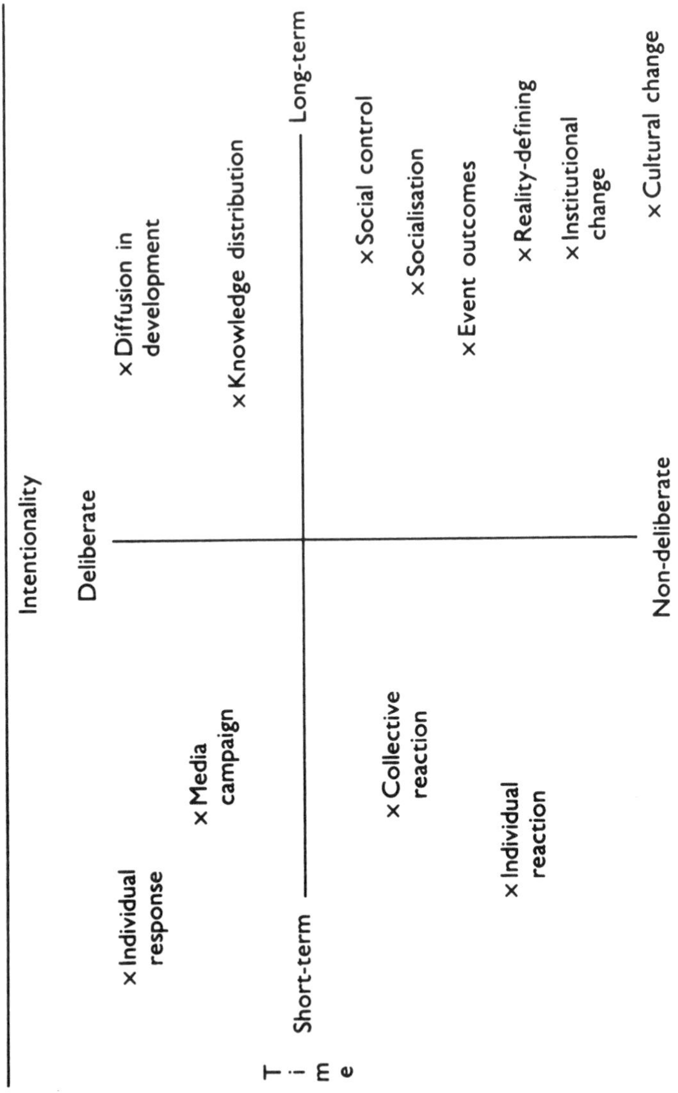

Intentionality

Deliberate

× Individual response

× Media campaign

× Diffusion in development

× Knowledge distribution

Time

Short-term

Long-term

× Collective reaction

× Individual reaction

× Social control

× Socialisation

× Event outcomes

× Reality-defining

× Institutional change

× Cultural change

Non-deliberate

Figure 9.2 **A typology of media effects** (Source: McQuail (1987), p. 258).

The mass media undoubtedly play a crucial role in the formation of public opinion, but there is no agreement about the precise nature of that role. Denis McQuail (1987) has produced a comprehensive typology of media effects, which is shown in Figure 9.2. He draws a basic distinction between short- and long-term effects and deliberate and non-deliberate effects. Many of the terms used are self-explanatory, but for greater clarity they are defined in Figure 9.3. McQuail acknowledges that the precise impact of different effects is difficult to measure, likely to vary over time and from one section of society to another, often a matter of dispute, and in need of further research. At the same time, the complexity of the effects of the media is clearly evident, important and pervasive.

Certainly the mass media are the most important source of information about political matters in countries like Britain. A poll

---

Individual response: change or resistance to change in response to messages designed to influence attitudes, knowledge or behaviour.
Media campaign: the use of the media to achieve a persuasive or informational purpose with a chosen population.
Collective reaction: the unplanned or unpredictable consequences of the exposure of many people to a media stimulus.
Individual reaction: the unplanned or unpredictable consequences of the exposure of a person to a media stimulus.
Diffusion in development: the planned introduction of change for the purposes of long-term development of society.
Knowledge distribution: the dissemination of news, information and knowledge.
Social control: the promotion of conformity to the established order and the reaffirmation of the legitimacy of existing authority.
Socialisation: the learning and adoption of established norms, values and expectations of behaviour in given social roles and situations.
Event outcomes: explaining and contributing to the results of major events in society.
Reality defining: the presentation of incomplete versions of 'reality' as a result of the nature of the media, commonly known as 'unwitting bias'.
Institutional change: unplanned adaptation by existing institutions to developments in the media.
Cultural change: shifts in the overall pattern of values, behaviour and symbols characterising a society or sector of a society.

Figure 9.3 A typology of media effects: definitions (Source: McQuail (1987), pp. 258–9).

conducted in 1974, for example, found that 63 per cent of respondents said that television or newspapers were the best means of getting information about politics, with only 10 per cent citing 'talking to people' and 9 per cent 'meetings'. For learning about the day's news the figure was no less than 89 per cent. The balance between television and newspapers has changed markedly since 1963, with 46 per cent citing newspapers as their principal source of news and 31 per cent television; in 1974 the figures were 34 per cent for newspapers and 46 per cent for television (Social Surveys (Gallup), September 1974). Measuring the influence of the media is more difficult, but it is worth noting the subjective finding of a MORI poll in 1989: 'Television was rated an important influence by more than 50 per cent of our respondents on twelve issues and newspapers on two' (Jacobs and Worcester 1990, p. 57).

The role of the media in agenda-setting also cannot be doubted. A classic example is the impact of Enoch Powell's speech in 1968 on immigration delivered to a tiny audience, but subject to massive coverage because he released copies to the media. The consequent publicity pushed the issue of race relations to a very high place on the political agenda (Seymour-Ure 1974, pp. 99–136). Another example is the attention focused by *The Sunday Times* in the 1970s on the adverse effects on unborn children of the tranquillising drug thalidomide. More recently, the media has played a major role in moving the complex of issues concerning AIDS up the political agenda, especially the plight of haemophiliacs who had become HIV-positive through blood transfusions.

Evidence of media effects is thus not difficult to cite, but it is often selective and anecdotal rather than systematic. No one doubts, for instance, that the media played an important role in the Watergate Scandal and the consequent fall of Richard Nixon, but just how important *The Washington Post* and the televised hearings of congressional committees were is more difficult to gauge. Furthermore, however important their role, the question of whether it was typical or atypical remains. Thus when it comes to exploring the effects of the media in areas such as social control, socialisation, or institutional or cultural change, the task is even more difficult (see Seaton 1988). Totalitarian regimes overtly use the media to exert social control and influence the socialisation process, but the relationship between the media and government in countries like Britain and the United States is infinitely more complex and subtle. Certainly,

Marxist writers such as Miliband (1969), Poulantzas (1973), and Westergaard (1977) regard the media as operating in the interests and maintenance of capitalist society, the evidence for which is compelling, not least because, as McQuail points out:

> It would be very difficult to argue that the media are, on balance, a force for major change in society, or to deny that a large part of what is most attended to is generally conformist in tendency ... [or] that the media are mainly owned and controlled either by (often large) business interests or (however indirectly) the state – thus the interests which do have political and economic power. ... [I]t is no secret that, most media most of the time do not see it as their task to promote fundamental change in the social system. They work within the arrangements that exist, often sharing the concensual goal of gradual social improvement.

But he adds:

> [the] media are committed by their own ideology to serving as a carrier for messages (e.g. about scandals, crises, social ills) which could be an impulse to change, even of a quite fundamental kind. They probably do stimulate much activity, agitation and anxiety which disturb the existing order, within the limits of systems which have some capacity for generating change. Ultimately, the questions involved turn on how dynamic societies are and on the division of social power within them and these take us well beyond the scope of media-centred theory. (McQuail 1987, pp. 288–9)

POLITICAL COMMUNICATION AND PUBLIC OPINION

The importance of communication in the study of politics cannot be exaggerated: without communication there is not only no politics, but no society. However, there are serious problems with the state of knowledge of political communication in general and public opinion in particular. The first, and perhaps most serious, is the absence of an adequate model. Many of the elements of such a model can be identified, but the relationship between them remains empirically underresearched; its complexity remains acknowledged but largely unexplored. In addition, some models concentrate on individual or interpersonal communication, others on mass communication, and somehow these two have to be adequately brought together.

The absence of an adequate model is also closely related to another problem: it is not clear theoretically, let alone empirically, how political attitudes fit in with other attitudes. Just as it is a mistake to isolate political behaviour from social behaviour, so it is a mistake to isolate political attitudes from wider, social attitudes. Common sense suggests that the two are inextricably linked, however possible it may be to separate them analytically, one from the other.

If theories of political communication are inadequate, then inevitably so are those of attitude or opinion-formation. Again the relevant elements of a model can be identified, but the problem of relating individual and mass opinion reappears. Identifying opinion characteristics, such as intensity, salience and consistency, is also far short of adequately measuring them. Opinion polls and surveys provide a mass of information about people's opinions, but do little to explain why they hold them. Where attempts are made to measure intensity and salience, the tools used are crude and the analysis all too often based on inferential data, especially socio-economic characteristics. What may be adequate for market research is woefully inadequate for serious hypothesising. Without necessarily intending to, polls and surveys can change opinion; indeed, the very act of asking a question may contribute to the formation of an opinion.

Above all the role of values needs to be addressed, especially whether individuals' values and attitudes constitute a coherent whole – an ideology. Not everyone may be an ideologist, but does everyone have an ideology?

Chapter 10

IDEOLOGY AND SOCIETY

WHAT IS IDEOLOGY?

The term 'ideology' was coined by the French philosopher Destutt de Tracy at the beginning of the nineteenth century to mean 'the science of ideas', but it did not enjoy widespread use until the posthumous publication of Marx and Engels' *The German Ideology* in 1927. They defined ideology as 'false consciousness', that is a distortion of reality – the reality being the class struggle, the distortion the prevailing ideas of the ruling class. This led Karl Mannheim (1936 [1929]) in *Ideology and Utopia* to develop his theories about the sociology of knowledge, that is, ideas about ideas and systems of thought in particular social contexts. He came to define ideology as 'styles of thought' about social phenomena and therefore posited that Marxism itself was an ideology. Mannheim further argued that ideologies may range from a limited or particular ideology, such as the ideology of small businessmen, to a total ideology, or *Weltanschauung*, that sought to explain everything.

Talcott Parsons (1951, p. 331) saw ideology as 'the belief system shared by members of a collectivity' and as an interpretative scheme used by social groups to make the world intelligible to themselves. This may well be a distortion of reality, but not in the Marxist sense in that such a distortion is not necessarily a reflection of the ideas of the ruling class, but may, for example, include religious beliefs. Others, such as the social anthropologist Clifford Geertz (1964), define ideology as one of a number of cultural symbol systems, others being religious, aesthetic and scientific, and regard ideology as essentially neutral in role.

There is, then, essentially a Marxist and a non-Marxist view of ideology, on the one hand as the prevailing ideas of the ruling class, and on the other as a number, possibly an infinite number, of available views of the world or part of the world. In the latter case, however, ideology should not be seen as synonymous with philosophy, which it differs from in two respects. First, philosophy is much broader in that ultimately it is thought about thought, even though it may offer explanations or views of ways of life. Philosophy thus involves epistemology, or the theory of knowledge, metaphysics, or the investigation of what exists, and ethics, or the investigation of morality. Second, ideology differs from philosophy in that it is clearly associated with action, insofar as it forms the basis or justification for action or a desire for action (or indeed, inaction). Daniel Bell (1960, p. 394) defines ideology as 'the conversion of ideas into social levers'.

THE CHARACTERISTICS AND FUNCTIONS OF IDEOLOGY

Ideology may be said to have four important, interrelated characteristics. First, the holding of a particular idea or belief is related to the holding of one or more associated ideas or beliefs. For example, a belief in freedom of speech will normally be associated with similar beliefs in freedom of association and freedom from arbitrary imprisonment. Second, such beliefs will, to a greater or lesser degree, have clarity, coherence and internal consistency. Thus, even though the ideas and beliefs constituting an ideology may be based on one or more false premises, the relationship between them is still logical and internally consistent, at least in the mind of the believer. Third, these ideas and beliefs are likely to reflect views about the nature of the human race as, for instance, egoistic, co-operative, rational, individualistic, communal, or social. Again, the accuracy of such a view, important as it may be when the ideology becomes the basis for behaviour, is not a precondition for the existence of a given ideology. Fourth, such beliefs are likely to be associated with a particular social situation or set of arrangements to be striven for, attained and maintained. Of course, such a state of affairs may be close to or far removed from reality, but ideology may range from the mundane to the messianic.

There are two broad schools of thought about the functions of ideology in society. One sees ideology as a reflection of personality, as meeting the individual's psychological needs; the other sees it as a group response, the way in which a group explains and itself understands its position or situation in society. There is, however, no reason why ideology should not fulfil both functions and it can be argued that ideology fulfils a series of related functions, as follows:

1. Providing the individual with a picture of the world (i.e. how the individual sees the world).
2. Implicitly or explicitly providing the individual with a *preferred* picture of the world (i.e. what the individual would like the world to become).
3. Providing the individual with a means of identity in the world (i.e. allowing the individual to place himself or herself in their society).
4. Providing the individual with a means of reacting to phenomena (i.e. allowing the individual to respond to what happens and what is said).
5. Providing the individual with a guide to action, particularly how to keep the world in or change it to a preferred state.

In short, ideology is a means by which individuals can come to terms with the world and their place in it, or alternatively, a means to change it.

THE MARXIST VIEW OF IDEOLOGY

As noted in Chapter 3, Marx and Engels (1976 [1845–6], pp. 59 and 60) argued in *The German Ideology* that the 'ideas of the ruling class are in every epoch the ruling ideas'. Thus once a class has achieved dominance, it will 'present its interest as the common interest of all the members of society, that is, expressed in ideal form: it has to give its ideas the form of universality, and present them as the only rational, universally-valid ones'. This is the dominant ideology thesis. But the Marxist view is more complex than arguing that it is false consciousness, a distortion of reality which masks the inherent contradictions in society. The relationship between the mode of production and the ideas prevalent in society is simple in conception but complex in practice, since it involves individual consciousness or perception: 'The mode of production of material life conditions the general process of social, political and intellectual life. It is not the consciousness of men that determines their existence, but their social existence that determines their consciousness' (Marx 1980 [1859]: 29–263).

The Marxist approach to ideology is essentially one of asking *why* do people want what they want? It is a rejection of the pluralist answer that people are the best judges of their own interests and wants. Thus even Herbert Marcuse, a leading neo-Marxist, who argues that ultimately individuals are the best judges of their own interests, also argues that this is so only when they are free to give an answer, that is, when they are not indoctrinated (1968 [1964]). It is important to be aware that Marxists define interest as 'an advantage' in the sense of having a stake in something.

It is also important to bear in mind that *The German Ideology* was not published until 1927 and was therefore unavailable to early Marxists, including Lenin. Marx and Engel's view of ideology is basically negative, although there are signs of a positive view in some of their writings. Lenin gave the concept of ideology a clearly positive thrust by acknowledging that *initially* ideology stems from the interests of the dominant class, but then goes on to argue that any critique of ideology has to stem from the interests of the *dominated* class. In Lenin's view it is therefore possible to speak of a bourgeois ideology and a proletarian ideology. In this sense ideology becomes the product of the political consciousness of classes and led Gramsci (1971 [1929–35], pp. 328 and 377) to define ideology as 'a concept of the world that is implicitly manifest in art, in law, in economic activity and in all manifestations of individual life', but that ideology is more than a system of ideas, being 'the terrain on which men move, acquire consciousness of their position'.

Althusser argues that ideology is the 'indistinguishable cement of social cohesion' (Anderson 1976, p. 84), a view not dissimilar from that of Parsons in that Althusser assigns ideology a quasi-functional role. In many respect Gramsci and Althusser hold views that are not that different from the non-Marxist view, except that non-Marxists regard Marxism itself as an ideology. Actually, the difference between the Marxist and the non-Marxist concepts of ideology is not as great as it might appear, given the widespread acceptance that ideology is a limited or distorted view of society. In perceptive study Jorge Larrain (1979; see also Larrain 1983) suggests that ideology can be seen in several ways – as a distortion of reality, as the world view of a social class, as particular ideas of individuals, classes or parties, and as applying to society as a whole or to only part of it. Larrain further argues that ideology may take many forms, for example, in 'feudal society ideology resorted to religion in order to justify class domination' (1979, p. 211), and points out that both Machiavelli and Hobbes stressed the importance of religion in the exercise of power and authority. Nor is science immune from ideology: 'The social determination of scientific knowledge does not make it an ideology, but it opens up the possibility for ideological penetration. ... Science is not itself ideological; but it may be ideological to claim it is' (Larrain 1979, pp. 210–11).

Abercrombie and Turner (1978, 1980) reject the traditional Marxist and the neo-Marxist view – the dominant ideology thesis – on the grounds that it is historically and empirically invalid: 'it is typically the case that subordinate classes do *not* believe (show, accept) the dominant ideology which has far more significance for the integration and control of the dominant class itself... the real significance of the dominant ideology lies in the organisation of the dominant class rather then the subordination of the dominated classes' (1978: 153 and 161). Parkin (1972) not dissimilarly argues that there are three competing ideologies: a dominant value system; a subordinate value system that underpins accommodative behaviour by subordinate classes; and a radical value system that stimulates opposition to the dominant class.

Ultimately, the conflict between the Marxist and non-Marxist views of ideology relates to its role: is it, as Marx originally asserted and neo-Marxists have reasserted with increasing sophistication, a major factor in the dominance of the ruling class? Or is it, as most non-Marxists believe, a number of coherent sets of ideas available about the world, characterised by varying distortions of reality? Is what has been called the dominant ideology thesis sustainable? Do most people have an ideology or think in ideological terms? Can a society exist without ideology? These questions are the subjects of the remainder of this chapter.

IDEOLOGY, POLITICAL CULTURE AND THE END OF IDEOLOGY THESIS

In one of several definitions of political culture Almond and Verba (1963, p. 12) offer one which could also serve as a definition of ideology: 'specifically political orientations – attitudes toward the political system and its various parts and attitudes toward the role of self in the system.' Marxist and political culture theories have one thing in common: both see political behaviour as the product of prevailing sets of ideas, but differ in that political culture argues that any number of sets of ideas are available or possible, whereas for Marxism ultimately only one set of ideas is important, that of the ruling or dominant class. Viewed thus, Marxism is not a set of ideas but the truth.

Political culture, however, should not be seen as synonymous with ideology, from which it differs in two important respects. First, political culture is normally seen as broader than ideology and, even though it may substantially reflect a particular ideology, it will usually include ideas and values which are outside that ideology or even drawn from other ideologies. For example, the existence and justification of conservative, liberal and socialist traditions in Britain can be seen as part of British political culture, broader than any one of the ideologies associated with these traditions. Second, political culture is not therefore characterised by a greater or lesser degree of clarity, coherence and internal consistency, but may include contradictory and conflicting elements as illustrated by the existence of different social and political traditions.

Some of the ideas that led to the development of political culture theory contributed significantly to what became known as 'the end of ideology thesis'. The developmental view of politics, with which theorists like Almond and Verba were strongly associated, argued that all societies are at different stages on a continuum of economic and political development culminating in liberal-democratic societies. 'The end of ideology thesis' was a powerful but separate sub-argument which reinforced the developmental view. Its principal proponents were Edward Shils, Raymond Aron, S. M. Lipset, but most of all, Daniel Bell (1960), author of *The End of Ideology: On the exhaustion of political ideas in the fifties*, published in 1960. Nearly twenty years after its publication *The End of Ideology* was reissued with an extensive 'Afterword' by Bell, in which he effectively agreed with the Marxist view that ideology is false consciousness:

> Ideology . . . deals with social movements that seek to mobilise men for the realisation of . . . [particular] . . . beliefs, and in this fusion of political formulas and passions, ideology provides a faith and a set of moral certitudes . . . by which ends are used to justify immoral means. The disillusion of individuals with such movements results in the dissipation of ideology among the adherents; or, when such movements are in power, ideology becomes a coercive force used by the rulers to maintain conformity. (Bell 1988, p. 437)

Bell began his 1988 reappraisal of the end of ideology thesis by wryly commenting: 'There are some books that are better known for their titles than their contents. Mine is one of them.' (1988, p. 409). He pointed out that he had originally argued 'that the old nineteenth-century ideologies and intellectual debates have become exhausted, the rising states of Asia and Africa are fashioning new ideas with a different appeal for their own people. These are ideas of industrialisation, modernisation, Pan-Arabism, colour and nationalism' (1960, p. 403). Essentially, what Bell was arguing in 1960 and reiterated in 1988 was that all ideologies outlive their usefulness. However, proponents and critics alike tended to focus not only on the title of Bell's book, but concentrated their attention almost exclusively on advanced industrial or capitalist societies, those that had a claim to be called liberal-democracies.

In most advanced industrial societies, it was argued, technology and modernisation had exhausted the old ideas, the traditional ideas, which had therefore lost their truth on the power to persuade. What had developed in these societies, was a democratic consensus, characterised by an agreement on ends and accompanied by some disagreement on the means to be used to achieve those ends. For Lipset (1960, 1966), for example, it meant that in the Western world 'the fundamental problems of the industrial revolution have been solved' (1960, p. 406) so that '[i]ntense ideologisation, sharp conflict is characteristic of politics in which new, emerging classes or strata are denied political, social or economic rights, but declines when those classes are admitted to full citizenship' (1966, p. 17). Lipset, in particular, inclined towards the view that under the impact of modernisation developing countries would eventually conform to a similar ideological pattern. Bell (1988), however, adopted a somewhat different view in that he did indeed look forward to the end of ideology, but not to the end of ideas and ideals as a force in politics and society: 'a moral order, if it is to exist without coercion or deceit, has to transcend the parochialism of interests and tame the appetites of passions. And that is the defeat of ideology' (1988, p. 447).

The end of ideology school arose out of the undoubtedly lower profile that ideology enjoyed in 'real politics' in the 1950s, especially in the form of consensus politics. In both the United States and Britain the ideological gap between the major parties seemed to lessen markedly. The Republicans under Eisenhower effectively accepted the New Deal legislation of Roosevelt and did not attempt any wholesale reversal of policy. Correspondingly, the Conservatives did not attempt wholesale denationalisation of the industries taken into public ownership by the 1945–51 Labour Government. Of course, it could be argued that internationally the ideological conflict between East and West, between communism and capitalism went on and even intensified, but equally it could also be argued that the end of ideology thesis has now penetrated the international sphere with the collapse of communism in Eastern Europe and in the Soviet Union. This may well be, but in the context of the role of ideology it is perhaps less important than to point out that the end of ideology thesis itself can be seen as an ideology. Viewed this way the end of ideology thesis assumes a position not unlike that of Marxism – it must be seen either as an ideology or the 'truth'. The ideological conflict may have subsided or even disappeared, but the significance of ideas and values in politics is in no way lessened. However, even if it is conceded that liberal-democratic values are the 'truth', this cannot prevent an ideological challenge emerging in the future. Indeed, the rise of Islamic fundamentalism could be seen as just such a challenge, not least in asserting that it, of course, is the 'truth'.

Ulf Himmelstrand (1962) has provided a way of putting the end of ideology school and perhaps ideology itself into a meaningful perspective. He argued that the end of ideology thesis was not really an assertion that ideology was dead, but that ideology was no longer the basis for political action and conflict. Himmelstrand used Sweden in the 1960s as an example of what he calls the depoliticisation of politics, in which political conflict is over matters such as rates of pay, prices and pensions, and not over the very nature of society. Using a two-dimensional approach which looks, on the one hand, at the extent to which ideology is important in political conflict – the salience of manifest ideology – and on the other, the extent to which political conflict reflects ideology in practice – the functional dissociation of ideology and practical politics – he argues that where salience is low and functional dissociation high, then genuine depoliticisation will occur.

The United States in the 1950s and 1960s is regarded by Himmelstrand as an example of genuine depoliticisation. Britain in the 1950s, however, may be seen as an example of spurious depoliticisation, in which there were low levels of the salience of manifest ideology and of the functional dissociation of ideology and practical politics. Thus it could be argued that the apparent ideological consensus between the Conservative and Labour Parties masked their continuing ideological differences, so that even if they promulgated or pursued similar policies they did so for different ideological reasons.

Himmelstrand's third category is that of no depoliticisation, characterised by high salience of ideology but low functional dissociation, and the Soviet Union in the years from 1917 until at least the completion of Stalin's programme of collectivisation could be seen as an example. A more recent example would be Iran since the overthrow of the Shah, particularly during the lifetime of the Ayatollah Khomeini. The fourth category – semi-depoliticisation – is characterised by high ideological salience and high functional dissociation and it could be argued that both Nazi Germany and the Soviet Union after the collectivisation of agriculture showed distinct signs of semi-depoliticisation. Ideological salience in both was high and political behaviour and policy was always justified in ideological terms, even though policy could be remarkably pragmatic and apparently at odds with ideology. The Nazi–Soviet Non-Aggression Pact of 1939 is a prime example, with enemies becoming friends, and friends enemies. All totalitarian regimes need to justify their existence and behaviour in ideological terms, but whether behaviour is always consonant with ideology is another matter.

The significance of Himmelstrand's argument is that it suggests that ideology plays a different role in different systems and at different times. This can be taken a stage further by comparing the relationship between ideology and values.

IDEOLOGY, VALUES AND ATTITUDES

There is no doubt that ideologies exist; to deny it is to deny that nationalism, conservatism, liberalism, socialism, national socialism, fascism, communism, anti-Semitism or apartheid have not powerfully influenced individuals' social and political behaviour. This does not mean, however, that people's basic values and attitudes necessarily constitute a personal ideology, even though they are inevitably associated with particular historical and social environments and experiences.

Research into political participation and political psychology suggests that there are essentially two views of the role of ideology – the minimalist and the maximalist. The minimalist view argues that individuals have low levels of political knowledge, do not use or even understand political ideas, have unstable political preferences, and that their political preferences are frequently inconsistent with one another. The maximalist view is that individuals have coherent packages of beliefs and that one or more of these packages constitutes an ideology. While there is a good deal of research evidence to support the minimalist view, especially on levels of political knowledge, it is a dubious assumption that such a view is true of all individuals. Certainly, there are many individuals whose ability to express themselves, and therefore presumably to think, in ideological terms is self-evident, chief among whom are many, though not necessarily all, politicians.

It is therefore more realistic to argue that many, perhaps most people, are closer to the minimalist than the maximalist view, but that both are valid and should be seen as the extremes of a continuum. This is the view of Sniderman and Tetlock, who see the two views not as alternatives but as complementary. Drawing on a variety of research they conclude:

> It cannot be argued, for example, that the mass public has a firm grip on liberalism and conservatism as complex political philosophies. Yet a substantial proportion of the public may have a clear preference for one against the other. ... [T]hese ideological differences are psychologically rooted in the widespread reliance on simple, easy-to-execute rules of thumb ... in policy reasoning. People's likes and dislikes of strategic political groups provide them with the

> clues they need in order to understand politics in terms of liberal versus conservative. ... [T]he resultant ideological understanding of mass publics may be a crude one; but so are most effective ways of understanding a complex world. (Sniderman and Tetlock 1986, p. 89)

In other words Sniderman and Tetlock see people's values and beliefs expressed in their likes and dislikes for both individuals and organisations, proposals and policies, which in most cases they do not articulate in ideological terms, but nevertheless often reflect what analytically can reasonably be described as an ideological position. A distinction is thus drawn between overt and covert ideological positions, the first recognised and acknowledged by the individual, the other not.

However, while there is evidence that many people are able to identify parties and themselves in ideological terms when asked appropriate questions in surveys, the evidence that they habitually think in such terms is far less strong. Butler and Stokes, for instance, found that only 25 per cent of their respondents thought of themselves in left–right terms and 'threequarters ... indicated that these concepts were not among their working stock of ideas when they thought about politics' (1969, p. 329). More pertinently, Whiteley, in a study of the Labour Party in the early 1980s, concluded:

> it is clear that the ideological structuring of attitudes only occurs to a significant extent amongst the Labour elite [i.e. local party activists]. In the case of ordinary Labour voters, and even strong Labour identifiers, there is only a weak level of attitude structuring, and this exists for only a small number of issues. By contrast, for the Labour elite attitudes are structured sufficiently to make it possible to identify a distinct left–right continuum of opinions underlying beliefs. (Whiteley 1983, p. 50)

On the other hand, while electoral studies in Britain suggest that to a significant extent electors vote for the parties they do out of self-interest, the same data can be interpreted as reflecting their values and therefore as an ideology underpinning their behaviour. Not surprisingly, the strongest support for the Conservative government elected in 1979 has been from those sections of the electorate who have benefited most from its policies and the strongest opposition from those who have benefited least or, who, even if they have benefited from them, have been alienated by them. Thus in the elections of 1979, 1983 and 1987 strong support for the Conservative government and its policies was found among the skilled working class, especially in the South of England, those who bought their council houses, and first-time owners of shares in privatised industries, but it was strongest among the self-made middle class and small businessmen. Conversely, it is much weaker among semi-skilled and unskilled workers, and council tenants, who still find the Labour party a more natural locus, and among university graduates and those working in the public sector, who have been alienated by the government's policies, and many of whom shifted their allegiance to the now-defunct Liberal–SDP Alliance (Butler and Kavanagh 1988; Heath *et al.* 1985, 1991; Rose and McAllister 1986; and Denver 1989).

In the context of ideology, however, of even greater interest is that neither the British electorate generally, nor even a substantial proportion of it, has been ideologically converted from a collectivist, welfare state society to an individualistic, free market society, from the consensus policies of the 1950s and 1960s to the Thatcherite policies of the 1980s. Conservative privatisation of state-owned or nationalised industries does not enjoy widespread support in principle (though neither does nationalisation), whereas support for a fully publicly funded health service, the maintenance of a wide range of welfare benefits, and the state funding of schools remains very high (Jacobs and Worcester 1990), so that, given a choice of the type of society they would prefer, a significant majority of the electorate would reject Thatcherism. However, the choice at general elections is seldom so simple and, in the elections of 1979, 1983 and 1987, sufficient of the electorate (though not a majority) responded to pragmatic self-interest, thus ensuring the election and re-election of the Conservatives. The apparent paradox can be explained by asking what is ultimately desired and what is currently attainable, that is, between long-term and short-term considerations.

In totalitarian societies this paradox may appear to be absent: belief in and conformity to the ideology seem absolute and the relationship between behaviour and ideology entirely congruent. This may well be so where socialisation and the control of political communication have been at their most successful, but where the relationship between ideology and experience becomes incongruent political behaviour is more likely to change. Such a change may involve societal change, sometimes of a fundamental sort, as occurred in Eastern Europe in 1989 and more recently in the Soviet Union, but there is strong evidence that fundamental change is preceded by a long period during which belief in the ideology declines markedly, but conformity to it continues. The outward appearance of the society remains unchanged, but beneath the surface a more cynical reality exists, graphically described by Vaclav Havel, a former dissident, now President of Czechoslovakia:

> one need not believe all these mystifications, but one must behave as if one did, or at least put up with them tacitly, or get along with those who use them. But this means living a lie. One is not required to believe the lie, it is enough to accept life with it and within it. In so doing one confirms the system, gives it meaning, creates it . . . and merges with it. (Quoted in Rupnik 1988, pp. 232–3)

It may therefore be circumspect to agree with Thompson when he asserts:

> There is little evidence to suggest that certain values or beliefs are shared by all (or even most) members of modern industrial societies. On the contrary, it seems more likely that our societies, in so far as they are 'stable' social orders, are stabilised by virtue of the diversity of values and beliefs and the proliferation of divisions between individuals and groups. The stability of our societies may depend not so much upon a consensus concerning particular values or norms, but upon a lack of consensus at the very point where oppositional attitudes could be translated into political action. (Thompson 1984, p. 5)

IDEOLOGY AND SOCIETY

The relationship between ideology and society is a complex one, not least because the relationship between ideology and values and between long-term and short-term behaviour is complex. The major reason for this is that ideology and reality are seldom totally at one. It is reasonable to argue that ideology operates at several different levels. At the highest and most overt level it informs the behaviour of those most active in politics. For those who aspire to power ideology is often at its most overt and coherent; for those who hold power ideology is invariably tempered by the need to compromise, which the taking of real rather than hypothetical decisions imposes. As Himmelstrand argues, the extent to which ideology is manifest or latent is likely to vary from society to society and over time, but no society exists in a value-free environment, no more than do a society's social and political institutions, a point eloquently expressed by Bernard Crick (1964, p. 199): 'All ideas seek institutional realisation; all institutions embody purposes.'

PART V

CHANGING SOCIETY: REVOLUTION, DEVELOPMENT AND MODERNISATION

INTRODUCTION

How and why societies change is of central concern to political sociology. It has been the subject of much theorising by those who wish to understand and explain the process of societal change and not a little action by those who have sought, and in some cases succeeded, in changing particular societies. Analytically it can be argued that societal change is the product of either revolution or evolution, revolution being defined, for the moment, as profound societal change precipitated by violence, and evolution as gradual societal change prompted largely though not exclusively by technological change. Such definitions, however, do no more than suggest contrasting forms of societal change and offer little by way of explanation. Moreover, it can be further argued that they are not necessarily alternative forms of change, but in certain circumstances, may be complementary. For example, revolution may lead to evolution by creating the circumstances for longer-term, evolutionary change; or evolutionary change may ultimately encounter social and political obstacles that can only be surmounted by revolutionary change. The Marxist view of revolution involves evolutionary change in the means of production creating the circumstances which render revolution inevitable.

This raises a further question: is societal change inevitable? The Marxist answer is, of course, unequivocally affirmative: bourgeois and proletarian revolutions are instrumental in attaining a communist society; the process may be slowed down or speeded up, but the outcome cannot be in doubt. Non-Marxist theorists see revolution as inevitable only when certain conditions exist, usually when other means of societal change have been unsuccessful and only violent and possibly prolonged upheaval will change the existing social and political order. If revolution is not necessarily inevitable, then what of other means of change? Certainly, some development and modernisation theorists regard societal change as inevitable; others regard it as inevitable once the development or modernisation process has started or reached a particular stage.

Historically, there is ample evidence that patterns of societal change exist, especially as a consequence of technological innovation. There is, for example, a clear and close association between industrialisation and urbanisation, but the links between material changes and values are less clear. That some link exists is hardly to be doubted and there is no shortage of theories, but that is far from establishing a universal theory of societal change leading to the universal and uniform society implicit in much development and modernisation theory. Even if such a society were the ultimate end, it is pertinent to ask whether the means to that end is uniform – the consequence of an inevitable linear process or progression. Development and modernisation theory often suggests that it is, but a number of neo-Marxists argue that industrialisation has created a world capitalist order, rather than simply a number of capitalist societies. In this world capitalist order 'developing' or 'Third World' societies have become *dependent* – hence the term 'dependency theory' – on advanced industrial societies. The Third World cannot develop or industrialise in the 'normal' way, since their economies are an integral part of a world capitalist system. Post-1945 political independence has not brought and cannot bring economic independence.

Dependency theory challenges both the traditional Marxist view of revolution, and development and modernisation theory. The relationship between advanced industrial societies and developing societies is vital to an understanding of societal change – a few societies survive in relative, occasionally significant, isolation, but most are profoundly affected by external as well as internal forces: In both cases the role of values looms large, but remains inadequately explored. Traditional Marxist theory regards values (in the form of ideology) as a consequence of the mode of production; neo-Marxists tend to resort to the dominant ideology thesis; and development and modernisation theorists invariably acknowledge the importance of values in societal change, but beyond that take them for granted.

Ultimately, an adequate theory of societal change needs to encompass and explain sudden and violent change and slower, more evolutionary change in both material and value terms. No such theory exists, but Part V examines theories of revolution, development, modernisation, and dependency with that need in mind.

Chapter 11

REVOLUTION

INTRODUCTION

'Revolution' is yet another widely used term in the political vocabulary and perhaps even more in political rhetoric, quite apart from its frequent literary use as in 'technological revolution', or its historical use, as in the 'agricultural revolution' or the 'industrial revolution'. It is also used in conjunction with other terms like 'rebellion', '*coup d'état*', and 'insurrection', often without drawing adequate conceptual distinctions between them. However, it is common to regard the English Revolution of the seventeenth century, the American Revolution of 1774–89, the French Revolution of 1789, the Russian Revolution of 1917, and the Chinese Revolution of 1949 as revolutions in the sense that they involved the violent overthrow of a regime followed by significant changes in society, and it is the latter – significant changes in society – which is normally taken to distinguish revolutions from rebellions, *coups d'état*, and insurrections.

There is also a particular rhetorical use of the term 'revolution' to which attention should be drawn and that is revolution as a necessary myth in the political culture or history of a society. This is where, definitionally, a revolution has not occurred, but those in power claim that it has in order to justify particular policies in 'the name of the revolution' or more generally to legitimise their claim to power. For example, the leaders of many developing countries refer to the winning of independence from the colonial power as a revolution, as in some cases it may have been, but in others clearly was not.

The idea of the revolution as myth has some analytical value, too, in that not only can it be used to explain and justify political actions in a positive sense, but its *absence* can also be used to explain other phenomena. It has been argued, for instance, that Canada has, unlike the United States, failed to develop a strong sense of national identity precisely because it *lacks* a revolution. Nigeria can be used to demonstrate both aspects: independence for Nigeria came largely through negotiation rather than as a result of a conflict between nationalist leaders and Britain, as is well illustrated by the speech of the Nigerian Prime Minister, Sir Abubakar Tafawa Balewa, on Independence Day in 1960: 'We are grateful to the British officers we have known, first as masters and then as leaders and, finally, as partners but always as friends.' Later Nigerian leaders have referred to the coup which overthrew the Balewa government in January 1966 and the second coup of July 1966, which installed a second military regime, as 'our revolution'.

For conceptual purposes, however, revolution is best confined to those events, or more accurately series of events, which go much further than producing a change of government personnel or even regime, but result in fundamental socio-economic changes in society. A. S. Cohan (1975, p. 31) surveyed the literature and argued that there is widespread agreement that a revolution has the following six characteristics:

1. The alteration of values or myths of the society.
2. The alteration of the social structure.
3. The alteration of institutions.
4. Changes in the leadership formation, either in the personnel of the elite or its class composition.
5. Non-legal or illegal transfer of power.
6. The presence or dominance of violent behaviour . . . in the events leading to the regime collapse.

A more recent observer, Jaroslav Krejčí (1983), basically agrees, arguing that a revolution must bring about changes in the ideology, the political regime, and the socio-economic structure of society. In practice, therefore, this means that the changes wrought by revolution occur over a prolonged period, often beginning well before the event commonly designated as *the* revolution – 1789 in France or 1917 in Russia, for instance. Thus in his study of six revolutions Krejčí describes the English 'Puritan' Revolution as beginning in

1628, with the Petition of Right, and ending in 1689, with the passing of the Bill of Rights on the Act of Toleration. The French Revolution he dates from 1751, when work began on the French Encyclopaedia which challenged the prevailing ideology, and ending in 1884, with the legalisation of trade unions. The Russian Revolution is dated from 1818, when the first secret revolutionary association was formed, and, at the time Krejčí was writing, was still continuing. The dates, and more especially the events, he chooses to denote the beginning and end of particular revolutions are open to question, but this is less important than acknowledging the prolonged nature and impact of revolutions.

Seen in these terms a revolution can only be identified with considerable hindsight, when it is clear that the sort of changes described have taken place. Thus a reasonable working definition of revolution is – the overthrow of a regime as a result of violence, the threat or perceived threat of violence, leading to or followed by significant changes in or the transformation of a society socially, economically and politically.

THE MARXIST VIEW OF REVOLUTION

Marx would not have disagreed with revolution defined in this way, but would have nevertheless regarded it as inadequate. In their earlier writings Marx and Engels (1976 [1845–6]) argued that revolution is the inevitable consequence of the conflict between different modes of production and the classes produced by them. According to Marx (1980 [1859]), the mode of production determines the structure of social relations between the classes in society. Essentially there are, in any society, two classes – a ruling class and an exploited class. The mode of production changes under the impact of technological development and an increasing division or specialisation of labour, but exploitation by the ruling class leads the exploited class to be alienated from that mode of production. Alienation makes the exploited class conscious of its exploitation and therefore of its class position, leading to a revolution led by the exploited class. Thus in Marxist terms the English, American and French Revolutions were bourgeois revolutions against aristocratic exploitation. They were led by the emergent middle class, motivated by the need to expand the capitalist mode of production. This mode of production creates a new exploited class – the working class or proletariat, which will become alienated and class conscious, and, in due course, will overthrow the bourgeois ruling class by revolutionary means. Revolution is therefore part of the natural order of things.

The logic of Marxist theory is clear enough, but it is complicated by a number of factors. First, Marx and Engels, and many of their contemporary associates, were not only theorists but political activists. Thus, apart from interpreting the history and events of their own lifetimes, they were actively engaged, directly or indirectly, in many of these events to the point that they were trying to bring about revolution as well as theorising about it. Second, a view from the latter part of the twentieth century is inevitably different from that of the nineteenth – hindsight complicates as much as it explains. Third, many of Marx's own theories were not fully developed at the time of his death in 1883 and, although Engels did much to elaborate them, important parts of their work did not become available until nearly fifty years after the death of Marx. Fourth, Marx's ideas have inevitably been subject to much interpretation and reinterpretation by later Marxists, many of whom have made their own significant contributions to Marxism.

Marx and Engels originally conceived a revolution as being a cataclysmic leap from one era to the next produced by the inevitable internal conflicts caused by the mode of production. While revolution was inevitable, its timing was not and there might be many attempts before a revolution actually took place. Marx argued that the revolution would occur only when the 'material conditions' were right, when the exploited class was conscious of its exploitation and the ruling class was unable to maintain its dominant position. A communist revolution, therefore, would occur only when the mass of the proletariat was ready to support it.

The Communist Manifesto, written by Marx and Engels, was published in 1848 in the midst of Europe's 'Year of Revolutions', but the latter disappointed and disgusted the *Manifesto*'s authors and led Marx to believe that the communist revolution would take the form of a long-drawn-out struggle, not a sudden event. Both Marx and Engels expected the revolution to take place first in the most advanced industrial societies. This, after all, was the essential logic of the Marxist model of revolution: the greater the level of industrialisation, the greater the level of exploitation; and the greater the level of exploitation, the greater the level of working-class alienation, the essential precondition of class consciousness. Conditions and events in many European societies gave Marx and Engels good reason to believe in the correctness of their theories and the accuracy of their predictions that revolutions would take place first in Britain, Germany and France, in all probability more or less simultaneously, one sparking off revolution in another. While rejecting the idea later advanced by Lenin of 'a vanguard of the proletariat' – a class-conscious 'elite' which could lead the working class to revolution, Engels conceded that a communist revolution might be possible in Russia because the tsarist regime was so unstable.

The predictions of Marx and Engels were not realised, of course, but later Marxists, notably Lenin, explained this by propounding the view that imperialism – the acquisition and exploitation of colonial territories by the industrialised societies – had staved off the revolution, which, of course, remained inevitable. Meanwhile, Lenin, a more active and ultimately much more successful revolutionary than Marx, put into practice his theory of 'the vanguard of the proletariat' in Russia, taking advantage of the chaos of the First World War and the aftermath of the February Revolution of 1917 to seize power. Once in power he instituted Marx's concept of the dictatorship of the proletariat, which Marx never really defined, except by citing the Paris Commune of 1870 as an example. Lenin and Trotsky confidently expected that the Russian Revolution would spark off other revolutions in Europe and this appeared a reasonable assumption in the last years of the First World War and in the light of many of the events that immediately followed it. There was widespread social unrest in Europe and communist revolutions seemed particularly possible in Hungary and Germany, while the Bolsheviks unsuccessfully sought to export the Russian Revolution by occupying Polish territory as German forces retreated and seeking support among Polish peasants and workers.

Later theorists have further adapted the Marxist view of revolution to explain both past and contemporary experience. As noted in earlier chapters, Gramsci, for example, developed the concept of hegemony – the dominance of one social class in terms of ideology as well as economic power, and Althusser developed similar views. The most dramatic adaptations, however, were made by practitioners, essentially following in the footsteps of Lenin. Part of the quarrel between Trotsky and Stalin that developed after Lenin's death was that Trotsky believed 'international revolution' – helping foster and support communist-led revolutions in other countries – was the only way of ensuring the survival of Russia's revolution. Stalin, quite apart from his power struggle with Trotsky, disagreed and ruthlessly pursued a policy of 'socialism in one country' to maintain the revolutionary impetus. Mao Zedong developed and put into practice the idea of a peasant-based guerrilla revolution, which particularly suited the conditions in China. Mao's peasant-based revolutionary model was followed by Fidel Castro in Cuba and Ho Chi Minh in Vietnam. Mao, like Trotsky, also stressed the concept of 'permanent revolution' – the idea that the revolution was in continuous need of renewal and reinvigoration. In short, it became necessary to adapt Marxist theory to the reality of what was possible, rather than what should happen.

Once in power, of course, Marxist regimes have had to explain why the revolution had not brought all the fruits its leaders and Marxist theory predicted. Explanations were not difficult to find: the Second World War and its aftermath is an obvious candidate, but far more important, of course, is capitalism, which always ruthlessly defends its interests. All developments and events must be explained in Marxist terms, so that the bitter quarrel between the USSR and the People's Republic of China (PRC) is accounted for by mutual accusations of 'revisionism'. By the same token, the participants in the demonstrations in Tiananmen Square in 1989 are described as 'counter-revolutionaries'. But the greatest problem has come with the collapse of communist regimes in Eastern Europe and the Soviet Union. Apart from dismissing the USSR, as some Marxists have done, as 'a deformed workers' state', traditional Marxist theory would have to describe the events in Eastern Europe as 'counter-revolutions', since there is little evidence that they are 'corrections' of 'perverted Marxist revolutions'.

All theories need to be tested against reality, but Marxism has this further dimension in that it is a theory which various practitioners of politics have sought and continue to seek to put into practice clearly and overtly. Marxists, theoreticians and practitioners alike, have had to adapt it further to changing circumstances. Marx would undoubtedly have welcomed this in principle, accepting not only that theories must be tested, but that they can and should be developed in the light of new knowledge. The development of Marxist theory does not therefore invalidate it, but it remains a matter of opinion whether Marxism can adequately explain how the world has changed since the death of Marx and, in particular, why revolutions take place. Marxist theory has been widely and, in many respects, successfully adapted; it remains a very significant strand of socio-political theory and should not be dismissed out of hand because the expectations of Marx and Engels have not been realised, nor because some of their ideas were not fully worked out. Marxism rightly places great stress on the relationship between society and politics, and especially between economics and politics, in seeking to understand the course of history and the occurrence of revolutions. What remains in dispute is whether that relationship is a causal one and, if so, whether it is the sole explanation.

A NON-MARXIST VIEW OF REVOLUTION

The non-Marxist view of revolution is more varied, but theorists of different types, such as system theorists, functionalists, and mass society theorists, agree that a revolution is a fundamental transformation of society involving a change of ideology, political regime, and socio-economic structures. They agree as well with the Marxist view that conflict is a natural part of society, but differ in believing that revolution is not inevitable. Not surprisingly, non-Marxists also have a different view about the causes of revolution, a matter to be examined in the next section. Essentially revolution is seen in terms of Cohan's six characteristics.

Various theorists have sought to delineate the stages of revolution. Certainly a number of revolutions appear to have several stages in common, most obviously the violent upheaval, not uncommonly a reign of terror, and a period of limited, but sometimes more substantial, retreat from the most radical changes introduced. However, this ignores at least one important stage common to all revolutions, that of the initial stirrings and events that precede the violent upheaval that usually accompanies a revolution. Krejčí (1983), in his examination of six revolutions ranging from the Czech Hussite Revolution in the fifteenth century to the Chinese Communist Revolution in this, has drawn up an elaborate morphology of revolution, from its very beginning to it ultimate conclusion.

The first stage he calls *onset*, which is 'a prolonged period of innovative, reformist moves within part of the society's cultural elite' (1983, pp. 17–18), leading to the defection of a number of intellectuals who provide the impetus for change. The *Encyclopédistes*, notably Diderot, Voltaire, Montesquieu and Rousseau, performed this role for the French Revolution, but particular individuals are less easily identified for the English 'Puritan' Revolution, although Calvinist and Presbyterian ideas underpinned many of the broader ideas about a limited monarchy and the role of Parliament. At this stage the process is reformist rather than revolutionary and the reformist forces embark on a second stage, which is *institutionalisation*.

Institutionalisation involves capturing some of the existing social and political structures to provide a power base for bringing about reform. In some cases, Krejčí argues, it may be necessary to create new institutions where existing ones cannot be adapted, such as the creation of the Russian Duma or constituent assembly in 1906. If at this point the reformist view prevails and significant societal change is set in train, the revolutionary process might abort. However, if the regime attempts to stop it, then the revolutionary process enters what Krejčí calls the *compression* stage, which may turn the reformist process into a clearly revolutionary one. Examples of the compression stage are Charles I's attempt to rule without Parliament after 1629 and the severe limitations placed upon the Duma after 1906.

Compression leads to the violent upheaval usually associated with revolution, which Krejčí calls the *explosion* – the outbreak of the Civil War in England in 1642 and the fall of the Bastille in 1789 are obvious examples. Once the explosion has happened and brought about the immediate overthrow of the regime, a new phase of *oscillation* starts, as differences between ideological groups produce a further struggle for power. The struggle between moderate Parliamentarians, who wished only to curb the excesses of Charles I, the more strongly committed Parliamentarians, who wanted a limited monarchy, and the extremists, represented by the Levellers and the Diggers, provide one example; the conflict between Girondins and Jacobins in France provides another, and that between the Mensheviks and Bolsheviks in Russia a third.

Eventually, one of the competing revolutionary groups wins power – in Krejčí's terminology this is *interception*. This is followed by a *tightening*, securing a stronger grip, usually through a revolutionary dictatorship – Cromwell's Protectorate, Jacobin rule in 1793–4,

Stalin's 'socialism in one country', collectivisation and industrialisation. The 'enemies' of the revolution are suppressed, invariably through the use of terror, and the revolutionary regime may further attempt to defend itself by the *expansion* of revolutionary rule abroad, illustrated by the English campaigns against the Scots and the Dutch, the French revolutionary wars between 1795 and 1799, and Stalin's annexation of the Baltic republics, part of Poland and the attack on Finland in 1939–40.

Krejčí argues, however, that expansion puts the resources available to the revolutionary regime under even greater strain, resulting in a limited retreat from the regime's revolutionary ideals or *reversal*. The march on London in 1660 by General Monck and the restoration of the Long Parliament constituted a reversal in the English Revolution; and the defeat of Napoleon at Leipzig in 1813 and Waterloo in 1815 were a reversal in the French Revolution. This reversal may then result in what Krejčí calls a *restoration compromise*, in which there is a partial restoration of the pre-revolutionary regime, as happened with Charles II in England and Louis XVIII in France, but because such a compromise is usually uneasy it may lead counter-revolutionaries to hope for or seek further concessions and create further *restoration pressure*. Again, the English Revolution provides a clear example in the latter part of the reign of Charles II after he had dissolved Parliament in 1681 and, of course, the pro-Catholic policies pursued by his successor, James II. The strengthening of the ultra-royalist forces under Louis XVIII and more especially Charles X provide a similar French example.

The culmination of the revolutionary process is that of *consolidation*, by which the changes brought about by the revolution are confirmed and a clear shift in ideology, political regime, and socio-economic structure has taken place. Where restoration pressure has occurred Krecjčí says this takes the form of *consolidation overthrow*, whereby the counter-revolutionary forces are ousted as part of the consolidation process. In the English case this was the Glorious Revolution of 1688, which brought William of Orange to the throne; for France it was the July Revolution of 1830, which brought Louis-Philippe to the throne. Krejčí suggests two versions of his morphology: one in which there is a restoration phase and one in which there is not. The latter is true of the Russian and Chinese Revolutions, but the consolidation process will normally follow – in the Russian case after Stalin's death and in the Chinese after the 'Cultural Revolution'.

Krejčí does not therefore suggest that every revolution goes through exactly the same process, hence his use of the term 'morphology'. There may be the recurrence of some stages, prolonging the revolutionary process over a considerable period of time. The French Revolution, for example, experienced its first *consolidation* with the 1830 'Revolution', but a second *explosion* and *oscillation* occurred with the 1848 'Revolution' and the election of Louis Napoleon Bonaparte as President, leading to a second *interception*, *tightening* and attempted *expansion* under the Second Empire between 1852 and 1870. This produced a second *consolidation* culminating in the failure of attempts to restore the monarchy and the clear establishment of the Third Republic.

In the case of more recent revolutions, including the Russian and Chinese, the revolutionary process is not or may not be complete, an observation which predates the changes in Eastern Europe and the Soviet Union. Krejčí does not argue that the revolutionary process is irreversible, but that it will inevitably leave its mark and that no society will revert fully to its pre-revolutionary condition. Thus whatever the eventual outcome of events in Eastern Europe and the Soviet Union, revolutions will have taken place and societies will have been transformed ideologically, politically, economically and socio-structurally.

What remains a fascinating question is whether the collapse of the communist regimes constituted revolutions. One answer is to test each against Cohan's six characteristics and come to at least a provisional assessment. It is quite clear that most of the criteria are met or show many signs of being met: there has been a shift in values or ideology; social structures show distinct signs of change; institutions certainly are being altered, especially political ones; changes in leadership have occurred and look to be doing so among the elites; but the transfer of power and the presence or dominance of violence are more problematic. In only one case, Romania, was the transfer of power clearly illegal and violence played a major role, although ironically doubt has been cast upon the extent of the changes resulting from that transfer of power. In the other Eastern Bloc states a legal transfer of power occurred and the pressure for that transfer came not from violence but almost entirely from peaceful demonstrations. Any violence which occurred was almost exclusively used by the regime rather that its opponents. The Soviet Union is a more complex case in that, while violence was used mainly by the opponents of change, it was also of some importance in republics like Georgia, Azerbaijan and Armenia, in which ethnic conflicts erupted. Despite this, there was a legal transfer of power within the Soviet Union to its constituent republics, including the recognition of the independence of the Baltic republics. These events would suggest a need to modify the nature of the transfer of power and the role of violence as defining characteristics of revolution.

Rather than asking whether the transfer of power was non-legal or illegal, it may be more appropriate to ask whether it was *normal* or *abnormal*, to which the answer was clearly the latter. In other words, although the legal processes were observed, it was not a *normal* transfer of power within each of the ruling communist parties. Rather than relying solely on the presence of violence or the threat of it by opponents of the regime, it may be more appropriate to ask whether the transfer of power was brought about by *abnormal* means, and again the answer is clear. Demonstrations of the sort that brought about the collapse of the communist regimes in Eastern Europe were not normal, and where attempts had previously been made to hold them, they were invariably suppressed by force. In Czechoslovakia, for example, the initial response of the regime to demonstrations calling for the liberalisation of the regime was violent suppression and arrests; this did not occur at later demonstrations. Similarly, Gorbachev's policies of *perestroika* and *glasnost* in the USSR led to expressions of opinion and demonstrations which would not formerly have been permitted, undermining the credibility of the communist regime and facilitating resistance to the unsuccessful coup of August 1991. Beyond that, of course, only time will tell whether these events are part of a revolutionary process in that they are part of a transformation of society, even though there are many indications that such a transformation is taking place.

A different perspective can be arrived at by applying a further feature of Krejčí's analysis to Eastern Europe. At the beginning of his study Krejčí draws a distinction between what he terms 'vertical revolutions' and 'horizontal revolutions'. The former are revolutions that take place as a result of forces within the society concerned, whereas the latter are revolutions which take place as a result of forces outside the society concerned. Thus the six revolutions Krejčí analyses in depth, including the English, French and Russian Revolutions, are 'vertical revolutions', but the revolt of the Netherlands against Spanish rule, the American Revolution, and most nineteenth-century Latin American revolutions are 'horizontal revolutions'. The same would be true of most Third World revolutions in that these and their historical predecessors involve breaking away from a foreign or colonial power and it is the presence of the foreign power which is the key causal factor in the revolution. The events which began in 1989 in Eastern Europe could be regarded as the *explosions* of 'horizontal revolutions', that is new revolutions whose status as revolutions cannot yet be fully determined. Alternatively, they could be seen as part of the Russian Revolution that spilled over into Eastern Europe in the process of that revolution's *expansion* and are therefore examples of further *oscillations*, *reversals*, and, perhaps, *restorations*. At this stage it is only possible to speculate, but it usefully illustrates the view that revolution needs to be analysed over a substantial period of time, that it involves complex changes, and that its path is seldom straightforward.

THE CAUSES OF REVOLUTION

In a study of the French, Russian and Chinese revolutions Theda Skocpol (1976, 1979) suggests that each of these revolutions was caused by the conjunction of three developments: first, the collapse or incapacity of the central administrative and military machines; second, widespread peasant rebellions; and third, what she termed 'marginal elite political movements'. In each case the administrative and military collapses were due largely to external pressures: France was under pressure throughout the eighteenth century in a series of conflicts with other European powers and the French success in helping the American colonists win independence was deceptive; Russia was under immense pressure in the First World War; and China came under European pressure initially, then plunged into civil war, and was finally faced with the Japanese invasion. Peasant insurrections deprived all three of crucial economic support and further undermined the ability of their governments to maintain order. These rebellions were based on traditional demands, but created the conditions for a greater social upheaval. The marginal elites to whom Skocpol refers were lawyers, teachers, students, and the offspring of state officials. They formed a radical vanguard of social and therefore revolutionary change. All this was in agrarian societies faced with considerable internal and external pressures to modernise.

In his broader analysis of revolution Krejčí relates the causes of revolution to a number of 'disproportions' or 'contradictions' derived from the observations of a variety of individuals as disparate as Weber and Marx, Aristotle and de Tocqueville, Pareto and Ibn Khaldun, a fourteenth-century Islamic scholar. In each case the reference is to a particular relationship in society: with Weber it is the relationship between social status, wealth and power, with Marx that between the forces of production and the means of production, with Aristotle that between actual inequality and a sense of injustice, with de Tocqueville that between achievement and expectation, with Pareto that between the elite and the non-elite, and with Khaldun that between the 'fighting spirit of the revolutionaries and of their opponents' (Krejčí 1983, p. 15).

From various studies of revolution it is possible to draw up lists of general or long-term causes and specific or immediate causes of revolution, as shown in Figure 11.1. The basic causes of revolution are societal rather than political in the narrow sense, in that the existing basis of society is undermined more or less simultaneously on several fronts. There is likely to be significant economic and socio-cultural dissatisfaction. Particular groups in society find themselves economically and socially disadvantaged to the point that they may

---

A. General causes
   1. *Economic:* a shift in economic power leading to economic dissatisfaction.
   2. *Socio-cultural:* dissatisfaction on ethnic, linguistic, religious, or regional grounds.
   3. *Ideological:* the prevailing ideology is challenged and undermined and rival ideologies emerge.
   4. *Political:* loss of efficiency, control and legitimacy by the regime.

B. Specific causes
   1. Persistent demands by a well-organised sector of society that a significant sector of the ruling elite is unwilling to meet.
   2. Visible dissension within the ruling elite between those favouring resistance and those favouring concessions.
   3. The credibility of the regime's ideology is undermined by its performance in the face of demands.
   4. Widespread loss of legitimacy by the ruling elite.
   5. Widespread loss of political control by the regime.

Figure 11.1 The causes of revolution.

be discriminated against. Underlying this is often a substantial shift in economic power. The prevailing ideology or values that underpin society come under challenge, negatively in that they no longer command as widespread support as they did, and positively in that one or more rival ideologies emerge. All this tends to undermine the ability of the regime or ruling elite to continue to govern effectively and, in particular, to maintain law and order.

It is at this point that the specific causes of revolution come into play. Persistent demands by a well-organised sector of society which sees itself as significantly disadvantaged, especially in the existing distribution of power, leads to growing dissension within the ruling elite between those who favour further repression and those who favour further concessions. The ideological credibility of the regime is undermined by its divisions and by its apparent inability to resolve the situation, resulting in a sudden loss in its legitimacy. This opens the regime to direct challenge, leading to a loss of political control in which the regime is either overthrown or faces civil war or guerrilla warfare.

In the case of the English Revolution, for example, the development of a market and monetary economy laid the foundations for a major shift in economic power, further enhanced by the break-up of the feudal system, especially under the impact of enclosure. The latter created a growing number of wage-labourers, who also contributed to the growth of towns. There was also an important religious conflict following the Reformation and the break with Rome, which added to the economic pressure for a shift in the distribution of political power in favour of the growing middle class or bourgeoisie. Prevailing values came under challenge and alternative ideologies emerged. The ruling elite sought to head off trouble by a combination of repression and concessions, fuelling dissatisfaction and further undermining its own credibility.

After ruling without calling a Parliament for eleven years and pursuing financial, religious and foreign policies against widespread opposition, Charles I was forced to summon Parliament in 1640 in order to raise taxes to impose his will on the Scots. Charles made limited concessions, but what became known as the Short Parliament was dissolved when it demanded the redress of grievances before agreeing to taxation. However, defeat by the Scots led to the calling later in 1640 of what was to be the Long Parliament. The demands of the king's opponents were far beyond what he was willing to concede, but the ruling elite was divided. Some of Charles' advisers urged the use of an army from Ireland, others that concessions to Parliament were necessary and inevitable. Charles' insistence on his absolute right to rule brooked no concessions, but the idea of a limited or constitutional monarchy ruling through Parliament offered a viable alternative ideology. In addition, the king and his opponents were also divided by religion. The whole legitimacy of the political system was called into question and it was now quite clear that Charles had lost political control. Both sides now took uncompromising positions: Parliament acted against the king's ministers, notably by impeaching the Earl of Strafford and issuing the Grand Remonstrance, a catalogue of Charles' illegal acts; and the king retaliated by attempting to arrest five of his leading opponents in Parliament. The scene was set for the outbreak of the Civil War.

A not dissimilar pattern can be traced in Russia, with the combination of the abolition of serfdom in 1861 and industrialisation leading to widespread agrarian and urban dissatisfaction, a growing ideological challenge, and alternate bouts of repression and concession. The Tsar's claim to rule by divine right did not admit the possibility of compromise and made the emergence of alternative ideologies inevitable. As the regime persisted in its resistance to extensive reform, the alternative ideologies became more extreme. Defeat in the war with Japan in 1904–5 and the suppression of the attempted Revolution of 1905 further undermined the legitimacy of the regime, while a policy of repression with concessions, notably in the form of a representative assembly, the Duma, did nothing to restore its credibility. The strains imposed by fighting the First World War were more that the regime could stand: military defeat and loss of political control at home made its overthrow inevitable. But was it inevitable?

The Marxist view is that revolution is inevitable, but revolution defined, of course, in Marxist terms. Mass society theorists believe that revolutions occur when a society's social structures are undermined or where there is 'disequilibrium' between different sections of society. This, by implication rather than explication, is also the functionalist view, but functionalists regard revolution as the exception to the general rule that societal change is brought about by society's self-adjusting mechanisms. Johnson (1964, 1966) is the leading proponent of a functionalist approach to revolution. He suggests that revolutionary change is the result of discordance between a society's values and its environment, producing what Johnson calls 'multiple dysfunction'. Such changes in values and the environment might be internally or externally triggered – the introduction of a new ideology, a growth in religious fervour, invasion, or a major population increase, for instance. The position of the society's elite would come under threat and, where its reaction is one of intransigence, the elite becomes vulnerable to direct and violent challenge.

Others have adopted what is essentially a psychological view, suggesting that a primary cause of revolutions is the relationship between people's expectations and reality, especially their economic expectations. This is known as the theory of rising expectations. It was first advanced by de Tocqueville in his study of the French Revolution (1966 [1856]), actually arguing that the revolution occurred when the economic situation was improving, but not enough to meet people's expectations. Brinton (1953 [1938], p. 33) made similar observations in a study of four revolutions – the English, the American, the French, and the Russian: '[they] were not born in societies economically retrograde; on the contrary, they took place in societies economically progressive.' More recent writers have elaborated on the rising-expectations theme, arguing, for example, that the interruption of economic improvement by a recession or a levelling off in improvement in an atmosphere of rising expectations will spark off a revolution: 'revolutions are most likely to occur when a prolonged period of objective economic and social development is followed by a short period of sharp reversal' (Davies 1962, p. 6), Tanter and Midlarsky (1967) further argue that the greater the gap between expectations and reality, the more extensive the ensuing revolution. Huntington (1968) offers a political variant of deprivation by suggesting that people's expectations of a greater participation or share in the distribution of power may exceed reality and precipitate revolution.

A related concept is that of relative deprivation, but here individuals or groups of individuals measure their situation *vis-à-vis* others in society. This concept is of importance to the Marxist theory of the proletarian revolution, in which increasing deprivation is a major factor in the working class becoming conscious of its subordination to and exploitation by the dominant class. It is not, however, a factor in a bourgeois revolution, since the bourgeoisie's class consciousness develops as it becomes aware of its improving material conditions, not their deterioration. The feudal ruling class is seen by the bourgeoisie as an obstruction to capitalist development, whereas under the consequent capitalist mode of production the working class is increasingly repressed and deprived. The theory of relative deprivation also has much wider implications than explaining revolution (Runciman 1966) and is also used to explain political violence generally (Gurr 1967–8, 1970).

Various criticisms have been made of theories of rising expectations and relative deprivation. One is methodological – that aggregate and macro-data are used to explain individual behaviour – but even more important is the criticism that neither theory is able to identify clearly the point at which 'people have had enough' and resort to violence, nor why this point varies from society to society. An attempt by Tilly *et al.* (1975) to link periods of collective violence with deprivation covering the years 1880 to 1930 found no clear pattern of strikes and riots when times were hard, or during periods of rapid urbanisation and industrialisation. Strikes and violence were more common whenever the opportunity of those concerned to advance and defend their interests presented itself and this depended primarily on the balance of power between workers and employers, rather than obvious deprivation. None the less, these ideas all reflect the importance of *perception* in political and social behaviour generally and revolution in particular.

It may well be that if a large enough gap opens up between people's material expectations and reality, it reaches a point where it is unbridgeable by normal social and political processes and revolution is then inevitable. In the same way, where a gap between one section of society and another becomes unbridgeable in terms of what one demands and the other is prepared to concede, then again revolution is inevitable. This ignores, however, another factor which seems common to most, possibly all, revolutions, that of *leadership*. In some cases revolutions are closely identified with a particular leader – John Pym in the earlier and Cromwell in the later stages of the English Revolution, Lenin with the October Revolution in Russia, Mao Zedong with the Chinese Communist Revolution, being obvious examples, but other revolutions generally are associated with a small group of identifiable leaders whose role is crucial to the success of the revolution. Thus George Washington, Alexander Hamilton, and James Madison were among the leading participants in the American Revolution and the Girondins and Jacobins in the French. Leadership, as in other aspects of politics, is a key factor in revolution, especially in terms of organisational and inspirational ability in both the initial overthrow of the old regime and in giving the revolution a directional impetus likely to bring about a transformation of society.

REVOLUTION AND SOCIETAL CHANGE

Clearly revolution is a major form of societal change, but only a particular form. Not all important societal change could be said to be the result of revolution. Further, there are events and circumstances which have or appear to have revolutionary potential, but do not lead to revolution itself. It is questionable, for instance, whether Nazi Germany was the product of a revolution. Hitler came to power in January 1933 legitimately: as head of the largest party in the Reichstag, he was invited to form a government by President Hindenburg, but the Nazis always referred to their coming to power as a *Machtergreifung* – a seizure of power – and the Nazis had made widespread use of violence and the threat of it remained. Hitler's real seizure of power was the immediate use he made of his authority as Chancellor to consolidate his position and outmanoeuvre his opponents. Once in power, Hitler embarked on a considerable societal change, involving policies based on a far-reaching ideological shift, and established what was widely regarded as a totalitarian society. Yet nothing of substance remains of the Third Reich – Hitler's vision of a thousand-year Reich collapsed in military defeat in 1945, but, had Germany won the Second World War, what might be described as a failed revolution would in all probability have been a successful one. Not only would Germany have been transformed but much of Europe as well.

Krejčí (1933, p. 3) is correct when he says of revolution that 'a view *ex post* provides a safer guide . . . than a view *ex ante*' and in his insistence on looking at revolution as a long-term process, not confined to the explosion of violence which topples a regime or to its immediate consequences. Most societies, in fact, do not experience revolution in the sense discussed in this chapter and, while it is common to refer in English history to the agricultural revolution and the industrial revolution which did indeed transform society, they are better seen as processes within their own right to be discussed in the next chapter, or as a consequence of the English Revolution and to that extent a *part* of the revolutionary process. It is important to place revolution in a proportional context historically: as Krejčí (1983, p. 10) observes, 'revolutions . . . are not the most frequent way in which comprehensive social change materialises. In the history of the world it is foreign conquest that has been the commonest agent of change'. Fair comment though this may be, it begs the question of what part is played by the processes of development and modernisation, to which attention is now turned.

Chapter 12

DEVELOPMENT AND MODERNISATION THEORY

INTRODUCTION

Theories of revolution do not, of course, purport to explain all change in society, even for Marxists, although the latter would argue that a great transformation of society can only come about by revolutionary means. It is not enough, however, to say that the converse of revolution is evolution. Even a Darwinian view of societal change needs greater elaboration than mere assertion of the survival of the fittest. Not only is there the possibility that a Darwinian view is no more than an analogy, but the processes by which societies change, other than by revolution, need to be explored in greater detail.

Significant theories of societal change arose after the Second World War, largely out of concern with the effects of decolonisation and the emergence of new states. Traditional political studies had concentrated primarily on liberal-democracies, with some attention being paid to the totalitarian regimes that emerged in Italy, Germany, and the Soviet Union, but little attention was paid to what is now variously described as the 'Third World', 'developing' or 'underdeveloped' societies. Moreover, the approach was widely institutional, concentrating on the three traditional branches of government – the executive, the legislature, and the judiciary, and the constitutional framework within which they operated. Attention was also paid to political parties and some aspects of electoral behaviour, and interest or pressure groups became an increasingly important area of research. However, the approach tended to be relatively static and change was seen as implicitly but simplistically developmental, often as an historical progression to liberal-democracy. Quite apart from the shortcomings that critics of this approach saw in its application to societies like Britain and the United States or those of Western Europe, it was not particularly fruitful when applied to Third World societies, at best often being sterile in its conclusions, at worst misleading.

These problems led a number of social scientists to look for alternative approaches which would seek to explain how societies changed socially, economically and politically. Most were explicitly non-Marxist, even anti-Marxist – W. W. Rostow (1960), an economic historian, subtitled one study 'A Non-Communist Manifesto'. Not all were, however, since Marxist theorists also had to grapple with the problem of explaining the Third World. The theories that emerged can be divided into four schools: the political development school, the nation-building school, the modernisation school, and the underdevelopment and dependency school. The last two could reasonably be divided into separate schools, but are more usefully examined together.

THE POLITICAL DEVELOPMENT SCHOOL

Early theorists, for example Bryce (1921) and Friedrich (1953 [1937]), saw political development as a progression towards liberal-democracy and this is implicit in the work of later theorists, such as Almond (Almond and Coleman 1960; Almond and Powell 1966), and explicit in others, such as Pye (1966). The essence of the developmental school is that all societies go through a series of stages of political development in which primitive, traditional societies eventually become modern, industrial societies. Considerable stress is laid upon increasing specialisation of roles in society or the division of labour, a change from local or tribal identification and loyalty, or particularistic views, to societal or national identification, or universalistic views, a change in societal status based on tradition or ascription to merit or achievement, and the development of appropriate processes and institutions to accommodate these changes. These views, whilst not always synonymous with functionalist theory, were strongly influenced by it, especially with the emphasis on differentiation or specialisation of roles and the development of appropriate processes and structures.

Prominent among political development theorists were Binder *et al.* (1971). They posited a development syndrome based on three variables, changes between which produce five types of developmental crises, as shown in Figure 12.1. As a basis for analysing societal change, theories of political development provide a useful means of isolating significant variables and factors. In addition, these variables do relate to a number of problems that arise as societies undergo significant change. The division of labour or tendency for growing specialisation in society, as human control of the environment increased and the ability of social structures to cope with changing circumstances developed, are clearly crucial to understanding societal change; but the case for equality is less clear, not least because the term lies uneasily between description and prescription. Equally, the crisis or problems concerned with conflict between national and other loyalties, with the legitimacy of rival claims to power, and with distributive or economic questions, have been identified in various theoretical contexts, but participation and penetration are less obviously commonplace. Implicit in both is that political development leads to demands for greater participation and that this, among other things, will take the form of demands for

---

A. Variables
   1. *Differentiation:* the progressive separation and specialisation of roles, institutional spheres, and associations in society.
   2. *Equality:* the development of national citizenship, a universalistic legal order, and achievement norms.
   3. *Capacity:* the ability of the polity to stimulate change and manage the resulting tensions.

B. Crises
   1. *Identity:* conflicts between national feelings of the masses and the elite, between ethnic and regional loyalties and national loyalties.
   2. *Legitimacy:* conflicting claims to power or rejection of a ruler's or ruling group's claim to power.
   3. *Participation:* conflict between the demands of the masses wishing to participate politically and of the elite resisting their participation.
   4. *Penetration:* pressure on the elite to make institutional or structural changes or other political changes.
   5. *Distribution:* conflict over resources, ideology, and environmental change.

Figure 12.1 Political development: variables and crises.

institutional change. Certainly, demands for greater participation are likely to be accompanied by demands for institutional change, but it is an assumption that demands for greater participation are inevitable.

Theories of political development have been widely criticised as being biased in favour of liberal-democratic values, that political development will lead inexorably to the establishment of a liberal-democratic society. Even if this were conceded as being the case, development theory does not provide any real explanation of *why* change takes place. The relationship between the various types of crises is not adequately explained. Above all, there is too much emphasis on political as distinct from other sorts of societal change.

THE NATION-BUILDING SCHOOL

The nation-building school represents a significant attempt to bring values into the developmental process, particularly as applied to the Third World. Nineteenth-century European nationalism, with its emphasis on ethnic, linguistic, cultural, and religious links and on a common historical heritage, was seen as an important force in the development of European states, especially in the unification of Italy under Cavour and of Germany under Bismarck, and further evidenced by the increasing nationalistic pressures on the Austro-Hungarian and Russian Empires. As discussed at greater length in Chapter 2, European nationalism gave rise to the concept of the nation-state, the idea that the nation (as defined in European terms) is the appropriate basis for society and therefore the state. Much of the rest of the world has, directly or indirectly, had the European concept of the nation-state imposed upon it, but for most states this has meant creating a sense of national identity within largely artificial boundaries and it this process that has been called nation-building.

That nationalism, especially in the context of the Third World, has been a major impetus for societal change cannot be doubted. Third World political leaders have sought to mobilise their followers in the name of 'national progress'. Symbols of national identity – a flag, a national anthem, a 'common heritage', a new name – have been adopted as part of the mobilisation process. Policies of the nationalisation of industry and the indigenisation of the workforce are pursued, and political structures – often involving one-party states and all-inclusive nationalist parties – are established. As an explanation of societal change, however, nation-building, while clearly important, is hardly an explanation of societal change. There is little evidence that where a strong sense of national identity already existed or was successfully developed, a greater transformation of society has occurred.

THE MODERNISATION SCHOOL

Theories of modernisation, like theories of political development, are based on the assumption that societal change is a linear process involving the transformation of traditional, agrarian societies into modern, industrial societies. Rostow (1960) and Organski (1965) argued that development or modernisation consisted of a series of stages, as shown in Figure 12.2. Rostow posited an essentially capitalist model built on the considerable assumption that such a model was equally available to any society. As noted earlier, Rostow's approach was explicitly anti-communist, constituting 'an alternative to Karl Marx's theory of modern history' (1960, p. 2). He was also quite clear that economic growth is 'only an automatic process if one can assume that society will respond actively and effectively to the potentials for growth available to it' (1960, rev. 2nd edn 1971, p. 194) and a traditional society is therefore defined as one which is unable or unwilling to take advantage of technological development.

A. Rostow: the stages of economic growth
1. Traditional society.
2. Pre-conditions for take-off.
3. Take-off.
4. Drive towards maturity.
5. Age of high mass-consumption.

B. Organski: the stages of political development
1. Primitive unification.
2. Industrialisation.
3. National welfare.
4. Abundance.

Figure 12.2 Theories of modernisation (Sources: Rostow (1950); Organski (1965)).

Significant and continuing economic growth would not happen unless or until a period of transformation – the preconditions for take-off – had taken place. This transformation involves changes in values (especially the belief that economic growth is not only possible but desirable), in economic institutions (leading to greater investment), and in the exploitation of raw materials, and the development of a transport and communications infrastructure and, invariably, of an effective, centralised political authority. Only then could society be said to have achieved 'take-off', defined as: 'the interval when the old blocks and resistances to steady growth are finally overcome. The forces making for economic progress, which yielded limited bursts and enclaves of modern activity, expand and come to dominate the society. Growth becomes a normal condition' (Rostow, 1960, p. 7). Take-off produces 'a drive to maturity', in which the economy becomes increasingly efficient, adapting rapidly to further technological innovation, and laying the basis for a high level of mass-consumption. The latter is characterised by an emphasis on the production of consumer goods and the provision of services, and the development of the welfare state.

Rostow's model was based upon a detailed analysis of the economic history of a number of major industrialised societies and, writing in 1959, he argued that, among Third World countries, Turkey, Argentina, Mexico, China and India had achieved take-off. While acknowledging that his approach was deliberately 'arbitrary and limited', Rostow claimed that it demonstrated 'the uniformities of the sequence of modernisation' (1960, p. 1) and vigorously defended his views in a second edition published in 1971. Since he argued that maturity was likely to be achieved some sixty years after take-off, the ultimate test of his model lies well into the twenty-first century. What it neglects is the relationship between advanced industrial societies and developing societies, other than pointing out that modernisation in the Third World has been brought about primarily by the impact and intrusion of industrialised societies.

A similar approach was adopted by Organski (1965). He emphasised the role that government played in development, defining political development as 'increasing governmental efficiency in utilising the human and material resources of the nation for national goals' (1965, p. 7), and suggests four stages of modernisation. The first of these is 'primitive unification', involving the establishment and maintenance of central political rule, facilitating economic unification, and leading to Rostow's 'take-off' – curiously the only reference to Rostow in Organski's book. The second stage is industrialisation, which transformed the economy, led to rapid urbanisation, the emergence of a new economic and political elite, and the consolidation of national identity. This sets the scene for the third stage – 'national welfare', similar to Rostow's age of mass consumption, with the development of the welfare state, but Organski then looks to a future produced by a 'revolution of automation'. This is the stage of 'abundance', in which there would be an enormous concentration of economic and political power threatening the existence of the nation-state and probably resulting in its replacement by regional or continental blocs as the major form of political organisation. Organski is unclear about the inevitability of the modernisation process: on the one hand he says, 'There is nothing inevitable about the stages here set forth', and on the other, 'No nation can skip these stages . . . [although it is possible to] speed up the pace, condense the stages, even overlap them' (1965, pp. 16 and 212).

Huntington (1965, 1968) defined development more specifically as the ability of society to cope with changes caused by modernisation, arguing that it was therefore necessary to develop institutions capable of controlling the modernisation process, which in certain circumstances could mean authoritarian or totalitarian regimes. Huntington and Organski thus shifted the focus of development and modernisation theory from a progression towards 'democracy' to a concern with political stability and the role of government in the modernisation process.

By explicitly or implicitly using a capitalist model, modernisation theory offers an explanation of how and why change takes place, but it is based largely on the assumption that the capitalist model is universally applicable. In so doing the 'second world' of the communist bloc was either ignored or assumed to be a temporary aberration to the capitalist model. The collapse of communist regimes in Eastern Europe and the Soviet Union make it tempting to assume the latter; that, however, is to assume a degree of inevitability every bit as strong as the traditional Marxist view, but without, of course, leading to the 'inevitable' communist revolution.

David Apter (1965) in *The Politics of Modernisation* adopted a structural-functional approach and sought to incorporate communist systems in one of two models of modernisation. He suggests modernisation requires three conditions: first, a social system able to adapt to changing circumstances; second, flexible social structures involving an extensive division of labour or structural differentiation; and third, a social framework capable of providing the skills and knowledge necessary for coping with technological change. On this basis he puts forward two models of modernisation, as shown in Figure 12.3.

In their universalistic form development and modernisation theories suffer from being ethnocentric, drawing too heavily on American experience and tending to look at the world from an American point of view. As explanations of particular societies over particular periods they may have a good deal of validity, but it is a very considerable supposition that all societies are simply at different stages of the same linear process. In a reassessment of his earlier work and later theoretical developments, Apter (1987, p. 13) remarks: 'the record of genuine accomplishment seems a good deal more meagre than the outpouring of books ... might attest. ... Too much of what passed for developmental 'science' was confusing. Too much that passed for political development was ideological; theories were overkill, obvious, or wrong.' When attempts are made to apply such theories universally, inadequate attention is paid to history: at best they represent an over-reliance on inductive reasoning, at worst the selective use of examples. Of equal significance is the assumption that a process of societal change that was open to one or more societies in the past is open to all societies in the present or future: the world has moved on politically and, more especially, economically, and the degree of mutual interdependence has changed beyond all recognition. It is this degree of interdependence that has produced the most effective criticism of development and modernisation theory – the related schools of underdevelopment and dependency.

A. The 'secular libertarian' or reconciliation system
   1. Characterised by a pluralistic, diversified distribution of power and leadership, pragmatic bargaining parties, and an emphasis on compromise.
   2. Examples: United States, Western Europe and other liberal-democracies.

B. The 'sacred collectivity' or mobilising system
   1. Characterised by political 'religiosity', personalised or charismatic leadership, and a single mass party.
   2. Examples: communist systems and most Third World countries.

Figure 12.3 Apter's two models of modernisation (Source: Apter (1965)).

UNDERDEVELOPMENT AND DEPENDENCY THEORY

The principal tenet of underdevelopment theory is that underdevelopment is not a stage on the road to a capitalist society, but a condition or symptom of capitalist domination: advanced industrial societies were therefore responsible for the economic and political underdevelopment of the Third World. This was not, however, initially a Marxist critique of development and modernisation theory, but an acknowledgement of how capitalism had transformed the world and come largely to dominate the world economy. At the same time, such a view is extremely close to the Marxist view put forward by writers such as Wallerstein (1974, 1979), Frank (1966, 1971, 1978) and Amin (1974, 1976).

Wallerstein argued that the world itself constituted a capitalist economy in the Marxist sense of the term and would therefore develop according to Marxist theory. The world, he argued, is divided into three groups – a world division of labour: a core of industrialised societies, peripheral societies (whose economies are based on primary products); and partly industrialised semi-peripheral societies who are therefore both exploiters and exploited. In Wallerstein's world the state is largely irrelevant and the differences between 'capitalist' and 'socialist' states more apparent than real.

Basing his conclusions on a detailed analysis of the economic and social history of underdeveloped societies, Frank too asserted that, while advanced capitalist societies were once *undeveloped* economically, they were never *underdeveloped*, and underdeveloped societies were the economic satellites of advanced capitalist societies or metropoles. Frank's ideas are known as centre–periphery theory – the domination of the periphery (the Third World) by the centre (advanced capitalist societies).

Amin, following Wallerstein, posits world capitalist system involving an international division of labour: at the centre is the world bourgeoisie, at the periphery the world proletariat, with the world's surplus value being extracted from the periphery by the centre. Even communist systems are, according to Amin, part of the world capitalist system – not, of course, socially and politically but as economically dependent upon the world capitalist system.

This Marxist view is widely known as dependency theory and has roots which go back to Lenin's theory of imperialism. One of the leading dependency theorists, Dos Santos (1970, p. 231), defined dependency as 'a situation in which the economies of certain countries are conditioned by the development and expansion of another area to which the former is subjected'. Dependent or underdeveloped societies are economically reliant on the export of primary products, various raw materials and agricultural products, the markets for which are controlled by capitalist economies and are therefore beyond the control of the producing countries. Any industry that does develop is also subject to capitalist control. Dos Santos argues that there are three stages of dependency, as follows:

1. *Colonial dependency* A monopoly of trade, land and manpower by the colonial power.
2. *Financial–industrial dependency* Capitalist societies invest in raw materials and agriculture in underdeveloped societies to support their own industrial development.
3. *New dependency* Underdeveloped societies become the markets for capitalist societies.

The non-Marxist underdevelopment theorists, particularly those associated with the United Nations Economic Commission for Latin America, such as Furtado (1964, 1970), believed that the only way for Third World societies to break out of the circle of underdevelopment was to pursue a policy of import substitution as a means of autonomous capitalist development. This meant developing indigenous industries in order to obviate the need to import manufactured goods. Efforts to implement a policy of import substitution have not, however, proved successful, including in Latin America where they were most strongly advocated. Marxist dependency theorists understandably scorned such a policy, asserting that only revolution could break the circle of underdevelopment, but revolution is couched in vague terms in the context of the centre–periphery relationship, since it is neither clear how a dependent society can break out of the circle on its own, nor yet how dependent societies can do so collectively, except possibly by following the example of the Organisation of Petroleum Exporting Countries (OPEC). The latter, however, is in many respects a special case and other raw materials do not lend themselves so easily to the OPEC strategy. Samir Amin has suggested an alternative strategy, 'self-reliant' development, which has much in common with the Soviet model and was successfully applied in North Korea after the end of the Korean War in 1953, but development was not sustained beyond the 1960s.

Underdevelopment and dependency theories imply that economic development of some sort would have occurred in the absence of capitalist domination, but it is neither clear that this is the case, nor, if it is, what sort of development would have occurred. The historical relationship between capitalist societies and the Third World is more complex than underdevelopment and dependency theories imply. Indeed, it can be argued that such theories are at odds with a Marxist view in that they regard capitalism as responsible for and continuing to obstruct the economic and social development of 'underdeveloped' societies. For Marx capitalism was the necessary means to a proletarian revolution and a communist society. Orthodox Marxism argues that, as part of a world capitalist system, the 'underdeveloped' societies would, as the world proletariat, ultimately become alienated, class conscious and thus progenitor of a proletarian revolution.

Without denying that economic motives were the key factor in the colonial expansion of Europe, other motives were also important and there is more than a grain of truth in the observation of the nineteenth-century historian, Sir John Seeley (1921 [1883], p. 10) that the English 'seem, as it were, to have conquered and peopled half the world in a fit of absence of mind'. Nor is it universally the case that the acquisition of colonies brought direct economic benefit to the colonial power concerned: Canada or New France brought little economic benefit to eighteenth-century France and in Britain colonies were widely regarded in the early part of the nineteenth century as a drain on economic resources, 'millstones round our necks', as the later arch-imperialist Disraeli described them in 1852. While Portugal and Spain benefited considerably from the exploitation of their colonies, it did not put them in the forefront of capitalist and industrial development. On the contrary, to use dependency theory terms, they became not only geographically but economically peripheral in Europe. J. A. Hobson (1954 [1902]), an economist and journalist, sought to demonstrate that the surplus capital produced by Britain was invested in her colonies. Yet although there was much British overseas investment in the latter part of the nineteenth century and early part of the twentieth, it was mostly not in British colonies but in other parts of the world, much of it in the United States.

Underdevelopment and dependency theories have little or nothing to say about the position of communist societies, except to say generally that they are part of the world capitalist system. Nor do such theories explain the economic relationships between advanced or metropolitan countries, between, for instance, the United States and Canada, or the richer and poorer members of the EC. Dependency theory in particular implies a one-way relationship, but there is little doubt that it is far more complex than that and it may be more accurate to describe the centre–periphery relationship as one of unequal interdependence. While it remains a matter of opinion whether all economic activity is somehow related to unified world economy, that Third World societies are to a significant degree economically dependent on industrial societies cannot be doubted. It is, however, a relationship which is in need of more research, not least to discover whether it is possible for that relationship to become less unequal.

It was suggested in Chapter 2 that the European model of industrialisation was not available or indeed applicable to Third World societies, but the European model is not the only possible path to industrialisation and it is worth exploring some alternative models.

MODERNISATION AND DEVELOPMENT AS INDUSTRIALISATION

The Soviet model

In 1917, immediately before the February Revolution which resulted in the overthrow of the tsarist regime, 80 per cent of the population of Russia lived in rural areas and 75 per cent were engaged in agriculture. None the less, Russia in 1917 was economically more advanced than Western Europe had been in 1800. The emancipation of the serfs in 1860 by Alexander II and Stolypin's later agrarian reforms stimulated an agricultural revolution, while in the last quarter of the nineteenth century the country embarked on rapid industrialisation. Russia possessed vast resources of raw materials and manpower, had a cadre of technically trained personnel, and was able to take advantage of the technological advances in Western Europe to establish modern plant and attract European investment. Even though the First World War had a disastrous impact on Russian economic development, so that in 1921 industrial production was only 21 per cent of its pre-war level and agricultural production less than half, the Soviet government was still considerably better placed than its Third World counterparts after the Second World War. Lenin made concessions to private enterprise by adopting the New Economic Plan and, in spite of enormous difficulties, output was considerably higher by 1926, but thereafter Stalin decided to force the pace of economic development by giving precedence to heavy industry. Agriculture was collectivised, the economy brought under central direction, and any challenges were met with force.

Underpinning Soviet industrialisation was a strong and coherent ideology, made all the stronger by Stalin's proclamation of 'socialism in one country'. The communist millennium of 'from each according to his ability, to each according to his needs' was held out as the goal to be attained through socialist planning directed by Stalin's 'state of the whole people'.

Industrialisation under Stalin was achieved by reducing consumption, reducing real wage levels, and by limiting investment in all sectors of the economy *except* heavy industry and technical education. The cost in human terms was enormous, but according to Soviet figures national production rose by 15.7 per cent per annum between 1928 and 1937 and by 20 per cent between 1945 and 1950. Even assuming that these figures exaggerate the real growth, Western observers have calculated that between 1928 and 1950 economic growth averaged between 5 and 7 per cent per annum, a figure higher than either Western Europe or the United States has achieved over a sustained period. Subsequently, of course, the Soviet economy developed severe problems, especially in meeting consumer demand, and major efforts to restructure the economy were set in train, but the Soviet model was applied in various forms in Eastern Europe after the Second World War and in a drastically modified form in the People's Republic of China (PRC) after the communist revolution of 1949. In none, however, has it had ultimate success and economic failure played a significant part in the collapse of communist regimes in Eastern Europe and the Soviet Union and in the difficulties faced by the PRC before and since the suppression of the demonstrations in Tiananmen Square in 1989.

The Japanese model

In the middle of the nineteenth century Japan looked a distinctly unpromising candidate for industrialisation: it had few mineral resources, only limited arable land for agricultural expansion, little surplus capital, and no cadre of technically trained personnel. Furthermore, limited but significant Western penetration had forced Japan to accept unequal trade treaties which the country was in no position to resist militarily. Japan was therefore faced with a choice of accepting Western domination or resisting as best it could.

In the event, Japan did possess a number of advantages which made resistance a credible alternative. There existed a small group drawn from the traditional samurai elite who were determined to modernise Japan and transform it into a great military power. This small elite therefore adopted a policy of adaptation and resistance and was willing and able to assume an entrepreneurial role. A merchant class already existed which had laid the foundations of a market economy and favoured modernisation. In addition, a shift from communal-based to individual, profit-based farming had also occurred and the introduction of new cultivation techniques, fertilisers and new crops produced a food surplus, to the extent that before the end of the nineteenth century Japan was a food exporter. Japan's major export, however, was silk, a commodity in which it was able to dominate production largely because of disease in the European silk-worm industry. The agricultural surplus yielded a capital surplus through central taxation and the limiting of consumption. The surplus was then invested substantially in technological development. Half the investment was directed by the government and could therefore be significantly channelled to appropriate sectors of the economy. Labour-intensive industry was facilitated by plentiful manpower and ready markets were available in Asia. The First World War produced an economic boom and gave Japan the opportunity to consolidate its position as the dominant economic and military power in Asia.

Japan's economic development was used to build up its military capability and this was put to the test in successful wars against China in 1894 and Russia in 1904–5. Although Japan was forced by the Western powers to surrender most of the territorial concessions on the Asian mainland it had wrung out of China, of Japan's military significance there could be no doubt, as events later in the twentieth century were to demonstrate only too effectively.

Perhaps the most crucial factor, however, was the skilful blending of the traditional basis of Japanese society with modernisation. In 1868–9 the Tokugawa shogunate, which had dominated Japan since

1603, was overthrown, and the Emperor Meiji was brought back from ceremonial exile to play a key role in the modernising process. The cult of reverence for the emperor became all-pervasive, and traditional family and community ties were retained, underpinning the development of a paternalistic pattern of employment. The innovating role of many members of the samurai elite epitomised this combination of the traditional and the modern. Modern political structures were also established in the form of a parliamentary system, a cabinet system of government, and a modern bureaucracy, but these were heavily imbued with traditional values. Not surprisingly, in terms of the exercise of power, these political structures did not operate in Western fashion. The cultural and ideological underpinning of the industrialisation of Japan was a vital part of the process and it is doubtful whether Western values would have produced similar economic results. This does raise the question, however, of whether the value systems found in some Third World societies can play a significant role in the industrialisation of those societies.

Alternative Third World models

Korea, Taiwan, Hong Kong, and Singapore are four Asian examples of successful industrialisation, but have they followed similar or differing paths? And what part did values play in the process?

Korea has a distinctive culture stretching back well over a thousand years and the Korean peninsula was a political entity from the middle of the seventh century until its *de facto* annexation by Japan following the latter's defeat of Russia in 1905. The Japanese developed Korea's mineral wealth, modernised its agriculture, and built its railways and a significant manufacturing base. There was little immediate benefit to Koreans: for example, although rice production was doubled, Korean consumption of rice was halved, the rest being exported to Japan, but the foundation for further development had been laid.

In 1945 Soviet and American forces occupied Korea and the peninsula was divided, followed in 1948 by the setting up of ideologically opposed regimes in North and South Korea. The Korean War broke out in 1950, precipitated by an invasion from the North. The war ended in stalemate in 1953, leaving both North and South in economic ruin, but both subsequently underwent considerable and successful industrialisation. Most of Korea's raw materials and industry were located in the north of the peninsula and, with extensive Soviet and Chinese aid, the regime of Kim Il-sung embarked on a major recovery programme based on rapid industrialisation. The success of the programme owed much to the ability of Kim's totalitarian regime to provide political stability and, crucially, to mobilise the population and resources, but that same regime stultified further development by the end of the 1960s.

South Korea was much slower to embark on a programme of industrialisation. Indeed, the economy stagnated until a military takeover by Park Chung Hee in 1960. With a strong agricultural base and backed by considerable American investment, South Korea increased its real GNP by an average of 9 per cent between 1961 and 1987. Heavy industry was developed first, particularly shipbuilding and then textiles, followed by a massive expansion in electronics, especially computers. As in North Korea, a strong authoritarian regime provided political stability and the impetus for mobilisation. Unlike North Korea, however, the South needed to compete in the capitalist world and this was facilitated by low wage levels, the expansion of the education system to provide a skilled workforce, and specialisation of products, which enabled South Korea to penetrate markets in the United States, Europe, and Japan.

Taiwan is a similar case to that of South Korea: after their ejection by the Communists from mainland China the Nationalists used massive American aid to industrialise, concentrating on textiles, electrical products, and a wide variety of consumer goods. Again industrialisation was much assisted by labour-intensive production and low wages, and by an authoritarian government providing political stability.

Singapore and Hong Kong provide somewhat different examples. Both have developed as major regional commercial and financial centres and both have excellent natural harbours and port facilities, but have also developed viable manufacturing bases in specialised products. Singapore began to develop mainly after its secession from the Malaysian Federation in 1965 and attracted considerable American investment, which increased tenfold between 1965 and 1975. Its main manufacturing areas are in electronics, oil refining, and transport equipment, especially shipbuilding and repairs. Hong Kong developed its manufacturing base after trade with China, for which Hong Kong was a major centre, was cut off by the Korean War, using financial expertise to attract investment and labour-intensive methods and low wages to establish a foothold in various markets. Both also benefited from political stability, provided in the case of Singapore by the one-party regime of Lee Kuan Yew and in the case of Hong Kong by the British colonial regime.

All five examples have two features in common – strong government (four authoritarian, the other colonial) providing political stability, and massive investment from outside. Also, in each case that investment was put to effective use in developing manufactures. North Korea differs from the rest, not only ideologically, but in failing to sustain its economic development. What the others have achieved points to two further common features: specialisation of products, that is, producing goods and offering services for which there is a market, and producing them at a competitive cost and sufficient quality to attract and hold a share of the market. It is also possible to argue that cultural values played a part in all five cases: three of the five were, of course, entirely or predominantly Chinese societies, which have a strong sense of identity and a long-standing entrepreneurial tradition, and Taiwan, Singapore and Hong Kong all became avowedly capitalist in orientation. Korea also has a strong sense of identity, but historically was much influenced by both the Chinese and the Japanese, while the establishment of rival regimes in north and south provided powerful ideological impetus for industrialisation.

It is doubtful, however, whether either the North Korean model or that illustrated by the other four is realistically available to the Third World in general. All five started from higher economic bases than are found in many Third World societies, they are all relatively small with a strong sense of identity, and they were able to concentrate their efforts in particular sectors of economic development. The task facing most Third World societies is much more formidable: many already have larger populations than they can adequately feed and house; their natural resources are either limited or firmly in the hands of small indigenous groups or overseas investors and multinational corporations; many have serious literacy problems at one end of the educational spectrum, yet are unable to provide employment for their graduates at the other; external aid and investment is often at best misdirected, at worst feeding widespread corruption; their societies are often divided on ethnic and religious lines; and above all many suffer from chronic political instability. Economic development requires greater resources and efforts than most of these societies can provide for themselves, even with external aid, and only greater co-operation between advanced industrial and Third World states is likely to make any significant impact.

CHANGING SOCIETY: AN OVERVIEW

As Krejčí points out, foreign conquest has been responsible for changing more societies than have revolutions, but the same could be said of the other means by which societies have changed. Industrialisation was possible in Europe and North America partly because much of the rest of the world provided the markets for manufactured products and the whole world has changed with it. Thus while the world market continues to expand, it does not mean that all other societies can follow the European–North American model; much of the world has, in effect, become part of that model. Similarly, although it is perfectly reasonable to describe industrialisation and its consequences as modernisation or development, it does not mean that the modernisation or developmental processes are themselves unchanged. Technological development may allow a speeding up of the process, but in the meantime advanced industrial societies have themselves changed, so that some theorists refer to a post-industrial society in which the service sector of the economy comes to predominate over the industrial or manufacturing sector (see Bell 1973).

Foreign conquest and economic penetration of much of the world by capitalist societies has been largely responsible for shaping the modern world and creating a world in its own image. The ideas of development and modernisation theorists may seem to be borne out by the collapse of communist regimes in Eastern Europe and the Soviet Union, not least the widespread introduction of the market economy. Nationalism has played an important role in these changes and is already largely responsible for the disintegration of the USSR. On the other hand, much of the Third World seems to be increasingly dependent on the 'first world', but it remains unclear whether the Marxist picture of an increasingly exploited and alienated 'international proletariat' is more accurate than a capitalist picture of gradual improvement. Elsewhere in the world, however, another major force is at work. Conscious attempts to modernise can be found in many oil-rich states, such as Saudi Arabia and the Gulf States, but these states are equally consciously striving to maintain the traditional values of their societies, principally in the form of the Islamic religion. Furthermore, Islamic fundamentalism has emerged in countries like Libya, Iran and Pakistan as a powerful force for change, combining traditionalism with economic development. What sort of world will eventually emerge is very uncertain.

As far as societal change is concerned, a clearer distinction needs to be drawn between what has happened in the past and why, and what may happen in the future and how. History doubtless has many lessons to offer, but it should not be assumed that they can simply be replicated. Too much of the theorising about societal change is at a level of abstraction that makes it difficult to test or to put into practice. Higgott (1983, p.103), in a comprehensive survey of development theory, rather pessimistically concludes: 'We might be methodologically more sophisticated and cautious than we were. . ., but we are as far as ever from developing an integrated theory of development and/or underdevelopment.' However, in his reappraisal of modernisation and dependency theory Apter (1987) is more positive, arguing that each can learn from the other. He looks for a synthesis which can draw on the functional emphasis on the extent to which social and political structures are responsive to societal needs; on the behavioural emphasis on how and why political, social and economic choices are made; on the emphasis dependency theory places on the economic disparities between societies; and on a renewed emphasis on the role of ideas and ideology in societal change. In short, Apter is seeking a version of modernisation theory in which 'ideology, motivation, and mobility become critical areas of discussion' (1987, p. 85). To achieve this, what is required is more detailed research into how societies have changed, and equally detailed studies of how applicable the findings of that research are to present societies, with the objective of developing a coherent theory of societal change in place of the plethora of existing alternative and rival theories.

PART VI

CONCLUSION

Chapter 13

WHITHER POLITICAL SOCIOLOGY?

INTRODUCTION

Political sociology seeks to explore and explain the relationship between social and political phenomena and to place politics within its societal context. As an interdisciplinary subject area it has built on the foundations laid by Marx and Weber, but it has done so spasmodically and haphazardly, and while much has been achieved, much remains to be done. Not all those who have contributed to the development of political sociology would necessarily wish to describe themselves as political sociologists, but this is less important than acknowledging the contribution that their work has made for those whose interests clearly fall within the ambit of political sociology. This is because the latter draws widely not only on the work of sociologists and political scientists, but also on many other disciplines, notably history, philosophy, economics, psychology, and communication studies. What, then, has been achieved and what remains to be done?

THE ACHIEVEMENTS OF POLITICAL SOCIOLOGY

Many writers on politics have argued that power is its key concept, but it was Max Weber who focused particular attention on the exercise of power in the form of authority and thus on the concept of legitimacy. Power, authority and legitimacy remain of central concern to political sociology, linking as they do the ability to take political decisions with the acceptance of those decisions and the methods by which they were made. Power is now seen as a much more complex phenomenon, partly because of its relationship to authority and legitimacy, but also because its exercise may be covert rather that overt, latent rather then manifest, with the realisation that the ability to control and influence the political agenda of decision-making is as important as decision-making itself. Power is now seen as a multidimensional concept related to the real and perceived values of those who exercise it and of those to whom it is applied.

Power is also of crucial importance to an understanding of the state: we live in a world of states, each of which claims to exercise power legitimately over defined territories and peoples. Much research has been done on the development of the modern state, both in its capitalist and non-capitalist forms and on the emergence of the nation-state as a role model. Consequently, the historical development of the state and its relationship to socio-cultural and economic factors is now better understood.

Within the societies upon which the modern state rests, far more is known about the political behaviour of individuals and groups of individuals and how this behaviour relates to their social milieu. Studies of political socialisation, participation, and recruitment have grown in number and scope, and a more rounded picture of political behaviour within its social context is emerging.

Political behaviour is also being seen in a wider context that takes account of the importance of political communication and the role of values. Rather that being taken for granted, political communication is receiving increasing attention, especially in attempts to unravel the formation of public opinion. Furthermore, the revival of ideological conflict in a number of Western countries under the impact of neo-liberal economic and political ideas has led to the role of ideology being brought into sharper focus.

Even before the collapse of communist regimes in Eastern Europe and the Soviet Union, there was also a better recognition that the political world does not stand still and that societies change, sometimes suddenly and rapidly, sometimes subtly and slowly. How societies innovate and change or adapt themselves to changing circumstances is now recognised as an important area for research. Indeed, the dramatic and far-reaching changes in Eastern Europe and the Soviet Union arguably present political sociology with its greatest challenge. This challenge relates not just to societal change, but to the role of the state, to all aspects of political behaviour, and to the role of values and ideology.

WHAT REMAINS TO BE DONE

There is no area of political sociology in which there is not a great deal more to be done. Were this merely because societies and their politics are subject to change, there might be room for complacency, but this is not the case, nor is it likely to be in the foreseeable future. What follows is an attempt to highlight those areas in greatest need of further exploration, even though in many cases much has already been achieved.

In the areas of power, authority and legitimacy there remain weighty definitional problems, but a more serious gap is the paucity of studies which link these three related concepts to social and political reality. Little is known about what people think and believe about the exercise of power, and the situation is only marginally better when it comes to popular perceptions of authority and legitimacy. Why do people accept the exercise of power over them? How far is it due to fear or a sense of helplessness? To what extent do people believe that others have a right to exercise power over them? And, where it exists, in what circumstances is such a right abrogated?

This question of what people think and believe is one which permeates the whole of political sociology and demands an answer. The concept of the state has long exercised the minds of academics and looms large in the literature of philosophy, history, sociology, and political theory and political science. Yet it has proved an elusive concept: can the state be adequately defined and, if so, what does it mean to members of the societies in which it operates? Is it no more than a useful analytical abstract, or does it have institutional reality? The fact that there are many who claim to act on behalf of the state, invoke its name in support of their actions, or who demand that the state act on their behalf, is testimony to the need for more research.

If the perceptions of the state by people in society have been neglected, their political behaviour has been widely documented. Much is known, in some societies at least, about who learns what and when in terms of political knowledge and values, about who participates in politics and who does not, and about who is recruited to political and administrative office and who is not. But far less is known about *how* people acquire political knowledge and values, about *why* people participate in politics, and *why* they aspire to high office. There is much speculation, but relatively little hard information. Some of that speculation focuses on the pychological needs and desires of individuals, but political psychology is at a very early stage of its development. Yet the psychological dimension of social and political behaviour is neglected at the peril of those who wish to explain political behaviour adequately.

Political communication is another area to which only a few political sociologists have paid more than cursory attention, and much of that has been in exploring the formation of public opinion. Communication studies, however, is an academic growth area and communication theory has long been there for any political sociologist who cared to look. Without communication there can be no society and no politics. Knowledge, values, attitudes, ideology – none can exist without communication. As long ago as 1963 Karl Deutsch in *The Nerves of Government* drew this fundamental fact to the attention of political scientists. His contribution was widely acknowledged and praised, but little acted upon; communication was regarded as a given variable, to be assumed rather than examined. Communication studies have produced much valuable research and many models have been developed, but theories are fragmented and no generally accepted model has materialised.

Public opinion and ideology have also received relatively little attention from political sociologists, although the literature on both is extensive and draws upon a wide variety of disciplines. These subjects need to be drawn more fully into the ambit of political sociology and examined within the context of both political behaviour and political communication. A wealth of data on public opinion exists, especially in the form of opinion polls and surveys, but its analysis often lacks sophistication and takes little or no account of the crucial characteristics of intensity, saliency, and consistency. Theories of opinion-formation also tend to be fragmented and difficult to test empirically. Much therefore remains to be done. Ideology has long held fascination for students of many disciplines, but remains a matter of much dispute. Attempts to place ideology in a broader context of political culture have not been conspicuously successful and the conflict between the Marxist and the non-Marxist view (as in many other areas of political sociology) continues. Above all, the relationships between ideology and public opinion and, ultimately, their role in political behaviour are largely unexplored, but offer an exciting prospect for future research.

If communication has been widely neglected in political sociology, societal change has been far from ignored. Theories of revolution abound and theories of underdevelopment and dependency have stimulated much discussion and writing. Likewise, theories concerned with more gradual change – development theory, nation-building, and modernisation – have received a great deal of attention, but no one has succeeded in developing, and few have sought to develop, a general theory of societal change which can account for both sudden and gradual change. This may be because revolution is all too often associated with a sudden, cataclysmic upheaval, when in reality it is part of a wider process of change. Societies have been utterly destroyed, but history records no society which has transformed so rapidly that its past has become utterly meaningless. The need for a general theory of societal change is even more important following the collapse of communist regimes in Eastern Europe and the Soviet Union.

A considerable obstacle to further progress in social science research generally and political sociology in particular is the fragmentation of knowledge. This takes two important forms. First, there are gaps in our knowledge of all societies, but even more important is the fact that so much more is known about some societies than others, to the point that gaps in knowledge are often greater than the knowledge itself. Social scientists sometimes complain about being faced with too much information when, in reality, the problem is frequently too little. Second, the academic development of the social sciences has been compartmentalised. As Sartori has cogently pointed out:

> Whatever is 'problem' for one discipline becomes a 'given', an external factor, for the neighbouring discipline. For instance, economists assume political structures to be given. Likewise, sociologists assume economic structures to be given. In a similar vein, political scientists assume social structures to be given. Each discipline throws light on a set of variables precisely because other factors are assumed to be external, distal and equal. (Sartori, 1969, p. 196)

Even so, the growth of interdisciplinary research is a hopeful sign for subject areas such as political sociology and, for those whose interest centres on the relationship between politics and society, it is appropriate to end this final chapter in the same way as the first, by arguing that we all are, or perhaps should be, political sociologists now.

BIBLIOGRAPHY

Square brackets [ ] indicate the original date of publication.

Abercrombie, N. and Turner, B. S. (1978), 'The dominant ideology thesis', *British Journal of Sociology*, vol. 29, pp. 149–70.
Abercrombie, N. and Turner, B. S. (1980), *The Dominant Ideology Thesis*, Allen & Unwin.
Adorno, T., Frenkel-Brunswick, E., Levinson, D. J., and Sandford, N. (1950), *The Authoritarian Personality*, Harper & Row.
Almond, G. A. and Coleman, J. S. (eds) (1960), *The Politics of Developing Areas*, Princeton University Press.
Almond, G. A. and Powell, G. B. (1966), *Comparative Politics: A developmental approach*, Little Brown.
Almond, G. A. and Verba, S. (1963), *The Civic Culture: Politlcal attitudes and democracy in five nations*, Princeton University Press.
Almond, G. A. and Verba, S. (eds) (1980), *The Civic Culture Revisited*, Little Brown.
Alt, J. (1979), *The Politics of Economic Decline*, Cambridge University Press.
Althusser, L. (1972), 'Ideology and ideological state apparatuses' in Althusser, *Lenin and Philosophy and Other Essays*, New Left Books.
Althusser, L. (trans. Brewster, B.) (1977 [1965]), *For Marx*, New Left Books.
Amin, S. (1974), *Accumulation on a World Scale*, Monthly Review Press.
Amin, S. (1976), *Unequal Development: An essay on the social formation of peripheral capitalism*, Harvester.
Anderson, P. (1974), *Lineages of the Absolutist State*, New Left Books.
Anderson, P. (1976), *Considerations on Western Marxism*, New Left Books.

Bibliography

Apter, D. E. (1965), *The Politics of Modernisation*, University of Chicago Press.

Apter, D. E. (1987), *Rethinking Development: Modernisation. dependency and postmodern politics*, Sage.

Arendt, H. (1951, rev. edn 1967), *The Origins of Totalitarianism*, Allen & Unwin.

Bachrach, P. (1967), *The Theory of Democratic Elitism*, Little Brown.

Bachrach, P. and Baratz, M. (1962), 'The Two faces of power', *American Political Science Review*, vol. LVII, pp. 947–52.

Bachrach, P. and Baratz, M. (1970), *Power and Poverty*, Oxford University Press.

Balandier, G. (trans. Sheridan Smith, A. M.) (1970 [1967]), *Political Anthropology*, Penguin.

Barber, J. D. (1965), *The Lawmakers: Recruitment and adaptation to legislative life*, Yale University Press.

Bauer, R. (1955), 'Some trends in sources and alienation from the Soviet system', *Public Opinion Quarterly*, vol. 19, pp. 279–91.

Bell, D. (1960), *The End of Ideology: On the exhaustion of Political ideas in the fifties*, Free Press.

Bell, D. (1973), *The Coming of the Post-Industrial Society*, Basic Books.

Bell, D. (1988), 'Afterword 1988: *The End of Ideology* revisited' in 2nd edn, *The End of Ideology*, Harvard University Press.

Bendix, R. (1964, 2nd rev. edn 1972), *Nation-Building and Citizenship: Studies of our changing social order*, Universiy of California Press.

Bendix, R. (1966), *Max Weber: An intellectual portrait*, Methuen.

Benn, R. S. and Peters, S. I. (1959), *Social Principles and the Democratic State*, Allen & Unwin.

Bentley, A. F. (1949 [1908]), *The Process of Government*, Principia Press.

Berrington, H. B. (1973), *Backbench Opinion in the House of Commons, 1945–55*, Pergamon.

Binder, L., Pye, L. W., Coleman, J. S., Verba, S., LaPalombara, J., and Weiner, M. (1971), *Crises and Sequences in Political Development*, Princeton University Press.

Bottomore, T. B. (1964), *Elites and Society*, Watts.

Bottomore, T. B. (ed.) (1979), *Karl Marx*, Blackwell.

Bottomore, T. B., Harris, L., Kiernan, V. G., and Miliband, R. (eds) (1983), *A Dictionary of Marxist Thought*, Blackwell.

Braudel, F. (trans. Siân Reynolds) (1981/1985 [1979]), *Civilisation and Capitalism, 15th–18th Century:* Vol. I – *The Structures of Everyday Life: The Limits of the Possible;* Vol. II – *The Wheels of Commerce;* Vol. III – *The Perspective of the World*, Collins/Fontana.

Brinton, C. (1953 [1938]), *The Anatomy of Revolution*, Cape.

Browning, R. P. (1968), 'The interaction of personality and political

systems in decisions to run for office: some data and a simulation technique', *Journal of Social Issues*, vol. 24, pp. 93–109.
Bryce, J. (1921), *Modern Democracies*, Macmillan.
Brzezinski, Z. K. (rev. edn 1967), *Ideology and Power in the Soviet Union*, Praeger.
Burke, E. (1883), *Works*, George Bell.
Burnham, J. (1942), *The Managerial Revolution*, Putnam.
Butler, D. E. and Stokes, D. (1969, rev. edn 1974), *Political Change in Britain*, Macmillan.
Childs, H. L. (1965), *Public Opinion: Nature, formation and role*, Princeton University Press.
Claessen, H. J. M. and Skalnik, P. (eds) (1978), *The Early State*, Mouton.
Cohan, A. S. (1975), *Theories of Revolution: An introduction*, Nelson.
Cohen, J. L. (1985), 'Strategy or identity: new theoretical paradigms and contemporary social movements', *Social Research*, vol. 52, pp. 663–716.
Cohen, R. and Service, E. R. (1978), *Origins of the State: The anthropology of political evolution*, Institute of Human Issues.
Connolly, W. (ed.) (1984), *Legitimacy and the State*, Blackwell.
Connolly, W. (1984), 'The Dilemmas of Legitimacy' in Connolly (ed.) *Legitimacy and the State*, Blackwell.
Crenson, M. A. (1971), *The Un-Politics of Air Pollution*, Johns Hopkins Press.
Crewe, I. M. (1984), 'The electorate: partisan dealignment ten years on' in Berrington, H. B. (ed.), *Change in British Politics*, Frank Cass.
Crewe, I. M., Sarlvik, B., and Alt, J. (1977), 'Partisan dealignment in Britain, 1964–74', *British Journal of Political Science*, vol. 7, pp. 129–90.
Crewe, I. M. and Sarlvik, B. (1980), 'Popular attitudes and electoral strategy' in Layton-Henry, Z. (ed.), *Conservative Party Politics*, Macmillan.
Crick, B. (1964), *In Defence of Politics*, Penguin.
Crick, B. (1966), 'The tendency of political studies', *New Society*, vol. 3, p. 683.
Curran, J. and Seaton, J. (rev. edn 1988), *Power Without Responsibility: The press and broadcasting in Britain*, Routledge.
Dahl, R. A. (1956), *A Preface to Democratic Theory*, University of Chicago Press.
Dahl, R. A. (1958), 'A critique of the ruling elite model', *American Political Science Review*, vol. 52, pp. 463–9.
Dahl, R. A. (1961), *Who Governs? Democracy and power in an American city*, Yale University Press.
Dahl, R. A. (1982), *Dilemmas of Pluralist Democracy*, Yale University Press.
Dahl, R. A. (1985), *A Preface to Economic Democracy*, Polity Press.
Davies, J. C. (1962), 'Towards a theory of revolution', *American Sociological Review*, vol. 27, pp. 5–19.

Dawson, R. E., Prewitt, K. and Dawson, K. P. (1977), *Political Socialisation*, 2nd edn, Little Brown.
Denver, D. (1989), *Elections and Voting Behaviour in Britain*, Philip Allan.
de Tocqueville, A. (trans. Lawrence, G., ed. Mayer, J. P. and Lerner, M.) (1966 [1835–40]), *Democracy in America*, Harper & Row.
de Tocqueville, A. (trans. Gilbert, S.) (1966 [1856]), *The Ancien Régime and the French Revolution*, Collins.
Deutsch, K. W. (1963), *The Nerves of Government: Models of political communication and control*, Free Press.
Deutsch, K. W. and Foltz, W. J. (eds) (1963), *Nation-Building*, Atherton Press.
Dos Santos, T. (1970), 'The structure of dependency', *American Economic Review*, vol. 60, pp. 231–6.
Downs, A. (1957), *An Economic Theory of Democracy*, Harper & Row.
Dowse, R. E. and Hughes, J. A. (2nd edn 1986), *Political Sociology*, Wiley.
Easton, D. (1953), *The Political System: An inquiry into the state of political science*, Knopf.
Easton, D. (1965a), *A Framework for Political Analysis*, Prentice Hall.
Easton, D. (1965b), *A Systems Analysis of Political Life*, Wiley.
Easton, D. and Dennis, J. (1969), *Children in the Political System: Origins of political legitimacy*, McGraw-Hill.
Eckstein, H. and Apter D. E. (1963), *Comparative Politics: A reader*, Free Press.
Eisenstadt, S. N. and Rokkan, S. (1973), *Building States and Nations* (2 vols), Sage.
EMNID Institute, Bielefeld (1967) – opinion polls.
Engels, F. (1975) [1884] *The Origins of the Family, Private Property and the State* in Marx and Engels, *Collected Works*, Lawrence & Wishart, vol. 26, pp. 129–276.
Eulau, H. (1963), *The Behavioural Persuasion*, Random House.
Eulau, H. (ed.) (1969), *Behaviouralism in Political Science*, Atherton Press.
Eysenck, H. (1954), *The Psychology of Politics*, Routledge & Kegan Paul.
Finer, S. E. (1962, rev. edn 1988), *The Man on Horseback: The role of the military in politics*, Pall Mall/Westminster Press.
Finer, S. E. (1970), *Comparative Government*, Penguin.
Finer, S. E., Berrington, H. B. and Bartholomew, D. J. (1961), *Backbench Opinion in the House of Commons, 1955–59*, Pergamon.
Fiske, J. (1982), *Introduction to Communication Studies*, Methuen.
Fortes, M. and Evans-Pritchard, E. E. (1940), *African Political Systems*, Oxford University Press.
Frank, A. G. (1967, rev. edn 1969), *Capitalism and Underdevelopment in Latin America: Historical studies of Chile and Brazil*, Monthly Review Press.
Frank, A. G. (1971), *The Sociology of Development and the Underdevelopment of Sociology*, Pluto Press.

Frank, A. G. (1978), *Dependent Accumulation and Underdevelopment*, Macmillan.
Franklin, M. (1985), *The Decline of Class Voting in Britain*, Oxford University Press.
Friedrich, C. J. (1953 [1937]), *Constitutional Government and Democracy: Theory and practice in Europe and America*, Harper.
Friedrich, C. J. (ed.) (1954), *Totalitarianism*, Harvard University Press.
Friedrich, C. J. (1969), 'The evolving theory and practice of totalitarian regimes' in Friedrich, Curtis and Barber (1969), *Totalitarianism in Perspective*.
Friedrich, C. J. and Brzezinski, Z. K. (1956 rev. edn 1965), *Totalitarian Dictatorship and Autocracy*, Harvard University Press.
Friedrich, C. J., Curtis, M. and Barber, B.R. (1969), *Totalitarianism in Perspective: Three views*, Pall Mall.
Fromm, E. (1941), *Escape From Freedom*, Holt, Rhinehart & Winston.
Furtado, C. (trans. de Aguiar, R. W. and Drysdale, E. C.) (1964), *Development and Underdevelopment*. University of California Press.
Furtado, C. (1970), *The Economic Development of Latin America: A survey from colonial times*, Cambridge University Press.
Geertz, C. (1964), 'Ideology as a cultural system' in Apter, D. E. (ed.), *Ideology and Discontent*, Free Press, pp. 47–76.
Gerbner, G. (1956), 'Towards a general model of communication', *Audio-Visual Communication Review*, vol. 4 pp. 171–99.
Giddens, A. (1971), *Capitalism and Modern Society: An analysis of the writings of Marx, Durkheim and Max Weber*, Cambridge University Press.
Gramsci, A. (ed. Hoare, Q. and Nowell Smith, G.) (1971 [1929–35]), *Selections from the Prison Notebooks*, Lawrence & Wishart.
Greenstein, F. I. (1968), 'Political socialisation' in *International Encyclopedia of the Social Sciences*, Macmillan and Free Press, pp. 551–5.
Greenstein, F. I. (1970), 'Research notes – a note on the ambiguity of "Political socialisation": definitions, criticisms, and strategies of inquiry', *Journal of Politics*, vol. XXXII, pp. 969–78.
Gurr, T. R. (1967–68), 'Psychological factors in civil violence', *World Politics*, vol. 20, pp. 245–78.
Gurr, T. R. (1970), *Why Men Rebel*, Princeton University Press.
Habermas, J. (trans. McCarthy, T.) (1976 [1973]), *Legitimation Crisis*, Heinemann.
Hall, J. A. (1985), *Powers and Liberties: The causes and consequences of the rise of the West*, Blackwell.
Heath, A. F., Jowell, R. M., and Curtice, J. K. (1985), *How Britain Votes*, Pergamon.
Heath, A. F., Curtice, J. K., Jowell, R. M., Evans, G., Field, J. and

Witherspoon, C. (1991), *Understanding Political Change: The British voter 1964–1987*. Pergamon.
Held, D. (1982), 'Crisis tendencies, legitimation and the state' in Thompson, J. D. and Held, D. (eds), *Habermas; Critical Debates*, Macmillan.
Held, D. (1984), 'Power and Legitimacy in Contemporary Britain' in McLennan, G., Held, D. and Hall, S. (eds), *State and Society in Contemporary Britain: A critical introduction*, Polity Press.
Held, D. (1987), *Models of Democracy*, Polity Press.
Herbele, R. (1945), *From Democracy to Nazism: A regional case study of political parties in Germany*, Louisiana State University Press.
Hermann, M. G. (1986), *Political Psychology: Contemporary problems and issues*, Jossey Bass.
Higgott, R. A. (1983), *Political Development Theory: The contemporary debate*, Croom Helm.
Himmelstrand, U. (1962), 'A theoretical and empirical approach to depoliticisation and political involvement', *Acta Sociologica*, vol. 6, pp. 83–110.
Hobbes, T. (1914 [1651]), *The Leviathan; or the Matter, Form and Power of a Commonwealth, Ecclesiastical and Civil*, Dent.
Hobson, J. A. (1954 [1902]), *Imperialism: A study*, Allen & Unwin.
Holland, M. (1986), *Candidates for Europe: The British experience*, Gower.
Hume, D. (ed. Selby, L. A., 2nd rev. edn Nidditch, P. H.) (1978 [1739–40]), *A Treatise on Human Nature*, Oxford University Press.
Hunter, F. (1953), *Community Power Structure: A study of decision-makers*, University of North Carolina Press.
Huntington, S. P. (1965), 'Political development and political decay', *World Politics*, vol. 17, 386–430.
Huntington, S. P. (1968), *Political Order in Changing Societies*, Yale University Press.
Hyman, H. (1959), *Political Socialisation: A study of the psychology of political behaviour*, Free Press.
Jacobs, E. and Worcester, R. (1990), *We British: Britain under the MORIscope*, Weidenfeld & Nicolson.
Jessop, B. (1982), *The Capitalist State: Marxist theories and methods*, Martin Roberston.
Johnson, C. A. (1964), *Revolution and the Social System*, Hoover Institution on War, Revolution and Peace.
Johnson, C. A. (1966), *Revolutionary Change*, Little Brown.
Katz, E. and Lazarsfeld, P. F. (1955), *Personal Influence; The part played by people in the flow of mass communication*, Free Press.
Katz, E. and Lazarsfeld, P. F. (1957), 'The two-step flow of communication: an up-to-date report on an hypothesis', *Public Opinion Quarterly*, vol. 21, pp. 61–78.

Kornhauser, W. (1959), *The Politics of the Mass Society*, Free Press and Routledge.
Krader, L. (1968), *The Formation of the State*, Prentice Hall.
Krejčí, J. (1983), *Great Revolutions Compared: The search for a theory*, Wheatsheaf.
Lane, R. E. (1959), *Political Life: Why people get involved in politics*, Free Press.
Lane, R. E. (1962), *Political Ideology: Why the American common man believes what he does*, Free Press.
Lane, R. E. and Sears, D. O. (1964), *Public Opinion*, Prentice Hall.
Langton, K. P. (1969), *Political Socialisation*, Oxford University Press.
Larrain, J. (1979), *The Concept of Ideology*, Hutchinson.
Larrain, J. (1983), *Marxism and Ideology*, Macmillan.
Lasswell, H. D. (1930), *Psychopathology and Politics*, University of Chicago Press.
Lasswell, H. D. (1936), *Politics: Who gets what, when, how*, McGraw-Hill.
Lasswell, H. D. (1948a), *Power and Personality*, Norton.
Lasswell, H. D. (1948b), 'The Structure and function of communication in society' in Bryson, L. (ed.), *The Communication of Ideas*, Harper.
Lazarsfeld, P. F., Berelson, B., and Gaudit, H. (1944, rev. edn 1948), *The People's Choice: How the voter makes up his mind in a presidential election campaign*, Columbia University Press.
Lenin, V. I. (1933 [1917]), *The State and Revolution*, Lawrence & Wishart.
Lindblom, C. (1977), *Politics and Markets*, Basic Books.
Lipset, S. M. (1960, 2nd edn 1983), *Political Man*, Heinemann.
Lipset, S. M. (1964), *First New Nation: The United States in historical and comparative perspective*, Heinemann.
Lipset, S. M. (1966), 'Some further comments on "The End of Ideology"', *American Political Science Review*, vol. 60, pp. 17–18.
Lipset, S. M. and Rokkan, S. (1967), *Party Systems and Voter Alignments*, Free Press.
Locke, J. (1924 [1690]), *Two Treatises on Government*, Dent.
Lukes, S. (1974), *Power: A radical view*, Macmillan.
Lukes, S. (ed.) (1986), *Power*, Blackwell.
McLellan, D. (1970), *Marx Before Marxism*, Macmillan.
McLellan, D. (1974), *Karl Marx: His life and thought*, Macmillan.
McLellan, D. (1979), *Marxism After Marx*, Macmillan.
McLellan, D. (ed.) (1983), *Marx: The first hundred years*. Fontana.
McLennan, G., Held, D., and Hall, S. (eds) (1984a), *The Idea of the Modern State*, Open University Press.
McLennan, G., Held, D., and Hall, S. (eds) (1984b), *State and Contemporary Society in Britain: A critical introduction*, Polity Press.
McNelly, J. T. (1959), 'Intermediary communication in the international flow of news', *Journalism Quarterly*, vol. 36, pp. 23–6.

McQuail, D. (1987), *Mass Communication Theory: An introduction*, Sage.
McQuail, D. and Windahl, S. (1981), *Communication Models for the Study of Mass Communication*, Longman.
Mair, L. (rev. edn 1977), *Primitive Government: A Study of the Traditional Political System in East Africa*, Solar Press. (First edition 1962: Penguin).
Maletzke, G. (1963), *Psychologie der Massenkommunikation*, Verlag Hans Bredow Institute.
Mannheim, K. (trans. Shils, E.) (1936 [1929]), *Ideology and Utopia: An introduction to the sociology of knowledge*, Routledge & Kegan Paul.
Marcuse, H. (1964), *One-Dimensional Man: Studies in the ideology of advanced industrial societies*, Routledge & Kegan Paul.
Marsh, D. (1971), 'Political socialisation:: the implicit assumptions questioned', *British Journal of Political Science*, vol. I, pp. 519–31.
Marx, K. (1980 [1859]), Preface to *A Contribution to the Critique of Political Economy* in Marx and Engels, *Collected Works*, Lawrence & Wishart, vol. 29, pp. 261–5.
Marx, K. (1989 [1875]), *Critique of the Gotha Programme* in Marx and Engels, *Collected Works*, Lawrence & Wishart, vol. 24, pp. 76–99.
Marx, K. and Engels, F. (1976 [1845–6]), *The German Ideology* in Marx and Engels, *Collected Works*, Lawrence & Wishart, vol. 5, 19–539.
Meisel, J. H. (ed.) (1965), *Pareto and Mosca*, Prentice Hall.
Michels, R. (1959 [1911]), *Political Parties: A Sociological study of the oligarchical tendencies of modern democracy*, Dover.
Milbrath, L. W. (1965), *Political Participation: How and why do people get involved in politics?*, Rand McNally.
Milbrath, L. W. and Goel, M. L. (1977), *Political Participation: How and why do people get involved in politics?*, University Press of America.
Milgram, S. (1974), *Obedience to Authority*, Tavistock.
Miliband, R. (1969), *The State and Capitalist Society*, Weidenfeld & Nicolson.
Miliband, R. (1970), 'The capitalist state: reply to Nico Poulantzas', *The New Left Review*, vol. 59, pp. 53–60; reprinted in Urry, J. and Wakeford, J. (1973), *Power in Britain: Sociological readings*, Heinemann, pp. 306–14.
Miliband, R. (1973), Review of Poulantzas, N., *Political Power and Social Class*, in *New Left Review*, vol. 82, pp. 83–92.
Mill, J. S. (1887 [1838]), 'Bentham' in *Dissertations and Discussions*, Longmans, Green, Reader & Dyer, vol. I, pp. 330–92.
Mill, J. S. (1887 [1840]), 'Democracy in America' in *ibid*, vol. II, pp. 1–83.
Mill, J. S. (1910 [1859]), *On Liberty*, Dent.
Mill, J. S. (1910 [1861a]), *Considerations on Representative Government*, Dent.
Mill, J. S. (1910 [1861b]), *Utilitarianism*, Dent.

Mills, C. W. (1956), *The Power Elite*, Oxford University Press.
Mosca, G. (trans. Kahn, H. D., ed. Livingston, A.) (1939 [1896]), *The Ruling Class*, McGraw-Hill.
Norris, P. (1991), 'Gender differences in political participation in Britain', *Government and Opposition*, vol. 26, 56–74.
Offe, C. (1984), *Contradictions of the Welfare State*, Hutchinson.
Offe, C. (1985), 'New social movements: challenging the boundaries of institutional politics', *Social Research*, vol. 52, pp. 817–68.
Olson, M. (1965), *The Logic of Collective Action*, Harvard University Press.
Organski, A. F. (1965), *The Stages of Political Development*, Knopf.
O'Sullivan, T., Hartley, J., Saunders, D. and Fiske, J. (1983), *Key Concepts in Communication*, Methuen.
Ostrogorski, M. (ed. Lipset, S. M.) (1964 [1902]), *Democracy and the Organisation of Political Parties*, Anchor.
Pareto, V. (1935 [1916]), *The Mind and Society*, Harcourt-Brace.
Parkin, F. (1972), *Class Inequality and Political Order*, Paladin.
Parry, G. (1969), *Political Elites*, Allen & Unwin.
Parry, G. (ed.) (1977), *Participation in Politics*, Manchester University Press.
Parry, G. (1977), 'The idea of political participation' in Parry (ed.) *Participation in Politics*.
Parry, G. and Moyser, G. (1984), 'Political participation in Britain', *Government and Opposition*, vol. 19, pp. 68–92.
Parry, G. and Moyser, G. (1990), 'A map of political participation in Britain', *Government and Opposition*, vol. 25, pp. 147–69.
Parry, G. and Moyser, G. (1991), *Participation and Democracy*, Cambridge University Press.
Parsons, T. (1937), *The Structure of Social Action*, McGraw-Hill.
Parsons, T. (1951), *The Social System*, Free Press.
Pollock, F. (1976), 'Empirical research into public opinion' in Connerton, P. (ed.), *Critical Sociology*, Penguin, pp. 225–36.
Polsby, N. W. (1963), *Community Power and Political Theory*, Yale University Press.
Poulantzas, N. (1969), 'The problem of the capitalist state', *New Left Review*, vol. 58, 67–78; reprinted in Urry, J. and Wakeford, J. (eds), *Power in Britain: Sociological readings*, Heinemann, pp. 291–305.
Poulantzas, N. (trans. O'Hagan, T.) (1973 [1968]), *Political Power and Social Classes*, New Left Books.
Presthus, R. (1964), *Men at the Top*, Oxford University Press.
Prewitt, K. (1970), *The Recruitment of Political Leaders: A study of citizen-politicians*, Bobbs-Merrill.
Pulzer, P. G. J. (1967, 3rd edn 1975), *Political Representation and Elections in Britain*, Allen & Unwin.
Pye, L. W. (1966), *Aspects of Political Development*, Little Brown.

Pye, L. W. and Verba, S. (eds) (1965), *Political Culture and Political Development*, Princeton University Press.

Radcliffe-Brown, A. R. (1940), Preface to Fortes, M. and Evans-Pritchard, E. E., *African Political Systems*, Oxford University Press, pp. xi–xxiii.

Rae, D. (1967), *The Political Consequences of Electoral Laws*, Yale University Press.

Rice, S. (1928), *Quantitative Methods in Politics*, Knopf.

Rose, R. and McAllister, J. (1986), *Voters Begin to Choose: From closed class to open elections in Britain*, Sage.

Rostow, W. W. (1960, 2nd edn 1971), *The Stages of Economic Growth: a non-communist manifesto*, Cambridge University Press.

Rousseau, J.-J. (1913 [1762]), *The Social Contract*, Dent.

Runciman, W. G. (1965, 2nd edn 1969), *Social Science and Political Theory*, Cambridge University Press.

Runciman, W. G. (1966), *Relative Deprivation and Social Justice*, Routledge & Kegan Paul.

Rupnik, J. (1988), *The Other Europe*, Weidenfeld & Nicolson.

Rush, M. (1969), *The Selection of Parliamentary Candidates*, Nelson.

Rush, M. (1986), 'The "selectorate" revisited: selecting candidates in the 1980s', *Teaching Politics*, vol. 15, pp. 99–113.

Rush, M. (1988), 'The Members of Parliament' in Ryle, M. and Richards, P. G., *The Commons Under Scrutiny*, Routledge, pp. 18–33.

Russell, B. (1938), *Power: A new social analysis*, Allen & Unwin.

Sartori, G. (1969), 'From the sociology of politics to political sociology', *Government and Opposition*, vol. 4, pp. 194–214.

Schramm, W. (1954), 'How communication works' in Schramm (ed.), *The Process and Effects of Mass Communication*, University of Illinois Press.

Schumpeter, J. (1943), *Capitalism, Socialism and Democracy*, Allen & Unwin.

Seaton, J. (1988), 'The sociology of the mass media' in Curran, J. and Seaton, J., *Power Without Responsibility: The press and broadcasting in Britain*, Routledge, pp. 222–45.

Seeley, Sir J. (1921 [1883]), *The Expansion of England*, Macmillan.

Seligman, L. G. (1961), 'Political recruitment and party structure: a case study', *American Political Science Review*, vol. 55, pp. 77–86.

Seligman, L. G. (1972), *Political Recruitment*, Little Brown.

Service, E. R. (1975), *Origins of the State and Civilisation: The process of cultural evolution*, Mouton.

Service, E. R. (1978), 'Classical and modern theories of the origins of government' in Cohen and Service (eds), *The Origins of the State*, Institute of Human Issues, pp. 21–34.

Seymour-Ure, C. (1968), *The Press, Broadcasting and the Public*, Methuen.

Seymour-Ure, C. (1974), *The Political Impact of the Mass Media*, Constable.

Seymour-Ure, C. (1991), *The British Press and Broadcasting Since 1945*, Blackwell.
Shannon, C. and Weaver, W. (1949), *The Mathematical Theory of Communication*, University of Illinois Press.
Shipler, D. K. (1985), *Russia: Broken idols, solemn dreams*, Futura.
Shirer, W. L. (1960), *The Rise and Fall of the Third Reich*, Secker & Warburg.
Skilling, H. G. and Griffiths, F. (eds) (1971), *Interest Groups in Soviet Politics*, Princeton University Press.
Skocpol, T. (1976), 'France, Russia, China: a structural analysis of social revolution', *Comparative Studies in Society and History*, vol. 18, pp. 175–210.
Skocpol, T. (1979), *States and Social Revolution*, Cambridge University Press.
Sniderman, P. M. and Tetlock, P. E. (1986), 'Interrelationship of political ideology and public opinion' in Hermann, M. G. (ed.), *Political Psychology: Contemporary problems and issues*, Jossey Bass, pp. 62–96.
Solomon, S. G. (ed.) (1983), *Pluralism in the Soviet Union: Essays in honour of H. Gordon Skilling*, Macmillan.
Talmon, J. L. (1952), *The Origins of Totalitarian Democracy*, Secker & Warburg.
Tanter, R. and Midlarsky, M. (1967), 'A theory of revolution', *Journal of Conflict Resolution*, vol. 11, pp. 264–80.
Thompson, J. B. (1984), *Studies in the Theory of Ideology*, Polity Press.
Thompson, J. B. and Held, D. (eds) (1982), *Habermas: Critical debates*, Macmillan.
Tilly, C., Tilly, L. and Tilly, R. (1975), *The Rebellious Century, 1830–1930*, Harvard University Press.
Truman, D. B. (1951), *The Governmental Process*, Knopf.
Verba, S. and Nie, N. (1972), *Participation in America: Political democracy and social equality*. Harper Row.
Verba, S., Nie, N. and Kim, J.-O. (1978), *Participation and Political Equality: A seven nation comparison*, Cambridge University Press.
Volgyes, I. (ed.) (1975), *Political Socialisation in Eastern Europe: A comparative framework*, Praeger.
Wallerstein, I. (1974), *Modern World System: Capitalist agriculture and the origins of the European world economy in the sixteenth century*, Academic Press.
Wallerstein, I. (1979), *The Capitalist World Economy*, Cambridge University Press.
Weber, M. (1930 [1904–5]), *The Protestant Ethic and the Spirit of Capitalism*, Allen & Unwin.
Weber, M. (trans. Henderson, A. M., ed. Parsons, T.) (1947), *The Theory of Social and Economic Organisation*, Free Press.

Weber, M. (trans. and ed. Gerth, H. H. and Mills, C. W.) (1948), *From Max Weber: Essays in sociology*, Routledge & Kegan Paul.

Weber, M. (trans. and ed. Shils, E. and French, H. A.) (1949), *The Methodology of the Social Sciences*, Free Press.

Westergaard, J. (1977), 'Power, class and the media' in Curran, J., Gurevitch, M. and Woollacott, J. (eds), *Mass Communication and Society*, Edward Arnold.

White, D. M. (1950), 'The "Gatekeepers": a case study in the selection of news', *Journalism Quarterly*, vol. 27, pp. 383–90.

White, G. (1977), *Socialisation*, Longman.

Whiteley, P. (1983), *The Labour Party in Crisis*, Methuen.

Wright, H. T. (1978), 'Toward an explanation of the origin of the state' in Cohen and Service (eds), *Origins of the State*, Institute of Human Issues. pp. 49–67.

Wrong, D. (1961), 'The over-socialised concept of man in modern society', *American Sociological Review*, vol. 26, pp. 183–93.

INDEX

Abercrombie, N., 185
absolutism, 71
Aden, 39
administrative office, 112–13, 128–9, 132, 143–4
See also political recruitment
Adorno, T., 11, 12, 47, 73, 74, 174
African Unity, Organisation of (OAU), 39
agenda-setting, 48, 69, 161, 175
agricultural revolution, 200, 217
Albania, 76
Alexander II, 230
Algeria, 54
alienation, 8–9, 115–16, 126–7, 202
Almond, G. A., 7–8, 50, 53, 54, 95, 186, 220
Alt, J., 172
Althusser, L., 12, 40, 50, 54, 101, 110, 161, 184, 204
Amin, S., 227, 228
Anderson, P., 12, 184
Angola, 39
anomie, 126–7
apathy, 111, 115–16, 126–7
Apter, D. E., 72, 225–6, 237
Arab League, 39
Arendt, H., 72–3, 74
Argentina, 224
aristocracy, 58–9
Aristotle, 58–9, 71, 79, 124, 212
Aron, R., 186
attitudes
definition of, 90
and ideology, 190–3
and political communication, 151–2
and political participation, 121, 122
and political parties, 113
and political socialisation, 90 96, 98
and pressure groups, 113
and public opinion, 173–4
Australia, 117, 118, 133
Austria, 29, 117
Austria-Hungary, 24, 35, 222
authority, 13, 18, 22, 47 50, 241–2, 243
definition of, 52
and legitimacy, 50–7
and political socialisation, 99

Bachrach, P., 48, 69
Balewa, Sir A. T., 201
Bangladesh, 22
Baratz, M., 48, 69
Barber, J. D., 130
behaviouralism, 5
Belgium, 35, 39, 117, 134
Bell, D., 182, 186–7, 236
Bendix, R., 38
Benn, S. I., 82
Bentham, J., 59
Bentley, A. F., 5, 68
Berrington, H. B., 146
Binder, L. *et al.*, 221
Bismarck, O. von, 44, 222
Bolsheviks, 35, 41, 74–5, 204, 207
Bottomore, T., 9, 36, 41
Braudel, F., 30, 31

Brehznev, L., 76
Brinton, C., 215
Britain, 22, 29, 32, 56, 95, 105–6, 116, 117, 121, 123, 128, 132–3, 134, 138–9, 140, 142, 143–4, 166–7, 178, 186, 188, 189, 201, 204, 220, 229
Browning, R. P., 130
Bryce, J., 220
Brzezinski, Z., 71–2, 76
Bulgaria, 35
Bund Deutscher Mädel, 93
Burke, E., 82–3
Burkina Faso (Upper Volta), 38
Burma, 38
Burnham, 61, 64–5
Butler, D. E., 105, 172, 191, 192

Campaign for Nuclear Disarmament, 114
Canada, 22, 37, 86, 103, 117, 139, 162, 201, 229, 230
capitalism, 30–9, 54–5, 179, 198, 202–3, 215–16, 225, 227–9, 236
Castro, F., 76, 205
Cavour, C., 222
Ceaucescu, N., 77
Charles I, 207, 213–14
Charles II, 208
Charles X, 208
Chiang Kai-shek, 75
Childs, H. L. 173
China, 10, 12, 23, 30–1, 73, 74, 75 76, 129, 131, 205, 211, 224 231, 232, 234, 235
civilisations, ancient, 23, 25–6, 28, 30–1
class
  consciousness, 110, 181 , 184, 203
  dominant, 22, 49–50
  and electoral behaviour, 105–6
  and elite theory, 60, 61–2
  and 'false consciousness', 22
  and ideology, 183–5
  Marxist theory of, 8–9, 22–3, 27–8, 39–40, 45, 49–50
  and power, 45, 49–50
  and revolution, 202–3, 203–4
  ruling, 22, 60, 61–2, 181, 182
  and the state, 22–3, 39–40
  Weber on, 10
Claessen, H. J. M., 26
Cohan, A. S., 201, 206, 209
Cohen, R., 26
Coleman, J. S., 7, 220
colonialism, 6, 33–4, 37–9, 227–9, 235
communication
  and coding and decoding, 156, 158
  definition of, 154
  and 'gate keeping', 157–8
  interpersonal, 154–5, 156–7
  mass, 154–5, 156–7
  models of, 154–5, 158–60, 163–5
  and 'noise', 155–6
  and perception, 156
  and political participation, 158
  and political socialisation, 158
  theories of, 154–60
  'two-step flow' theory, 157, 161
  See also political communication
Communist Party, 41, 70, 76, 84, 108, 110, 131, 140, 162
compliance, social and political, 55–7, 71
Comte, A., 3
conflict theory, 26–7
Congo, the, 38, 39
Connolly, W., 55
Conservative Party, 105, 132, 167, 169–70, 172, 188, 191–2
contract theory, 26–7, 51–2, 79–80
Corsica, 80
Crenson, M., 48, 69
Crewe, I. M., 105, 172
Crick, B., 5, 194
Cromwell, O., 53, 207, 216
Cuba, 76, 205
Cultural Revolution, 84, 131
cynicism, 126–7
Cyprus, 39
Czechoslovakia, 21, 36, 103, 193, 210

Dahl, R. A., 45, 47–8, 67–8, 69, 85
Darwinism, social, 27, 28, 219
Davies, J. C., 215
Dawson, K. P., 96
Dawson, R. E., 96
de Gaulle, C., 54
democracy, 58, 59, 78–83, 83–6
  and consent, 80–1
  and control, 80–1
  definition of, 78–9, 80, 81, 83
  direct, 79, 80
  and economic development, 82
  and elections, 80

democracy (*continued*)
and elite theory, 62
and majority rule, 81–2
and political communication, 151–2
and political participation, 110, 125
and public opinion, 82
and representation, 80
and rights, 79, 82–3
and totalitarianism, 70, 80
Denmark, 35, 117
Dennis, J., 98
Denver, D., 192
dependency theory, 13, 39, 226, 245
and societal change, 198–9, 220, 227–9, 236–7
See also development theory; modernisation theory; underdevelopment theory
de Tocqueville, A., 80, 124, 212, 215
de Tracy, D., 181
Deutsch, K. W., 38, 153, 158, 244
'developing societies', 219
See also development theory; Third World politics
development theory, 13, 218, 245
and societal change, 197–9, 220–2, 236–7
See also dependency theory; modernisation theory; underdevelopment theory
dictatorship of the proletariat 41, 71, 83
Dinka, the, 24
Disraeli, B., 230
Djilas, M., 41
dominant ideology thesis, 183–5
Dos Santos, T, 228
Downs, A., 125
Dowse, R. E., 127
Duric, 36
Durkheim, E., 3, 4, 25

Eastern Europe, 11–12, 21, 41, 73, 74, 76, 78, 84, 108, 129, 163, 188, 193, 205, 209, 210, 211, 225, 231, 236, 242–3, 245
East Germany, 93–4, 108
Easton, D., 6–8, 53, 54, 98
Eckstein, H., 72
Egypt, 23, 28, 38, 117
Eisenhower, D. D., 188
Eisenstadt, S. N., 38
electoral behaviour, 11, 12, 105–6, 119–20, 128, 169–70, 172–3, 191–2
electoral systems, 80, 133–4
elections, 80, 133–4, 139–40
elites
definition of, 59–60, 61, 63
recruitment of, 61–2, 64
and revolution, 211–12
See also elite theory
elite theory, 11, 12, 19, 45, 46
critique of, 65–7
and democracy, 62
and distribution of power, 83–6
economic approach 61, 64–5
institutional approach, 61, 65
and Marxist theory, 60
meaning of 59–60
organisational approach, 60–3
and political communication, 152
and political participation, 110, 117
psychological approach, 61, 63–5
and the state, 65
testing, 65–8
empires, 23, 24, 31, 35, 44, 222
end of ideology thesis, 68, 186–9
Engels, F., 22, 36, 49, 181, 183, 184, 202, 203–4, 206
England, 29, 32–3, 34, 71, 166–7, 207
See also Britain
Eulau, H., 5
Europe, 32–4, 34–6, 71, 229, 234
See also Eastern Europe; Western Europe
European Community, 17, 21–2, 230
European Parliament, 134
executive office, 128, 131, 132, 133, 137–9, 141, 142–3
experience
definition of, 90
and political participation, 121, 122
and political socialisation, 90, 97, 98, 106–7
and public opinion, 173–4
Eysenck, H., 47, 174

Fascism scale, 73
Fascist Italy, 73, 74, 76, 78
Federal Republic of Germany, 107
feudalism, 23–4, 26–7, 32–3, 51–2, 215–16
Fifth French Republic, 54, 134, 137–8
Finer, S. E., 82, 131, 146

Finland, 35, 36, 208
First World War, 36, 71, 72, 93, 204, 211, 214, 230, 232
Fiske, J., 155
Foltz, W. J., 38
Fourth French Republic, 54, 107
France, 22, 35, 39, 54, 73, 85, 107, 134, 137–8, 143, 144, 201, 204, 229
Frank, A. G., 227
Frankfurt School, 12
Franklin, M., 105
Friedrich, C. J., 71, 72, 76, 220
Fromm, E., 73
functionalism *see* structural-functionalism
Furtado, C., 228

Gaddafi, M., 53
Gandhi , M., 53
Geertz, C., 181
Gerbner, G., 156
Germany, 34, 35, 44, 54, 72–4, 75, 76, 78, 83, 93, 95, 103, 104, 107, 114, 131, 134, 151, 163, 189, 204, 217, 219, 222
Ghana, 38, 39
Giddens, A., 9, 10, 126
Girondins, 207, 216
Goel, M.L., 99, 111, 117, 118, 120, 125, 126
Gold Coast, 38, 39
Gorbachev, M. S., 41, 117, 210
government
  'minimal', 25
  role of, 5
Gramsci, A., 40, 49, 101, 110, 160, 184, 204
Greek city-states, 58–9, 79, 80, 131
Greenstein, F., 92–3
Griffiths, F., 70
Gulf States, 237
Gurr, T. R., 216

Habermas, J., 12, 54–5
Hall, J., 30, 46–7
Hamilton, A., 216
Harcourt, Sir W., 13
Havel, V., 193
Heath, A. *et al.*, 105, 192
Hegel, G. W., 8
hegemony, 49, 50, 101, 160
Held, D., 19, 56–7, 82
Herbele, R., 11
Hermann, M. G., 47
Herrschaft, 49, 53
Higgott, R. A., 237
Himmelstrand, U., 188–9, 194
Hindenburg, P. von, 217
Hinduism, 23, 30, 31, 38
Hitler, A., 53, 54, 74, 75, 76, 83, 93, 131, 217
Hitler Jugend, 93
Hobbes, T., 26, 51–2, 59, 71, 185
Hobson, J. A., 229
Ho Chi Minh, 76, 205
Holland, M., 134
Home, Lord, 132
Hong Kong, 233, 234–5
Horkheimer, M., 12
House of Commons, 101, 145–6
House of Lords, 101, 131, 138–9
Hoxha, E., 76
Hughes, J. A., 127
Hume, D., 8, 52
Hungary, 21, 204
Hunter, F., 66–7, 69
Huntington, S. P., 215, 225
Hyman, H., 92

'ideal types', 10, 53, 56, 61, 77, 126
'ideological state apparatuses', 40, 50, 54, 101
ideology, 9, 12, 13, 30, 36, 38, 40, 49–50, 54–5, 57, 69, 151–2, 242–3, 244–5
  and attitudes, 190–3
  characteristics of, 182–3
  definition of, 181–2
  dominant, 183–5
  end of, thesis, 68, 186–9
  functions of, 183
  and industrialisation, 231, 232–3, 235
  Marxist view of, 181, 182, 183–5, 188
  maximalist view of, 190–1
  minimalist view of, 190–1
  and political communication, 165, 192
  and political participation, 190
  and political psychology, 190–1
  and political socialisation, 93, 95, 99–100, 101, 103–4
  and politics, 188–9

ideology (*continued*)
and public opinion, 170–1, 178–9, 180
and revolution, 201, 206
and societal change, 192–3, 237
and Thatcherism, 192
and totalitarianism, 71–2, 76–8, 189, 192–3
imperialism, 49, 95, 227, 229
India, 10, 30, 31, 38, 224
Indo-China, 39, 54
Indonesia, 38
industrialisation, 31–4, 39, 217, 223–4
European model of, 31–4, 230, 236
Japanese model of, 231–3
Soviet model of, 230–1
Third World models of, 233–6
industrial revolution, 31–4, 200, 217
input–output analysis, 6–7
integrative theory, 26, 27–8
interest groups *see* pressure groups
Iran, 78, 189, 237
Ireland, 29, 81, 214
Ireland, Republic of, 22
Islam, 30, 31, 78, 237
Israel, 103
Italy, 32, 34, 35, 73, 74, 76, 78, 95, 117, 219, 222

Jacobins, 207, 216
Jacobs, E., 116, 178, 192
James II, 208
Japan, 118, 214, 231–3, 233, 234, 235
Jessop, B., 12
Johnson, C., 214–15
judicial office, 128, 129, 132–3, 144–5
See also political recruitment
Jungvolk, 93

Katz, E., 157
Kavanagh, D., 192
Kerensky, A., 74–5
Khaldun, I., 212
Khomeini, Ayatollah, 189
Kim Il-sung, 76, 95, 234
Kim, J.-O., 111
King, Martin Luther, 119
Kinnock, Neil, 143, 167
knowledge
definition of, 90, 96, 97
and political communication, 151
and political participation, 121, 122
and political socialisation, 90
and public opinion, 173–4
Komsomol, 94
Korea, 76, 95, 100, 228–9, 233–4, 235
Kornhauser, W., 63, 85–6, 152
Krejčí, J., 201, 206–9, 210–11, 212, 217–18, 236
Krushchev, N S., 41, 76

Labor Party, Australian, 133
Labour Party, 105, 120, 133, 140, 167, 169–70, 172, 188, 191, 192
Lane, R. E., 126, 169
Langton, K. P., 96
Larrain, J., 185
Lasswell, H. D., 11, 47, 154, 155
Latin America, 210–11, 228
Lazarsfeld, P., 11, 157
Lee Kuan Yew, 235
legislative office, 128, 131, 133–4, 137–9, 138–9, 141, 143
legitimacy, 10, 13, 17–18, 221, 241–2, 243
and authority, 50–7
bases of, 20–2, 53–7
charismatic, 53
and compliance, 55–7
definition of, 53
Marxist view of, 54–5
and political recruitment, 129, 130
and political socialisation, 106–8
rational–legal, 53
and the state, 29–2, 53–5
traditional, 53
Weber on, 20, 53
Lenin, V. I., 12, 22, 40, 41, 70, 74–5, 84, 93 110, 184, 204–5, 216, 227, 231
liberal democracy, 12–13, 80–3, 107, 117, 145, 187, 219–20, 222
Liberal Democrats, 105, 169–70
Libya, 237
Lincoln, A., 78
Lindblom, C., 85
Lipset, S. M., 11, 37, 82, 186, 187–8
Locke, J., 26, 51–2, 59, 79
Louis Napoleon, 209
Louis XVIII, 208
Lukes, S., 48–9, 69

McAllister, J., 105, 192
McCarthy, J., 85
Macdonald, R., 143
Machiavelli, N., 59, 64, 185

McLellan, D., 9, 41
McLuhan, M., 162
Macmillan, H., 132
McNelly, J. T., 158
McQuail, D., 164, 176, 177, 179
Madison, J., 216
Mair, L., 24
Major, J., 142–3
Malaysia, 234
Maletzke, G., 165
Mannheim, K., 181
Mao Zedong, 12, 75, 76, 84, 205, 216
Marcuse, H., 12, 184
Marsh, D., 108–9
Marx, K., 3, 12, 36, 49, 59, 71, 83, 181, 183, 184, 202, 203–4, 206, 212, 223, 229
  and political sociology, 4, 8–10, 241
  and sociology, 3–4
  See also Marxist theory
Marxist theory
  and alienation, 8–9
  and class, 8–9, 22–3, 27–8, 39–40, 45
  criticism of, 9–10
  and dependency, 227–9
  and economics, 8
  and ideology, 9, 12, 40, 49, 54–5, 69, 181, 182, 183–5, 188
  importance of, 9
  and legitimacy, 54–5
  and mode of production, 8–9, 202–3
  and nationalism, 36–7
  neo-, 9, 12, 39, 40, 44, 54–5, 184–5, 198, 204
  and political participation, 110
  and political socialisation, 100, 101–2
  and power, 45, 49–50, 59, 69, 83–4
  and revolution, 39, 41, 110, 197–9, 202–6, 214
  and societal change, 197–9, 220, 236–7
  and the state, 22–3, 39–42
  and underdevelopment, 227–9
  and values, 9
  and Weber, 9–10
mass society theory, 63, 85–6, 152, 214
media *see* public opinion
Meiji, Emperor, 233
Meisel, J., 60
Mensheviks, 207
Mesopotamia, 23, 28
Mexico, 96, 131, 224
Michels, R., 11, 60, 62–3, 66, 68
Midlarsky, M., 215
Milbrath, L. W., 99, 111, 117, 118, 120, 125, 126
Milgram, S., 73, 74
Miliband, R., 12, 40, 179
military office, 128, 129–30, 144–5
  See also political recruitment
Mill, J., 59
Mill, J. S., 59, 81–2, 124
Mills, C. W., 45, 60, 61, 65
modernisation theory, 13, 187, 245
  and societal change, 197–9, 218, 220, 223–6, 236–7
  See also dependency theory; development theory; underdevelopment theory
Montenegro, 35
Mosca, G., 11, 45, 60–2, 64, 83
Moyser, G., 112, 118, 119, 121, 123
Mozambique, 39
Mussolini, B., 49, 76, 83
Mynamar (Burma), 38

Napoleon, 208
Nasser, G. A., 38, 53
national identity, 38–9, 221, 222
    nationalism, 34–9, 187, 222–3, 236
nation-building, 38–9, 222–3, 245
National Socialist Party, 73, 74
nation-state, 34–9
Nazi Germany, 54, 73, 74–8, 83, 93, 94, 103, 104, 114, 131, 151, 163, 189, 217
neo-Marxist theories, 9, 12, 39, 40, 44, 54–5, 184–5, 198, 204
Netherlands, 35, 117
New England townships, 79
new social movements (NSMs), 85, 123–4
Nie, N., 111, 121
Nigeria, 201
Nixon, 178
Nkrumah, K., 53
Norris, P., 119
Northcote–Trevelyan reforms, 132
Northern Ireland, 81
North Korea, 76, 95, 100, 228, 233–4, 235
North Vietnam, 76, 129
Norway, 35, 117

Nuer, the, 24

obedience, social and political, 24, 50–7, 71
Offe, C., 55, 123, 124
oligarchy 58, 66
Olson, M., 125
OPEC, 39, 228
opinion
 definition of, 166
 formation of, 173–9
 types of, 168–9
 See also public opinion
Organski, A. F., 223, 224–5
Ostrogorski, M., 11, 62
O'Sullivan, T. , 155
Ottoman Empire, 31
 See also Turkey

Pakistan, 22, 237
Pareto, V., 11, 45, 60, 63–5, 83, 132, 212
Paris Commune, 83, 204
Park Chung Hee, 234
Parkin, F., 185
Parry, G., 60, 61, 111, 118, 119, 121, 123, 124
Parsons, T., 6, 53–4, 181, 184
People's Republic of China (PRC), 73, 74, 75, 76, 84, 129, 232
personality, 11, 47
 authoritarian, 11, 12, 47, 73, 74, 126
 and Marxist theory, 110
 and political communication, 151
 and political participation, 120, 121
 and political socialisation, 90, 97, 98, 106–7, 110
 and public opinion, 173–4
Peters, R. S., 82
Plato, 58, 71, 79
pluralist theory, 12, 19, 45, 46, 47–9 84–5
 critique of, 48–9, 69–70
 and elite theory, 67–8
 meaning of, 48, 67–9
 and political participation, 110, 124
Poland, 35, 36, 76, 103, 204
police, recruitment of, 128, 129–30, 144–5
 See also political recruitment
political behaviour, 8, 13, 242–3, 243–5
 and political communication, 151–2
 and political participation, 111–27
 and political recruitment, 147–8
 and political socialisation, 96–8, 104–9
 and societal change, 192–3
political communication, 11, 13, 151–2, 242, 244
 and agenda-setting, 161, 175
 channels of, 161
 characteristics of, 160–1
 definition of, 153
 factors influencing, 161–3
 nature of, 153–4
 patterns of, 163
 problems of, 179–80
 and public opinion, 157, 179–80
 and society, 153–4, 160
 'two-step flow' theory of, 157, 161
 See also communication
political culture, 7, 13, 50, 95, 108, 186, 200, 244–5
political efficacy, 54, 99, 125–6
political obligation, 50–7
 See also compliance, social and political
political office, 112–13, 128–90, 132, 137–43
 See also political recruitment
political organisations, 112–16, 121, 123
political participation, 11, 13, 54, 70, 89, 90–1, 95, 221
 and alienation, 115–16, 126–7
 and apathy, 111, 115–16, 126–7
 and attitudes, 116
 definition of, 110–11
 and demonstrations, 114–15, 115–16, 123
 developmental theory of, 124–5
 economic theory of, 125
 and elite theory, 110, 117
 and experience, 121, 122
 explanations of, 120–7
 extent of, 116–20
 forms of, 111–16
 hierarchy of, 111–16
 and ideology, 190
 instrumental theory of, 124–5
 intensity of, 111
 interest in, 116
 and knowledge, 121, 122
 model of, 121–2, 158
 modes of, 111

political participation (*continued*)
  and new social movements, 123–4
  and non-involvement, 111–12, 115–16, 126–7
  and personality, 120, 121, 126, 126–7
  and political communication, 158
  and political discussion, 115
  and political parties, 112–14
  and political recruitment, 112–13, 127, 147
  and political socialisation, 98, 109
  and pressure groups, 112–14
  quality of, 111
  rational choice theory of, 125, 126
  and socio-economic characteristics, 117–20, 123, 126
  and values, 121, 122
political recruitment, 11, 13, 65–6, 70, 158, 242, 244
  administrative office, 128–9, 143–4
  'agency-recruited', 130–1
  'aspirants', 134, 135–7
  and 'de-recruitment', 148
  definition of, 128
  on demand factors, 135–7, 141, 148
  eligibility, 130, 134, 135–7
  and elite theory, 145–6
  executive office, 128, 131, 132, 133, 137–9, 141, 142–3
  judicial office, 128, 129–30, 144–5
  legislative office, 128, 131, 133–4, 137–9, 138–9, 141, 143
  machinery of, 131–5, 148
  Marxist view of, 144–5
  military office, 129–30, 144–5
  model of, 135–7, 148
  and opportunity structures, 130, 135–7, 138, 141, 143, 148
  patterns of, 145–7
  and police, 128 129–30, 144–5
  political office, 128, 129, 137–43
  and political participation, 112–13, 127, 147
  and political parties, 139–40
  and political socialisation, 109
  and political violence, 131–2
  problems of, 147–8
  and psychology, 135, 141
  and resources, 135–7
  scope of, 128–30
  'self-starters', 130–1
  and socio-economic characteristics, 134–5, 137, 145–7
  and supply factory, 135–7, 141, 148
  and the state, 130, 144–5
political parties, 12, 62–3, 101, 112–13, 139, 146–7, 161, 169–70, 175, 191–2, 219
political science
  development of, 5–7, 219–20
  and sociology, 3–8
political socialisation, 11, 13, 39, 50, 54, 57, 70, 242, 243–4
  adolescent, 97, 102
  adult, 96–8, 99–100
  agencies of, 96–7, 100–1, 102–4
  and attitudes, 96–8, 102
  in Britain, 105–6
  childhood, 96–8, 100, 102
  covert, 92, 95–6
  critique of, 108–9
  definition of, 92–3, 96
  in Eastern Europe, 95
  and electoral behaviour, 105–6
  and experience, 97, 98
  and ideology, 93, 95, 99–100, 101
  interactionist view of, 100, 102
  and knowledge, 96–8, 98–9
  legislative, 101
  and legitimacy, 106–8
  Marxist view of, 100, 101–2
  mechanisms of, 96, 97, 104
  and the media, 103–4
  model of, 96–8, 158
  in Nazi Germany, 93, 94
  overt, 92, 93–5
  and perception, 96–8, 174
  and personality, 90, 97, 98, 106–7
  and political behaviour, 96–8, 100–2, 104–9
  and political communication, 158
  and political culture, 95, 108
  and political efficacy, 99
  and political participation, 98, 110
  and political socialisation, 109
  and public opinion, 173–5
  and reinforcement, 97, 98, 100, 102
  and religion, 102–3
  and resocialisation, 97, 98, 99–100, 101
  and societal change, 106–8
  and socio-economic status, 99, 102
  stages of, 102
  theory of, 96–109
  in totalitarian societies, 93–5, 178
  in the United States, 98–9, 102, 103

political socialisation (*continued*)
in the USSR, 93, 94, 107
and values, 96–8, 102
in West Germany, 107
political sociology
achievements of, 241–3
definition of, 8
founding fathers of, 4, 8–11
future of, 243–6
origins and development of, 8–12
remit of, 12–13, 241
political violence, 116, 123, 127, 131–2, 197, 199, 200, 201, 203, 204, 206, 207–8, 209–10, 214–15, 216, 217
politics
definition of, 4–5, 18
'minimal', 24
Pollock, F., 166, 167
Polsby, N., 68
polyarchy, 68
Portugal, 33, 39, 229
Poulantzas, N., 12, 40, 49–50, 54–5, 179
Powell, E., 178
Powell, G. B., 7, 95, 220
power, 10, 12, 13, 17–19, 20, 22, 241–2, 243
analysing, 43–50
and authority, 49, 50–7
'blocking', 30, 47
and class, 45
definition of, 43–5, 50
distribution of, 83–6, 215
elite view of, 45, 59–67
'enabling', 47
exercise of, 45–50, 51–7, 112–13
and force, 46
and ideology, 46–7
and legitimacy, 52–7
Marxist view of, 45, 49–50, 59
pluralist view of, 45, 47–8, 67–70
and probability, 44–5
and revolution, 215
three dimensions of, 48–9, 69
totalitarian view of, 70–8
types of, 30, 46–7
variable sum concept of, 45
Weber on, 44–5, 49
zero-sum concept of, 44–5
power elite, 65
pressure groups, 112–14, 161, 175, 219
Presthus, R., 69
Prewitt, K., 96, 130
primary elections, 134, 139–40
Prussia, 44
psychology, 3, 5, 11, 106
and elite theory, 47, 190–1
political, 61, 63–5, 244
and political participation, 125, 126–7
and political recruitment, 135, 141
and public opinion, 174
and revolution, 215–17
and totalitarianism, 73
public opinion, 13, 59, 82, 151–2, 242, 244
and agenda-setting, 175
and consistency, 170–3
definition of, 166–9
and direction, 169
and 'don't knows', 166–7, 179–80
formation of, 173–9
and ideology, 170–1, 180
and information, 167–8, 175
and intensity, 169–70, 175
and the media, 176–9
model of, 173–5
and perception, 173–4
and political communication, 157, 179–80
and political socialisation, 173–5
problems of, 180
and salience, 170, 175
Pulzer, P. G., 105
Pye, L. W., 220
Pym, J., 216

quasi-political organisations, 112–16

Radcliffe-Brown, A. R., 24
Rae, D., 133
recall, the, 80–1
referenda, 80–1
Reformation, the, 33, 34, 213
relative deprivation, theory of, 215–17
'repressive state apparatuses', 40
revolution, 13, 110, 245
American, 37, 200, 210, 211, 215, 216
Bolshevik, 35, 41, 74–5
causes of, 211–17
characteristics of, 201–6
Chinese, 200, 205, 206, 208, 209, 211, 216

revolution (*continued*)
communist, 203–4, 204
definition of, 200–2
English, 200, 201–2, 207, 208, 210, 211, 213–14, 215, 216, 217
French, 35, 200, 201, 202, 207, 208, 209, 210, 211, 215, 216
functionalist view of, 214–15
'horizontal', 210–11
Hussite, 206
and ideology, 201, 206, 212, 213
in Latin America, 210–11
Marxist view of, 39–41, 110, 197–9 202–6, 214
as a myth, 39, 200–1
non-Marxist view of, 206–11
and political violence, 197, 199, 200, 201, 203, 204, 206, 207–8
psychological view of, 215–17
and relative deprivation, 215–17
and rising expectations, 215–17
Russian, 35, 41, 74–5, 200, 201, 202, 204, 207, 208, 209, 210, 211, 214, 215, 216, 230
and societal change, 197–9, 200–2, 217–18, 219
in the Third World, 200–1, 211
'vertical', 210–11
See also societal change
Rhodesia, 38
Rice, S., 11
rights, 79, 82–3
rising expectations, theory of, 215–17
Rokkan, S., 38, 82
Roosevelt, F. D., 107, 188
Rose, R., 105, 192
Rostow, W. W., 220, 223–4, 225
Rousseau, J.-J., 51, 52, 55, 59, 73, 83, 124, 207
ruling class, 22, 60, 61–2, 181, 182
See also elite; elite theory
Romania, 21, 35, 77, 163, 209
Runciman, W. G., 5, 216
Rupnik, J., 193
Rush, M., 140, 146
Rushdie, S., 121
Russell, B., 43, 44
Russia, 35, 74–5, 201, 204, 207, 222, 230–1, 232, 233

St Augustine of Hippo, 59
St Thomas Aquinas, 59
Sarlvik, B., 172
Sartori, G., 8, 245
Sartre, J.-P., 12
Saudi Arabia, 237
Schramm, W., 156
Schumpeter, J., 83
Scotland, 29, 32, 166–7
Sears, D. O., 169
Seaton, J ., 18
Second World War, 71, 74, 75, 205, 217, 219, 231
Seeley, Sir J., 229
Seligman, L. G., 130
Serbia, 35
Service, E. R., 26
Seymour-Ure, C., 178
Shannon, C., 155
Shils, E., 186
Shipler, D. K., 94
Shirer, W. L., 104
Singapore, 233, 234–5
Skalnik, P., 26
Skilling, H. G, 70
Skocpol, T., 211
Sniderman, P. M., 190–1
social Darwinism, 27, 28, 219
socialisation, 39, 50, 89, 90–1
See also political socialisation
societal change, 13, 57, 197–9, 236–7, 242–3, 245
Darwinian view of, 219
and dependency theory, 198–9, 220, 227–9, 236–7
and development theory, 197–9, 218, 219–20, 220–2
and foreign conquest, 218, 236
and ideology, 192–3
and modernisation theory, 187, 197–9, 218, 219–20, 223–6
and nation-building, 38–9, 222–3
and political socialisation, 106–8
and revolution, 197–9, 200–2, 217–18
and underdevelopment theory, 227–9, 245
societies
communist, 22–3, 40–1, 65, 66, 76–8, 83–4, 114, 163, 229
feudal, 23–4, 32–3, 51 –2
liberal-democratic, 68, 80–3, 117
primitive, 23, 24–5, 26, 220
stateless societies, 18, 23
totalitarian, 70–8

society
  definition of, 3
  mass, 85–6
  and political sociology, 8, 13, 241–6
  and the state *see* Ch. 2, 20–42 *passim*
  See also societal change
sociology
  definition of, 3, 4
  and political science, 3–8
Soloman, S. G., 70
South Korea, 233–4
South Vietnam, 76
Soviet Union *see* Union of Soviet Socialist Republics
Spain, 33, 230
Spencer, H., 3, 25
'spoils system', 131, 132, 144
Stalin, J., 36, 41, 76–7, 83, 84, 131, 189, 204–5, 208, 231
state, the, 10, 12, 13, 17–19, 22, 243
  administrative organisation of, 20, 21, 23–4
  capitalist, 30–4, 45
  and class, 22–3, 39–40, 54–5
  compulsory nature of, 20, 22
  definition of, 17, 20, 21–2, 22, 23
  formation of, 25–9
  and the industrial revolution, 31–4
  and legitimacy, 20–22, 53–5
  Lenin on, 22, 40–1
  Marxist view of, 22–3, 26, 27–8, 39–42, 54–5, 205
  modern, 29–39
  and monopoly of force, 17, 20–2
  nation-, 34–9
  neo-Marxist view of, 40, 54–5
  neutrality of, 41–2
  non-Marxist view of, 20–1
  origins of, 23–9
  and political recruitment, 130, 144–5
  pre-modern, 23–9
  role of, 42
  territorial nature of, 17, 21–2, 23, 25
  totalitarian, 70–8
  Weber on, 20–2
  'withering away' of, 22–3, 41
state-formation, theories of, 25–9
stateless societies, 18, 23
Stokes, D. E., 105, 172, 191
Stolypin, P., 230
structural-functionalism, 6–7, 53–4, 101–2, 108, 214–15, 220, 225–6
Sweden, 35
Switzerland, 117
systems theory, 6–7, 53–4

Taiwan, 233, 234, 235
Talmon, J. L., 72, 73, 74
Tanter, R., 215
Tanzania, 38
Tetlock, P. E., 190–1
Thatcher, M., 142, 167, 172, 192
Third French Republic, 209
Third World politics, 6, 7, 12, 29, 34, 37–9, 86, 106, 117, 118, 131, 144, 162, 187, 198, 219–20, 222–3, 224, 226, 229, 231, 233–6, 236–7
Thompson, J. B., 193
Tiananmen Square 1989, 205
Tilly, C., 216
Tito, 76
totalitarianism, 19, 83–6, 178, 219, 234
  definition of, 71–2
  and democracy, 70, 80
  and ideology, 71–2, 76–8, 189
  origins of, 72–5
  in practice, 76–8
Trotsky, L., 12, 204–5
Truman, D. B., 68
Turkey, 35, 224
tyranny, 58, 71

underdevelopment theory, 226, 227–9, 245
  See also dependency theory; development theory; modernisation theory
Union of Soviet Socialist Republics (USSR), 11, 21, 41, 43, 65, 70, 73, 74–8, 83, 84, 86, 94, 107, 108, 117, 129, 145, 151, 162, 163, 188, 189, 193, 205, 209, 210, 219, 225, 230–1, 233–4, 236, 242, 245
United Kingdom *see* Britain
United Nations, 17
UN Economic Commissions for Latin America, 228
United States, 11, 22, 23, 33, 34, 37, 43, 61, 65, 70, 79, 80–1, 85, 86, 95, 98–9, 102, 103, 111–12, 117, 129, 131, 132–3, 134, 137, 139–40, 141, 142, 162, 178, 188, 189, 201, 220, 226, 230, 233–4
utilitarianism, 59, 124

values, 9, 10, 50
definition of, 90
and ideology, 190–4
and political communication, 151–2
and political participation, 121, 122, 126
and political socialisation, 90, 96–8
and public opinion, 173–4
Verba, S., 7, 50, 54, 95, 111, 121, 186
Versailles, Treaty of (1919), 35, 36
Verstehen, 10
Vietnam, 76, 129, 205
violence *see* political violence
Volgyes, I., 95, 99
voting, 111, 115, 121
See also electoral behaviour

Wales, 29, 166–7
Wallerstein, I., 227
Washington, G., 216
Weaver, W., 155
Weber, M., 3, 12, 212
and class, 10
and 'ideal types', 10, 53, 126
and legitimacy, 10, 53, 241
and Marx, 9–10
and power, 44–5, 49, 241
and political behaviour, 126
and political participation, 126
and political recruitment, 129
and political sociology, 4, 9–11, 241
and social stratification, 10
and sociology, 4
and the state, 17–18, 20–2, 24, 130
and values, 10
and *Verstehen*, 10
Weimar Republic, 54, 75, 85, 107
Westergaard, J., 179
Western Europe, 31, 32–4, 220, 226, 230, 231
West Germany, 95, 107, 117, 134
White, D. M., 157
White, G., 89, 100
Whiteley, P., 191
William of Orange, 208
Windahl, S., 164
Worcester, R., 116, 178, 192
Wrong, D, 90

Young Pioneers, 94
Yugoslavia, 36, 41, 76

Zaïre, 38
Zimbabwe, 38